TRAGEDY & TRIUMPH

CANADA IN THE 20TH CENTURY
1930 TO 1953

PAUL STANWAY

CANMEDIA INC.
EDMONTON
2007

Author and Editor
PAUL STANWAY

Layout and Design
DEAN PICKUP

Proofreading
NICOLE STANWAY

Index
MOIRA CALDER

Published By
CanMedia Inc.

President
CURTIS STEWART

Publisher
RODNEY DIETZMANN

Suite 202,
10479 - 184 Street,
Edmonton, Alberta.
T5S 2L1
Phone (780) 486-6735
Fax (780) 486-6726
Toll Free: 1-888-301-2664
www.cdnhistory.com

Printed in Canada
By Friesens Corporation, Altona, Manitoba

TRAGEDY AND TRIUMPH
CANADA IN THE 20TH CENTURY
1930 - 1953

Tragedy And Triumph
Canada In The 20th Century.
Includes bibliographical references and Index.
ISBN 0-9736530-6-X
ISBN 978-0-9736530-6-9
EAN 9780973653069

1. Canada - History - 1930-1953
11. Stanway, Paul, 1950- .

ISBN 978-0-9736530-6-9

FOREWORD

The turbulent years between the onset of the Great Depression and the end of the Korean War were the most influential of the 20th century, giving birth to so many of the attitudes and institutions later generations of Canadians take for granted. In 1930 Canada was technically independent but still struggling to cast off the shackles of Edwardian colonialism. Yet over the next two decades - the span of a single generation - we can clearly see a modern country take shape. And what decades they were, encompassing the worst depression of the century, the most destructive war in human history, the beginning of the nuclear age, the Baby Boom, and the arrival of television and the Consumer Society! Recent generations of Canadians have been encouraged to believe that the history of their country encompasses none of the national tragedies and triumphs that marked the development of the great republic to the south: that Canada was a smooth, almost effortless construct. As I hope this volume demonstrates, nothing could be farther from the truth.

By almost any economic measurement, the 1930s encompassed the worst years of the 20th century - and Canadians, so reliant on exports and international trade, suffered more than most. The Depression was a disaster that seemed beyond the power of government to remedy. On a more personal level, for many it became a conglomeration of set-backs and family tragedies that seared an entire generation. It finally demolished the boundless optimism of the age of Laurier, when Canadians had been encouraged to believe the 20th century would belong to their rapidly developing country. A measure of that optimism had survived the Great War and the turbulence of the 1920s, but it did not survive the Depression. For a minority - those with secure employment or wealth - the '30s were a happy time, when money went a very long way indeed, but for most Canadians it was at best an ordeal and at worst a disaster. It was also a decade that forever changed the relationship between revenue-rich Ottawa and the impoverished provinces - enhancing the role of the first at the expense of the second. The resulting jurisdictional arguments would, in one form or another, bedevil federal-provincial relations into the 21st century.

The abrupt end of the Depression came at a terrible price. For a generation that had endured the Great War, an even greater global conflict seemed unthinkable. Yet that was not the case for the European fascists, for whom aggression was part of a perverted philosophy that brought on the most destructive war in history and resulted in the deaths of countless millions. Battered by the Depression, Canada was even less prepared for war in 1939 than it had been in 1914, yet the country was called upon to assume a much greater role than in the earlier war. That it did so is a triumph not fully appreciated by Canadians today. From the fall of France in 1940 until the U.S. entry into the war, Canada was Britain's major ally and arsenal in the fight against Hitler. During the Battle of Britain and the Battle of the Atlantic, Canadians helped stall the seemingly unstoppable German juggernaut - and in the process laid the foundations for eventual victory. Canadian forces played an important role in the battle for Italy, and fully one fifth of the troops who took part in the D-Day landings wore the maple leaf. In 1944 and 1945 the Canadian Army liberated a huge swath of northwest France, Belgium, and Holland from the Nazi tyranny. And at home the war involved a supreme national effort with a level of organization that still boggles the mind. That effort revolutionized Canadian industry and made possible an economic recovery that obliterated the ravages of the Depression.

The post-war years ushered in a period of such widespread prosperity that even Wilfrid Laurier would likely have been astonished. For the first time home ownership and a family vehicle became the norm for working Canadians, many of whom now joined the swelling ranks of the middle class. The Baby Boom, the Consumer Society, and the Welfare State all date from the great post-war boom. Those years also saw the establishment of Canadian citizenship and the onset of a second great wave of immigration that would swell Canadian cities and forever change the national character. They also marked the onset of the Cold War and the transformation of the Soviet Union from ally to enemy. This confrontation with yet another brand of totalitarianism led to involvement in a new war - one Ottawa preferred to label a "police action." The distinction was often lost on the men who fought and died in Korea.

In bringing this story alive with stunning photographs I am once again indebted to designer Dean Pickup. My friend and former colleague Mike Jenkinson (a historian as well as a journalist and editor) was kind enough to read an early version of the book and made a host of helpful suggestions. And in the uncertain world of Canadian publishing Curtis Stewart of CanMedia continues to demonstrate the nerves of a poker champion. I am indebted to them all.

Paul Stanway
Edmonton, Alberta,
December, 2006.

TABLE OF CONTENTS

PART THREE – 1946-1953

A Brave New World
The Post-War Baby Boom And The Age Of Materialism

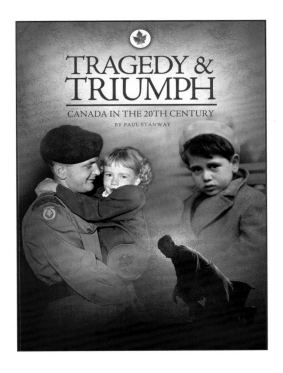

The Cover:

From the hardships of the Great Depression and the Prairie dustbowl, through the perilous years of World War Two, to the astonishing post-war boom and the arrival of a new wave of hopeful immigrants: The dramatic collage of images on the cover, created by graphic designer Dean Pickup, captures the tragedy and triumph of a turbulent quarter century during which Canada matured into an independent and prosperous nation.

PART ONE

1930-1939

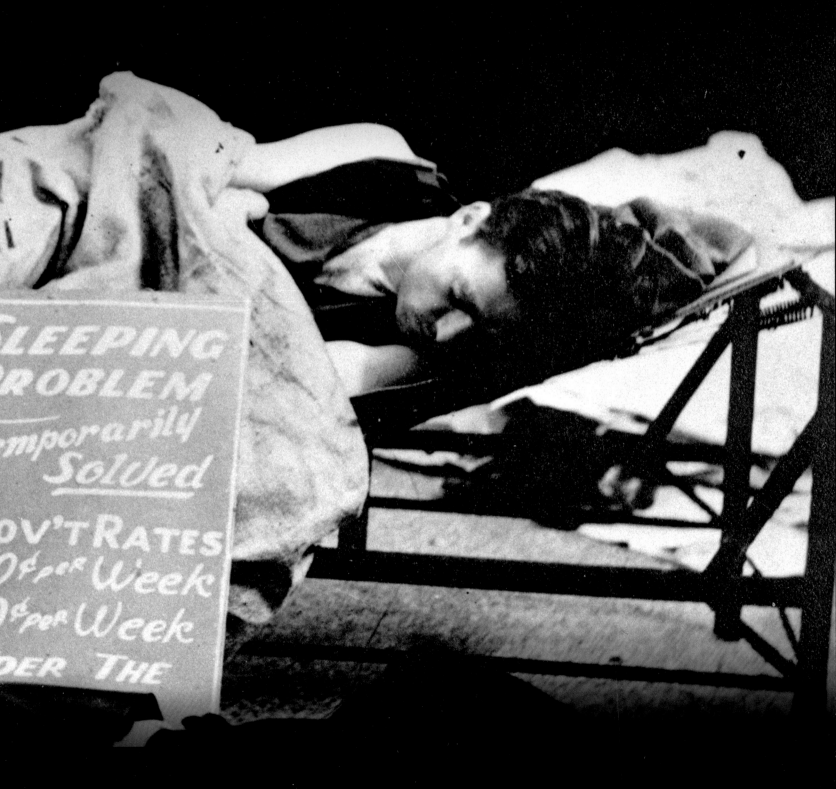

A place to sleep and something to eat became the daily goals of hundreds of thousands of Canadians during the Great Depression, particularly single men. It was, by almost any measure, the worst decade of the 20th century.

National Archives of Canada

A Bitter Harvest

Optimism, Prosperity Give Way
To A Decade Of Lost Dreams

'Men have been swindled by other men on many occasions.
The autumn of 1929 was, perhaps, the first occasion when men
succeeded on a large scale in swindling themselves.'

John Kenneth Galbraith

Two members of the growing number of unemployed (opposite page) wait to jump a freight train in Edmonton's Calder rail yards. They were part of an army of jobless who roamed Canada and the U.S. during the 1930s.

Provincial Archives of Alberta

*I*n the years between 1900 and 1929, Canada had the world's fastest growing economy, with only a brief recession after the Great War. There was international demand for the Dominion's products and resources: the country by now supplied half the world's wheat and 60% of its newsprint. Its growing cities hummed with industrial activity, and suburban development and the automobile were busy creating a new urban environment that would become the hallmark of the 20th century. Since the end of the war a decade of immigration had filled the vast internal empire of the Canadian Prairies, and in an age of furious innovation, aviation, the railways, radio, and the telephone had helped shrink the enormous distances and solitudes that had traditionally separated Canadians. Old-timers complained that the pace of life had become too hurried, the world too noisy, and people too preoccupied with material possessions. Yet there was a general sense of optimism and a firm belief that the coming decade would be one of growth and prosperity. Canada - Sir Wilfrid Laurier's "shining star" of the 20th century - would continue on its steady march toward the greatness predicted for it.

In fact the 1930s were destined to become a decade of lost hopes and shattered dreams, in Canada and across the industrialized world. The "Dirty Thirties" would forever alter the course of a tumultuous century and become a byword for deprivation, dislocation, and hardship. Canada, so dependent on exports, is by many historians considered to be the country hardest hit by what became known as the Great Depression. The economy fell further than that of any nation other than the United States, and Canada took longer to recover than did its neighbour.

The economic collapse affected Canadians in markedly different ways, barely touching some while searing the lives of others, but the terrible decade left no community or institution completely unscathed. As the global economy sputtered, much of Canada's newly-expanded industrial and agricultural production found itself suddenly unwanted and adrift. The economic setbacks were especially cruel for the newly-settled Prairies, where prolonged drought added to the woes of tens of thousands of farmers - not to mention the towns and cities that had grown up to provide them with goods and services.

There were many who believed that the Depression was the end result of a decade of rampant social change ("falling morals and rising hemlines") and self-indulgent materialism that encouraged people to live flagrantly beyond their means. Yet with the benefit of hindsight economists and historians now argue that the opposite was true. Less had actually changed since the Great War than most people thought, with the economic vitality of the 1920s being less substantial than it appeared. As the British economist John Maynard Keynes discerned early on, the problem was that modern technology allowed the industrialized nations to produce far more than people could yet afford to buy. As was the case across the developed world, the post-war prosperity of Canadians proved to be a mile wide and an inch deep, with most people only marginally better off than their parents or grandparents had been. In 1930 most of Canada's working class (60% of the population) earned a good deal less than $1,000 a year, yet the federal Department of Labour estimated that the average family needed $1,200 to $1,500 annually to ensure a "minimum standard of living." Too few consumers could actually afford the new household appliances, automobiles, and suburban affluence upon which economic growth increasingly depended.

None of this was readily apparent to the government in Ottawa, which at the time collected

Empty desks (above) at a school in Coaldale, Alberta. By the spring of 1930 school administrators and teachers across the country were becoming concerned about undernourished students. In Calgary the city council approved a plan to continue providing free milk to children through the summer holidays. Reports of the destitute rifling through garbage dumps began to appear in newspapers. The luckier unemployed might find seasonal work, like these people harvesting potatoes (opposite right) on a farm outside Ottawa.

Above: Glenbow Archives
Right: National Archives of Canada

few reliable statistics that might indicate where the economy was going. Why should it? Its role in the economy was limited. There was no central bank through which the government might have stimulated an expansion of credit. There was but one full-time economist in the federal civil service, and he worked for the Department of Foreign Affairs. Ottawa's responsibility for economic management was essentially limited to the setting of taxes and tariffs. Of course, then as now, politicians were not averse to claiming credit for a healthy economy. In fact, early in 1930 Prime Minister William Lyon Mackenzie King's government boasted of record employment levels - which had been true in 1929, but by the spring of 1930 employment was already falling sharply. Such "corrections" in the labour market were not surprising, argued the prime minister. There had been two brief economic downturns in 1920 and 1923, and they had not halted growth for long, so King resisted calls for Ottawa to aid the provinces in providing expanded unemployment relief, arguing that if they wanted to spend money on social programs they could raise it themselves. He found the notion of giving federal aid to provinces governed by Conservatives to be particularly distasteful. "With respect to giving monies out of the federal treasury to any Tory government in this country, for these alleged unemployment purposes, with these governments situated as they are today, with politics diametrically opposed to those of this government - I would not give them a five-cent piece!" he vowed.

Yet there were clear signs that the economy was turning sour. "The unnerving stock market declines since Thursday paled into insignificance beside the tidal wave of liquidation which flooded the Toronto and Montreal stock exchanges yesterday, and set prices crashing downward

in the greatest collapse ever witnessed in Canada," the *Toronto Globe* had breathlessly reported on October 30, 1929. "To see so many young men looking for work in town is most regrettable," noted the *Ponoka Herald* newspaper in Alberta. "The change has come so suddenly... How work is to be found for our unemployed is a great big problem." Auto registrations across the country -soaring during the late 1920s - suddenly went into free-fall. The operators of streetcar systems in Canada's larger towns and cities also noticed a sudden downturn in revenues as people decided to walk to work, or had no work to go to. Reports began to appear in newspapers of the destitute trolling through city garbage dumps. In Calgary the city councillors were asked to approve a plan to continue providing milk to children through the 1930 school holidays, since many of the youngsters "were clearly undernourished."

There were also mounting difficulties with Canada's largest trading partner, the United States. Some years earlier President Warren Harding had praised the deepening relationship between the two nations, trumpeting the development of a continental economy and culture. "We think the same thoughts, live the same lives, and cherish the same aspirations of service to each other in time of need," Harding enthused. "Since the end of the (1914-18) war, Americans have invested $2.5 billion in Canada. It's a lot of money, and I don't doubt is it being used wisely for us and in very useful ways for you." At least from a Canadian perspective, that would be a question that would come to dominate the relationship between the two nations. More than half of Canadian industry was by now American owned, two thirds of Canadian union members belonged to associations headquartered south of the border, and it was predominantly American radio and movies that entertained Canadians. But in the wake of the Wall Street Crash of October 29, 1929, all that was forgotten as $30 billion in stock value suddenly vanished from the U.S. economy - as if it had never existed! The protectionist Smoot-Hawley trade bill passed by the American Congress in the summer of 1930 dealt Canada's trade-dependent economy a lethal blow, eventually cutting exports to the U.S. by 60%.

Unperturbed by the deteriorating economy, Prime Minister King decided to call an election that summer, cutting the federal sales tax to 1% to ensure the expected positive result at the ballot box. He recorded in his diary that he had also consulted a Kingston, Ontario psychic, a Mrs. Bleaney, who found the omens more promising for 1930 than 1931 - and had predicted a great Liberal victory, with massive support from the West. During the campaign King virtually ignored the floundering economy, and also the advice of Labour Minister Peter Heenan to tackle head on the issue of 400,000 unemployed. King thought it "wiser to leave (that) matter alone." It was a fatal mistake. In Regina, Calgary, and Edmonton, crowds of unemployed workers drowned out the prime minister's speeches, roaring "Five-cent-piece! Five-cent-piece!" These were not the only disruptions. During a campaign visit to Halifax a horse pulling a garbage cart broke away from its driver and joined the prime minister's parade, much to the delight of accompanying reporters. Then, as King was about to speak, part of the grandstand collapsed, and by the time repairs had been made half the audience had gone home.

By contrast, the energetic new Conservative leader, R.B. Bennett, made the faltering economy the central issue of a slick campaign. In Moncton, New Brunswick, the Calgarian boldly predicted "the Conservative Party is going to find work for all those who are willing to work - or perish in the attempt." Sixty-year-old Bennett, wealthy and supremely confident, radiated businesslike competence. He promised emergency relief, and a big hike in import tariffs (a home-grown Smoot-Hawley bill). Restricting imports would bring Canada's trading partners to their senses and, according to Bennett, "blast a way into the markets of the world" for Canadian goods. The Tory leader's campaign was a model of energy and activity. He travelled 20,000 kilometres,

It was common in the 1920s for banks to bolster public confidence by advertising their capital and reserves, as on the windows of this branch of the Bank of Nova Scotia in Calgary (opposite page). There were those who suggested the economy was, in fact, vulnerable to collapse, but few Canadians paid them any attention.

Glenbow Archives

crossing the country twice and visiting every province. He delivered an amazing 107 major speeches, each one a torrent of condemnation aimed at a "group of mercenaries holding office by shame and subterfuge". His speeches may not have been models of oratory, but they radiated self-confidence and can-do enthusiasm.

At the end of the election campaign the popular vote was split between the two major parties, but a Tory breakthrough in Quebec and the Prairies handed Bennett a majority. The new prime minister quickly recalled Parliament and passed legislation providing for $20 million in emergency relief. It seemed to be a good start, but in reality Bennett had seriously underestimated the extent of the growing depression, and in common with many other political leaders he failed to see the contradiction in suggesting increased protectionism as a tonic for failing international trade. If enthusiasm and confidence could have defeated the Great Depression, Canada's economy would have been quickly revived. It was not.

In the 1931 federal election Labour Minister Peter Heenan urged the government of Prime Minister Mackenzie King to tackle head on the plight of the unemployed - by then numbering over 400,000 (including these men, below, sleeping in emergency accommodation). King thought it wiser to remain silent on the matter and let it blow over.

Glenbow Archives

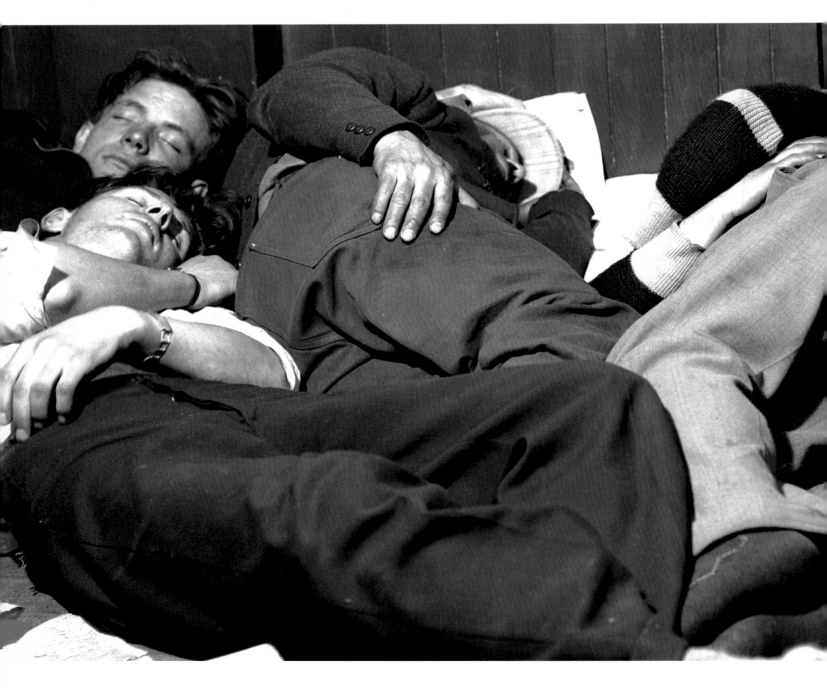

World trade declined dramatically as credit dried up, which was disaster for Canada - then as now heavily dependent for its prosperity upon the export of natural resources and manufactured goods. The U.S. raised duties on Canadian cattle, dairy produce, and poultry, which hit farm incomes across the country. Newsprint demand fell 45%. The export value of non-ferrous metals dropped 60%. The Atlantic fishery was also hit hard when Spain, Portugal, and Italy restricted the import of dried fish, and the sudden glut of cheap meat and eggs that could no longer be exported cut fresh fish prices in half. But nowhere was the impact of the Depression more immediate or dramatic than on the Prairies, heavily dependent on wheat exports. The price of wheat began a rapid descent to an all-time low of 45 cents a bushel (25 cents below the cost of production). An optimistic Canadian Wheat Pool had set its interim payment to producers at a much higher rate than the actual market price, while a large part of the 1929 crop remained unsold. Prairie governments covered the shortfall for a time, but with their economies in turmoil they were running short of money.

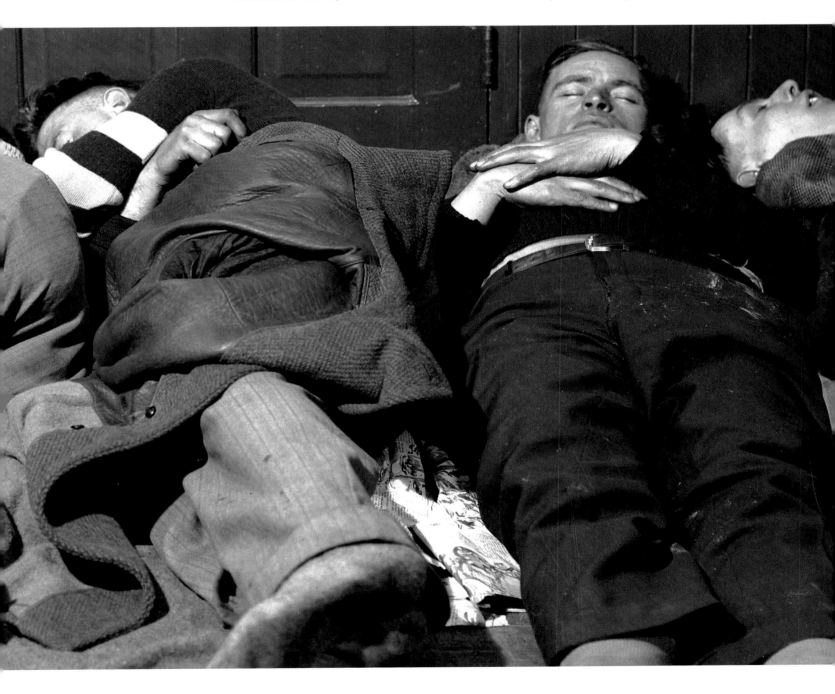

Calgary's 8th Avenue in the late 1920s. The bustling city was typical of the optimism and growth in the decade after the Great War, but all of that was about to change as the economy collapsed and the West in particular found that markets for its exports disappeared in a matter of months.

Glenbow Archives

In the midst of all this economic gloom and doom, Canada quietly celebrated the final and most significant political landmark in its development as an independent nation. Prime Minister Bennett attended the 1930 Imperial Conference in London and on behalf of Canada put his signature to the Statute of Westminster, which granted formal independence to the empire's self-governing dominions (Canada, Newfoundland, Australia, New Zealand, South Africa, and the Irish Free State). The British had been waiting impatiently since 1927 to adopt the new legislation, while Ottawa argued with the provinces (primarily Ontario and Quebec) over an amending formula for a new Canadian constitution. When Bennett arrived in London there was still no deal (and there wouldn't be one for another half century), and so it was agreed that the document confirming the nation's independence would remain in London - safely beyond the reach of federal-provincial arguments. It was a bitter-sweet moment for the young country, though few Canadians appreciated it at the time.

Not surprisingly, though, the main item on the agenda at the Imperial Conference was the looming economic crisis. Bennett argued - unsuccessfully - for the creation of an imperial trade zone. His timing was off. The British were willing to support trade within the Empire, but as the world's biggest exporter they were still trying vainly to revive global free trade. The prime minister's trip to London meant he had missed "Canadian Prosperity Week," a morale-boosting event that featured inspirational talks by business leaders appearing at Famous Players cinemas across the country. Bennett contributed a short, cheery, filmed speech in which he assured Canadians that the economy was "fundamentally sound" and sure to improve rapidly with his energetic new policies. It did not.

Canada at the beginning of the 1930s was already well on its way to becoming a very different country than the one created by the Fathers of Confederation. At the time of the country's first national census, 1871, more than 90% of the population lived on farms and in small rural villages. The only communities that could rightly be called cities were Montreal (107,000), Quebec City (60,000), and Toronto (56,000). In 1931 a new census confirmed Montreal was still Canada's largest metropolis, with a population of 819,000, but at 631,000 Toronto had unqestionably become the nation's second city - and that number did not take into account the 200,000 people who now lived around Toronto in bustling suburbs such as York, Scarborough, and Etobicoke. The census showed that for the first time a majority of Canadians lived in urban centres, and of those there were now more than two dozen with populations in excess of 50,000. Vancouver had been little more than a village in the last decade of the 19th century, but by 1931 it had surpassed Winnipeg (219,000) to become Canada's third largest city with a quarter of a million inhabitants. Edmonton had been a trading post for well over a century, but its population numbered only about 4,000 when Alberta entered Confederation in 1905. It had by now grown to almost 80,000, and Calgary was even larger at 85,000. By contrast, Halifax (59,000) and St. John (48,000) had been the fourth and fifth largest urban centres in the country at the time of Confederation, but by 1931 had slipped to 13th and 15th place respectively. The urbanization and westward movement of Canadians had become well-established trends.

However, the emergence of this new Canada would be put on hold as the Great Depression halted economic growth and stalled immigration and development. The impact of all this upon ordinary Canadians varied greatly by region and individual circumstance. In the first three years of the new decade prices fell faster than wages, so if you had a steady job you might actually have had a little more purchasing power. Even a 10% wage cut for civil servants imposed by the federal government - and imitated by most provinces and large companies - failed to seriously damage living standards for the employed. In eastern Canada farmers suffered from falling commodity

STATUTE OF WESTMINSTER

An Act to give effect to certain resolutions passed by Imperial
Conferences held in the years 1926 and 1930.

11th December, 1931.

WHEREAS the delegates to His Majesty's Governments in the United Kingdom, the Dominion of Canada, the Commonwealth of Australia, the Dominion of New Zealand, the Union of South Africa, the Irish Free State, and Newfoundland, at Imperial Conferences holden at Westminster in the years of our Lord nineteen hundred and twenty six and nineteen hundred and thirty did concur in making declarations and resolutions set forth in the Reports of the said Conferences:

And whereas it is meet and proper to set out by way of preamble to this Act, inasmuch as the Crown is the symbol of the free association of the members of the British Commonwealth of Nations, and as they are united by a common allegiance to the Crown...

NOW, THEREFORE, BE IT ENACTED by the King's Most Excellent Majesty, by and with the advice and consent of the Lords Spiritual and Temporal, and Commons, in this present Parliament assembled, and by the authority of the same, as follows:

1. The Colonial Laws Validity Act, 1865, shall not apply to any law made after the commencement of this Act by the Parliament of a Dominion.

2. No law and no provision of any law made after the commencement of this Act by the Parliament of a Dominion shall be void or inoperative on the ground that it is repugnant to the law of England, or to the provisions of any existing or future Act of Parliament of the United Kingdom... and the powers of the Parliament of a Dominion shall include the power to repeal or amend any such Act, order, rule or regulation in so far as the same is part of the law of the Dominion.

3. It is hereby declared and enacted that the Parliament of a Dominion has full power to make laws having extra-territorial operation.

4. No Act of Parliament of the United Kingdom passed after the commencement of this Act shall extend, or be deemed to extend, to a Dominion as part of the law of that Dominion, unless it is expressly declared in that Act that the Dominion has requested, and has consented to, the enactment thereof...

The Statute of Westminster, enacted just before Christmas, 1931, began Britain's long process of voluntarily dismantling the largest empire in history. For the first time it officially recognized the existence of the British Commonwealth as the Empire's successor, and gave full political independence to the countries named - including the right to enter into international treaties on their own behalf. For Canada it was the culmination of a steady march to independence from Britain - but the moment passed with little public interest at home, and as it would be half a century before the document confirming Canada's sovereignty was officially "repatriated" from Britain to form the basis of a new Canadian Constitution.

prices and the occasional foreclosure, but there was enough food to eat and the rural population actually increased. By contrast, in the West the 1930s brought collapsing grain prices, drought, grasshoppers, and literal starvation. On the parched southern Prairies there was often no living at all to be made, and in many cases the only possible choice was to abandon the land. Some 30,000 farm families were forced to make that awful choice. It was a setback of monumental proportions. The settling of Canada's great hinterland had been the country's proudest achievement of the first three decades of the century. At the end of the 1920s the residents of the new provinces of Alberta and Saskatchewan (founded in 1905) were among the most prosperous Canadians. Alberta's annual per-capita income, $548, was number two in the country, and Saskatchewan's, $478, was fourth. Those numbers were now cut by two-thirds. Saskatchewan became the poorest province in the country, and the governments of both Saskatchewan and Alberta were facing bankruptcy.

The situation was just as dire in Newfoundland, like Canada a self-governing Dominion (since 1907) struggling to further its own nationhood. Without outside assistance, welfare payments amounted to just six cents a day, and when the fishery collapsed many people were faced with destitution and starvation. There was talk of selling off Labrador, but there were no takers. An angry crowd of 10,000 people marched on the Colonial Building in St. John's intent on overturning the government of Prime Minister Richard Squires - and perhaps do him physical harm. Squires went into hiding, but the demonstration did force an election. When Newfoundland's banks failed the new government called on Britain to resume responsibility for its former colony, which London reluctantly did. A Royal Commission, headed by Scottish peer Baron Amulree, issued a gloomy report on Newfoundland's prospects. It advocated a return to direct rule from Britain. Acting on the report's recommendations, Newfoundland's legislators voted to abandon self-government. For a fiercely proud and independent people it was an unmitigated disaster.

On the Prairies the problem of collapsing grain prices was compounded by a worsening drought. Between Cadillac and Kincaid, Saskatchewan, this farmer (below) seems helpless as he contemplates the topsoil drifting off his fields.

National Archives of Canada

Members of the Single Men's Unemployed Association parade along Toronto's Bathurst Street in 1930. Correctly reading the public mood, energetic Conservative leader R.B. Bennett promised swift action to tackle unemployment - and led his party to a solid majority victory.

Across Canada, for the growing number of unemployed, and for farmers who were forced off the land, there was no alternative but relief. Distributed by municipalities in the time-honoured traditional of local responsibility for the destitute, this was most often cumbersome and ineffective. The Bennett government's Relief Act of 1930 attempted to create a national framework for aiding the unemployed, but it was a good idea badly implemented. The $20 million set aside for relief was distributed on the basis of population rather than need, resulting in some absurd anomalies. In the Vancouver area, for example, working-class Burnaby received $54,000, or $67.50 for each of its 800 unemployed. Upscale West Vancouver collected much less, $15,000, but with only 35 residents on relief that amounted to $428.57 for each one! These inequalities were national in scope. In prosperous London, Ontario, for example the average payment to families on relief was around $40-a-month, while in Halifax it was $18, and in Toronto, Montreal, or the mining towns of Cape Breton it could be less than $10.

To make matters worse, Ottawa's portion of the relief (40%) took months to trickle through federal and provincial bureaucracies, forcing municipalities to go into debt to feed and

A group of unemployed men (below) arriving at an emergency relief camp at RCAF Station Trenton in southern Ontario. In its first year in office the Bennett government spent an unprecedented $20 million on such projects, without making a serious dent in the unemployment problem.

National Archives of Canada

clothe residents. At the end of the day, interest and administration costs - all borne by the municipalities - often ate up half of the money made available. And with no trained staff to distribute relief, and no money to hire any, the front-line responsibilities fell to a ramshackle collection of private charities and hastily-organized emergency relief committees. It was far from being a well-oiled machine.

The qualifications imposed on the unemployed were often also very harsh, demanding the liquidation of virtually everything a family owned: automobiles, telephones, appliances, furniture, electric lights (one light bulb was allowed), and even pets. Once a family was deemed to be without assets, municipalities provided food vouchers, basic clothing, and sometimes access to an overworked doctor. Since most women didn't work outside the home, there was often no provision at all for their clothing or personal needs. The new profession of social work found an immediate niche within these government relief programs, weeding out alleged fraud and waste, rather than improving distribution. In Montreal, where 30% of the population was on relief, schools distributed free milk to children who weighed 10% or more below the norm for their age. But only if the family was deemed to be truly in need. After the weeding out process only half the malnourished children actually got free milk.

For many who endured relief it was a never-to-be-forgotten experience. Winnipeg journalist and historian James H. Gray later wrote about the frustrations of life on what was known dismissively as the dole. "The closest any of us on relief ever got to socially useful labour was sawing cordwood, but we were drafted periodically for all the make-work projects, like raking leaves, picking rock, digging dandelions, and tidying up back lanes. These 'boondoggles' as the *Chicago Tribune* was later to christen them, were devised to enable us to work off the assistance we received, and our services were demanded for a couple of days once a month. It was all justified on the grounds that the exercise would be good for us, that working would improve our morale, and that by providing us with a token opportunity to work for our relief, we would be freed of the stigma of accepting charity. None of these dubious propositions had much validity. The fatuous nature of the projects the authorities invented quickly brought the entire make-work concept into disrepute."

Gray made another astonishing discovery about relief when his weight dropped to 54 kilograms and it was thought he had tuberculosis. He was declared "medically unfit" for work and moved from the ranks of the unemployed to those on welfare. "We thought little of the change, until a box of groceries arrived to keep us for a month." He was also moved to a tuberculosis sanatorium for treatment, where he was well treated and well fed - at least until it was discovered that he did not have tuberculosis after all. "I made this shattering discovery," he later recalled. "As long as I was a broken-down liability to society I got lavish attention. Once I was restored to the status of a healthy asset, able and willing to work, nobody wanted me. Least of all the Relief Department."

Tuberculosis, the highly contagious "white death", was a dreaded disease in the 1930s. Every city had a sanatorium, where patients were sent to recover or die. Isolation had long been the only method of prevention endorsed by government. The disease was known to spread through fresh milk from infected herds of cattle, and some doctors had for years been advocating the pasteurization (flash boiling) of all milk. That was strenuously opposed by dairy farmers, but finally Ontario Premier Mitch Hepburn (a farmer himself) backed the move and his government ordered the pasteurization of all milk sold in that province. Other provinces eventually adopted similar legislation. It added slightly to the cost of milk, but saved thousands of lives each year.

The 1931 census confirmed that bustling Montreal, with just over 800,000 people, remained Canada's largest city. But by that year 30% of the city's population was on relief, and for many soup kitchens such as this one were the only source of a hot meal.

The Favero family (opposite page), after a successful fishing expedition near Nordegg, Alberta. Left to right, Jelindo, Edward, mother Jean, and family friend Howard Price. Price and Jerry Favero (the children's father) were coal miners, but like so many during the 1930s they were forced to supplement the family larder with fishing, hunting, and perhaps a garden plot. For those without work, sawing cordwood was often "the closest any of us on relief ever got to socially useful work," recalled Winnipeg journalist and historian James H. Gray. The photo above shows men on relief delivering wood near Valcartier, Quebec, in January 1932.

National Archives of Canada Photos

Inefficient relief may have been, but inexpensive it was not. In his speeches Prime Minister Bennett continued to fiercely resist the idea of widespread government welfare. "I will not permit this country, with my voice or my vote, to ever become committed to the dole system," he thundered. But in reality there was no other solution at hand. Between 1930 and 1937 the cost of relief and associated public works totalled close to $1 billion. It was the first time such a gargantuan number had been associated with Canadian government spending. It was also the first time government, at any level, had been called upon to maintain public welfare on such a scale. Relief payments from Ottawa, plus loans to the four western provinces so they could avoid bankruptcy, went far beyond the traditional transfers provided for in the constitution.

Nevertheless, nothing governments did seemed to have much impact on the growing number of unemployed, which topped 500,000 at the end of 1931 and would eventually peak at 713,000 - one in every three of Canada's non-agricultural workforce. Barter became commonplace and ingenuity thrived in an economy where money was in short supply. The pre-Depression boom in automobile ownership, for example, left many farmers with vehicles they couldn't sell and could no longer afford to operate. Rather than leave them useless, many removed the engine and hitched the chassis behind a horse, which was much cheaper to run. The resulting transportation, known derisively as the "Bennett buggy", came to define an era in which you made do with what you had.

The prime minister's inability to deal with the Depression steadily ate away at him, as did the constant criticism that he was unfeeling and impervious to the hardship all around him. The latter was far from true. Bennett received thousands of letters from Canadians pleading for help, which often reduced him to tears. Many of the letters still survive. War veteran Richard O'Hearn, of Southwark, Alberta, wrote to inform the prime minister that he had but two loaves of bread in his home to feed his wife and three children - and nothing to spread on the bread. One of his children was already severely malnourished. There were eggs to be had, wrote O'Hearn, but the

family had eaten almost nothing else for days and could no longer keep them down. With no broader solution to offer, Bennett often replied personally to such pleas with an encouraging note and a $5 or $10 bill from his own pocket. Mrs. Thomas Perkins, of Kingdom, Saskatchewan, wrote to the prime minister to ask if he could order her husband some underwear from the Eaton catalogue. "I have patched and darned his old underwear for the last two years, but they are completely done now," she reported. Bennett duly paid for Thomas's new underwear. Other letters, such as one signed "Sudbury Starving Unemployed," expressed the popular view that Bennett had somehow single-handedly caused the Depression and had it within his power to fix the situation. "Since you have been elected, work has been impossible to get. We have decided that in a month from this date, if things are the same, we'll skin you alive first chance we get."

By 1932, unemployment was so high that the Bennett government brought down a second Relief Act, which among other measures established camps to provide unemployed single men with a subsistence living and regular work. These men had been at the end of the line in terms of public assistance. It was still widely believed - particularly among politicians - that there was work out there, if only you searched diligently for it. As a result many thousands of men were refused relief and joined the army of unemployed riding railway boxcars across the country in search of a job or, more immediately, a meal. First the provinces and now the Department of Defence opened camps to control this human tide, paying men a dollar a day to clear bush, build highways, or restore public buildings. After food, accommodation, and other expenses were deducted, these relief workers were usually left with around 20 cents a day.

Some 20,000 unmarried, unemployed men would eventually spend time in these miserable camps. They were also supposed to keep young men out of trouble and defuse any possibility that the unemployed could be organized to open revolt. "In these ragged platoons, here are the prospective members of what Marx called the 'industrial reserve army,' the storm troopers of the revolution, "warned Gen. Andrew McNaughton, the government's military chief. Such suspicion of the unemployed was widespread, but ironically the camps had the effect of politicising many

Ladies of the relief society of the Church of Jesus Christ of Latter-Day Saints (above), Calgary chapter, in the early days of the Great Depression. Volunteer groups such as these played a major role in both collecting donations for the poor and distributing government relief.

National Archives of Canada

of the men. "In those bunkhouses there were more men reading Marx, Lenin, and Stalin than there were reading girlie magazines," wrote Ronald Liversedge, a jobless British immigrant who spent time in the camps.

During the first two years of its mandate the Conservative government had actively promoted spending on public works and had gone into deficit to do it. Potentially the largest job creation project the Bennett Tories proposed was the creation of a waterway navigable by ocean-going vessels to link the Atlantic with the industrial hinterland around the Great Lakes. U.S. President Herbert Hoover's administration also supported the idea of a St. Lawrence Deep Waterway, but it eventually foundered in the U.S. Senate, where representatives from the Atlantic states were concerned about its impact on East Coast ports. But by the spring of 1932, faced with the growing cost of his public works policy, Bennett's resolve seemed to evaporate (a recurring problem). Alberta Premier John Brownlee spoke for the cash-strapped western provinces when he pointed out that direct relief to the unemployed would be much cheaper than expensive public works - even if Ottawa loaned the provinces their share of the relief money. "I do not see how we can go on piling up capital expenditure," argued Brownlee. "People cannot expect the state to supply work for everyone." So the Bennett government reversed itself. There would be no more money for public works, but Ottawa would contribute to direct relief. Single men who did not qualify could be deployed as farm labourers, and urban families were offered $600 (spread over three years) if they agreed to settle vacant farmland. Immigration and Colonization Minister W.A. Gordon confidently predicted that 200,000 of the "unemployed and surplus city population" would be resettled, but the actual number was closer to 20,000.

There was an Imperial Trade Conference in Ottawa in the summer of 1932, which the prime minister used to once again promote his idea of an Imperial economic union. It would be "the

Fruit pickers line up for work (below) in Vancouver, B.C. The province's largest city became a hotbed of protest, with a number of violent confrontations between the unemployed and police. At one point Mayor Gerry McGeer was forced to read the Riot Act to disperse angry crowds besieging City Hall.

foundation of a new economic Empire in which Canada is destined to play a part of ever-increasing importance," he enthused. Sunday, July 17, was designated a "national day of prayer" so that concerned Canadians could implore the Almighty to lend a hand in the negotiations. The conference was the first substantial international event hosted by the Canadian capital, and for almost a month a parade of dignitaries from all corners of the Empire were chauffeured in a fleet of Buick limousines between official meetings, banquets and receptions. The $300,000 price tag raised eyebrows, but the endless public professions of Imperial solidarity from the various delegations suggested real progress was being made.

The truth was rather different. By this time Britain's efforts on behalf of global free trade had utterly failed and a coalition government was in power that was inclined to make trade agreements where it could. Britain agreed to lower tariffs for a range of Canadian exports, while Bennett agreed not to raise Canadian import taxes any higher than the 50% he'd already imposed. It was hailed as good news for Canadian exporters of wheat, lumber, apples, and bacon, but in reality the desire among all participants to protect domestic industries had trumped any real commitment to substantially lower trade barriers. Behind closed doors the negotiations had often degenerated into mean-spirited and nasty haggling. British politicians grumbled that the

Relief workers toil on a road project (below) near Drumheller, Alberta. Originally proposed to keep the unemployed too busy to cause trouble, the concept of work camps backfired when they became breeding grounds for political agitation.

Glenbow Archives

hard-nosed and demanding Bennett had tried to take advantage of the deepening economic crisis, while the Canadians complained of British arrogance and divisions among representatives of the coalition government of British Prime Minister Ramsay MacDonald. It was not the Empire's finest hour.

The failure to secure a meaningful Imperial trade deal at the Ottawa conference shattered Bennett's vow to restore prosperity by improving demand for Canadian exports, and left his legendary confidence seriously dented. Not only had his boundless energy and 16-hour work days failed to blunt the Depression, things were actually getting much worse. Work began to pile up on the prime minister's desk, mail went unanswered, and for the first time it was acknowledged within government that perhaps the great man did not have all the answers to the economic crisis. An editorial in the *Lethbridge Herald* noted that "the chastening hand of the Depression is beginning to tell on the prime minister".

In 1933 there were signs on the southern Prairies that the drought might be breaking, but in the better weather grasshoppers thrived. They stripped every farm and garden between Brandon and Calgary. Official surveys found 18 million acres of Prairie farmland, one quarter of all the arable land in Canada, stricken by drought. As many as six million acres had been seriously damaged by wind erosion as a result of the drought, and 300,000 acres were deemed to have become desert. All in all, land which had previously supported some 900,000 prosperous people now struggled to provide a minimal livelihood. The Red Cross estimated that 125,000 Prairie farm families were destitute. James Gray had found himself a job as a reporter on the *Winnipeg Free Press* and was

sent across the Prairies to describe conditions. His reports made grim reading. "The cloud of dust that trailed after us began to seep into the car. Our clothes stuck to us, and the seat of the car was damp with sweat. I could feel blisters developing on my feet from the concentrated heat of the floorboards. From Lethbridge to Winnipeg, temperatures rose to the 100 degree [F] mark [37 C], and stayed there for days on end. Each day seemed hotter than the day before. The hot winds grew stronger and the dust clouds that hung over the whole of the mid-continent grew thicker and thicker. By the second week in July the crop was gone."

Immigration dropped to levels not seen since the 1880s, and for the first time in the 20th century the country saw a net decline in population due to emigration, mostly to the U.S. Two million people were surviving on government assistance - the hated relief. Canada's national income had been cut by almost 45%, and almost one in four working Canadians was officially unemployed. Not surprisingly, the Depression also increased tension between employers and workers, and labour relations - not the best even before 1930 - increasingly turned violent. The shortcomings of capitalism seemed obvious, and talk of overthrowing liberal democracy and replacing it with revolutionary socialism put governments on edge.

Radical labour organizations had sprung up across Canada after the Great War, but until the 1930s trade unions in Canada had been generally conservative and dominated by "craft" organizations representing carpenters, railwaymen, metal workers and other tradesmen. But in the face of wage reductions and unemployment, radicalism now prospered and new unions emerged that

Frontier College, an organization dedicated to bringing education to remote work camps, continued its work through the grim Depression years. In this photo (opposite left), taken in 1930, a group of Northern Ontario workers are attending a class in a converted railway boxcar. The demand for automobiles dropped off sharply with the onset of the Depression, but the army of unemployed provided a workforce for expanding and improving Canada's fledgling road system. In this photo (above) relief workers are widening the highway between Calgary and Banff.

National Archives of Canada Photos

organized entire factories or industries. In the U.S. these industrial unions had organized themselves into the Congress of Industrial Organizations (CIO), and they became very active in Canada.

The expanding labour movement needed organizers, and first in the U.S. and then in Canada it often found them among members of the Communist Party - which further unsettled governments concerned by talk of overthrowing the established order. It was a combustible situation. In Estevan, Saskatchewan, Mounties opened fire on demonstrating miners, killing three people. In Stratford, Ontario, the militia - complete with armoured vehicles - were deployed against striking furniture workers. Protests against unsafe working conditions in B.C.'s lumber industry led to several violent confrontations between workers and police. Demonstrations were common, and sometimes degenerated into violence. In one typical commotion a group of the unemployed occupied and damaged the Hudson's Bay store in downtown Vancouver, before marching on City Hall. Mayor Gerry McGeer read the Riot Act and the police moved in. The ensuing running battle lasted several hours before order was restored.

Most people found it hard to believe their Canadian-born fellow citizens would actually foment revolution, but they weren't so sure about those born abroad. Newspaper accounts covering demonstrations and labour unrest invariably noted the foreign accents and backgrounds of the demonstrators, whether they were Polish, Ukrainian, Italian, or - as in the case of Canadian Communist leader Tim Buck - British. Some 28,000 foreign-born "agitators" would eventually be deported, most to Europe. An unknown number were deported to Nazi Germany, where some were jailed and tragically a few were even lost to Hitler's concentration camps. Ottawa outlawed communism and Communist Party leaders were arrested, including Buck who was jailed for five years for sedition.

Packaging A Miracle

The Tragic Tale Of The Dionne Quints

Babies Annette, Emilie, Yvonne, Cecile and Marie attracted worldwide attention after their birth at Corbeil, Ontario, to Elzire Dionne on 28 May, 1934. The quintuplets were two months premature, and together weighed less than 14 pounds. Each of the babies could be held in an adult palm. With only two previous cases of quintuplet births on record, they were the first to survive for more than a few days. But survive they did. They were put by an open stove to keep warm, and mothers from surrounding villages brought breast milk for them. Against all odds, they made it through their first critical days. This miracle, plus their baby cuteness, the poverty of their parents, and a controversy over their guardianship, made them an international media sensation during the 1930s.

Citing a threat of exploitation by their parents (it was said their father, Oliva, had talked about exhibiting them for money), the Ontario government assumed guardianship and placed them in a special hospital - built across the road from the Dionne farmhouse - under the care of Dr. Allan Roy Dafoe, the physician who had delivered them. Whether there was a real threat of family exploitation has long been a matter of dispute, but the girls' subsequent public exploitation cannot be in doubt. The hospital was turned into a tourist attraction, called Quintland, with up to 6,000 people a day viewing the girls from behind a one-way screen. Their parents, made unwelcome, became irregular visitors.

The Dionne quintuplets were a medical miracle when they were born two months premature on May 28, 1934, and subject for scientific study when they became the first quintuplets to survive beyond a few days. But it was their undoubted cuteness (readily seen in these three photos) that made them an international media phenomenon. They were the subject of several movies, and the province of Ontario turned them into a multi-million-dollar tourist attraction. Among their many visitors was Queen Elizabeth (the Queen Mother), who paid them a visit during the 1939 royal tour of Canada.

The quintuplets with their father Oliva (right). Within weeks of their birth, their poverty-stricken parents had allegedly signed a contract with an American company giving them the rights to tour the girls as an exhibition. Ontario Premier Mitch Hepburn stepped in to have any contract annulled, and the girls were made wards of the province - with Labour Minister David Croll as their legal guardian. The parents, the father in particular, had limited access as they grew up (below), but after a bitter nine-year custody battle they were eventually able to bring their children home (shortly after the photo on the opposite page was taken).

Ontario Provincial Archives Photos

Between 1934 and 1943, about 3 million people visited Quintland. The government and local community made an estimated half-billion dollars from the girls' commercial exploitation. Under Dafoe's supervision, the sisters became Canada's biggest tourist attraction. All aspects of their behaviour, from the food they ate to their emotions, were studied by medical staff under the dubious guise of scientific research. Cecile later said she learned the word "doctor" before she learned "mother." It was dehumanizing, she told a British newspaper in a 1995 interview. "It was a circus." Hollywood fictionalized their story in three movies, and dozens of commercial endorsements - everything from corn syrup to Quaker Oats - swelled a trust fund for the girls to nearly $1 million.

After nine years and a bitter custody fight between their parents and the Ontario government, the girls finally moved back home. They lived at home until they were 18, after which they moved to Montreal and broke off almost all contact with their parents. Three - Annette, Cecile and Marie - eventually married. Emilie, an epileptic, entered a convent and died of a seizure in 1954. The four survivors told their often bitter story in a best-selling book, *We Were Five*, published in 1965. Marie died of a stroke in February 1970. The remaining three girls shared the final instalment of the much depleted trust fund a few years later. In 1995, a new biography (*Family Secrets*) contained suggestions that the girls were abused by their father after their return home, although they were never substantiated. Three years later the Ontario government announced that it would pay the three surviving quints - Yvonne, Cecile, and Annette - $4 million in compensation for the years spent on display as a public attraction. ■

A troop of RCMP officers (below) ride down Victoria Avenue in Blairmore, Alberta. Blairmore gained much attention in 1935 when it elected the country's first communist town council and school board. Victoria Avenue was renamed after Canadian Communist Party leader Tim Buck, shown in the photo opposite speaking to a crowd in Blairmore. Buck was jailed for five years for his political activities, and for many working people he became something of a folk hero. Released from prison (after serving half his sentence), he was welcomed at a rally in Toronto that drew 17,000 people.

Glenbow Archives Photos

The mining town of Blairmore, Alberta, gained national attention in 1935 when it elected Canada's first Communist town council and a Communist school board. One of the council's first acts was to declare a civic holiday on November 9, the anniversary of Russia's Bolshevik revolution, and to rename the town's main thoroughfare, Victoria Avenue, after Tim Buck - whose birthday also rated a civic holiday. But there was some question as to just how Communist Blairmore's council and school board actually were. All the elected officials had been nominated by the Mine Workers Union of Canada, which was indeed a Communist controlled union, but the town's new mayor, Bill Knight (like Buck, a British immigrant), claimed he was not a Red. "There is not a real Communist on either the council or the school board," the mayor told the *Lethbridge Herald*. "We are in sympathy with the Communist Party, that is true, and I think the way out (of the Depression) lies in communism, but this is a workers' government that Blairmore has."

And an exemplary government it proved to be, keeping the community debt-free, buying a new snow plough and an automatic fire alarm, rebuilding its water system, and improving roads and sidewalks. There was also a new municipal bathhouse, again named after Buck. Even the town's business leaders thought Knight's council was doing a pretty good job, although they didn't much like the additional civic holidays. Mayor Knight's reticence regarding membership of the Communist Party might have had something to do with the fact that such membership was technically illegal in any province that cared to enforce Section 98 of the Criminal Code of Canada (a draconian measure originally designed to terminate the Winnipeg General Strike of 1919). Alberta did not, and within two years Blairmore's communist experiment was fading and Tim Buck Boulevard was once again Victoria Avenue.

The Great Depression forever altered the Canadian political landscape and public perceptions of the role of government in economic and social life. The inability of either the Liberal or Conservative parties to respond to the economic collapse encouraged many people to consider alternatives at the federal and provincial level. While the new parties and personalities proved no better at tackling the Depression, they did widen the political debate to challenge previous notions of limited government involvement in the economy and social issues. The Depression appeared to many people to be a failure of both capitalism and limited government, and there began a steady shift towards interventionist public policy that would frame national debate and public expectations for the next half century.

The leaders of both national parties were generally sceptical about demands for government to take greater responsibility for the economy or become permanently involved in social welfare programs.

This dramatic photo graphically illustrates the disaster that befell so many farmers on the southern Prairies during the 1930s. Some 18 million acres - one quarter of all the arable farmland in Canada - were stricken by drought, with six million severely damaged by wind erosion, and an astonishing 300,000 acres deemed to have become desert.

Glenbow Archives

Those demands were most vigorously expressed by the new Co-operative Commonwealth Federation (CCF), a coalition of farmer and labour groups formed in Calgary in 1932 under the leader of Christian socialist J.S. Woodsworth. Influenced by heady blend of political radicalism, social democracy, and the "social gospel" of the Protestant reformists - not to mention a significant dash of communism - the CCF held its first annual convention in Regina a year later, and endorsed a Regina Manifesto calling for a "new social order" that included centralization of government, public control of financial institutions, nationalization of key industries, a vastly expanded range of public programs and pensions, and world peace through the establishment of a non-competitive global economy.

Summer drought was in many places in the West followed by massive winter snowfalls, often drifting to the top of telegraph poles - a fact many Canadians raised in the 1930s would later recall to the disbelief of their grandchildren. However, the documentary evidence is abundant, as in this photo of a snowplow clearing roads around Crowley, Alberta.

Glenbow Archives

Depression-era school transport (above), with a makeshift wagon drawn by farm horses. Public transportation was still in its infancy, and non-existent in rural areas.

Glenbow Archives

Montreal lawyer and poet Frank Scott had been influential in the creation of the CCF, but he later wrote that he had serious misgivings about some of the people attracted to the new party. "There are dangerous movements in the CCF. B.C. has some queer people. Then members of the Communist Party are known to be in the CCF... and are taking their orders from the party to which they really give their allegiance. The result is a good deal of suspicion all around." Nevertheless, he reported that the Regina convention "showed a general unity that was quite encouraging... I shall not forget the denunciations of capitalism, hour after hour, and the raging thunderous applause afterwards." Eugene Forsey, then a young socialist and later a senator, wrote about the difficulties of uniting the Canadian left. "There were a lot of characters representing very different interests in Regina, and in the party. Bill Irvine, of the United Farmers of Alberta, had been touched by Social Credit and was anxious to get some Social Credit stuff into the manifesto. Ernie Winch, from British Columbia, wanted to get something in about nudism. The rest of us were somewhat leery... Winch was a dear old soul, a rip-roaring Marxist but the gentlest of men. In the B.C. legislature his great subjects were people in mental hospitals and animals in the zoo."

The CCF was formed as a party to represent the views of farmers and workers - the Canadian proletariat - but from the first it had trouble finding broad national support. There was significant support among Prairie farmers, among workers in the ports and mines of British Columbia, and in the factories of industrial Ontario. From the beginning Canadian socialism also appealed to the urban middle class: Protestant clergy, teachers, professors and other white-collar professionals. Historian Donald Creighton suggested this gave Canadian socialism its "earnest, slightly sanctimonious air". Catholic Quebec in particular never warmed to the party, and at the national level it struggled to achieve the broad appeal similar socialist parties would find in Europe and elsewhere.

Faced with the practical issues of regulating and delivering services to an increasingly complex society, Canada's provincial governments were often less reticent than Ottawa in their efforts to promote economic recovery and provide social welfare. The Liberals were elected to government in Nova Scotia and B.C. in 1933, and committed themselves to more activist policies to battle the Depression.

The Kernaghan kids (above), of Langdon, Alberta, aboard their horse, Black Diamond. Mechanization of Canadian farms was in full-swing during the 1920s, but slowed dramatically during the Depression, ensuring plenty of work for the likes of the Kernaghan horse.

Glenbow Archives

Mitch Hepburn led the Liberals to victory in Ontario the following year, promising an Ontario version of Roosevelt's New Deal. The CCF formed the official opposition in B.C. and Saskatchewan, and in Quebec the Union Nationale appeared as a populist left-wing alternative. Yet by far the most radical and unusual provincial government of the era was elected in Alberta. By the middle of the decade the poorest Prairie province was effectively bankrupt, running a $5 million deficit and relying on the federal government for bailouts. Yet it was not economics or unemployment which would prompt the demise of the province's United Farmers government under widely respected Premier John Brownlee. It was sex and a pretty 22-year-old government typist.

In 1933 Brownlee and his family rented a lakeside summer cottage in central Alberta. On August 3 a letter arrived from the Edmonton law firm of Maclean, Short and Kane. Addressed to the premier, it announced the beginning of legal proceedings. "We have been instructed to commence action against you for damages for seduction of Miss Vivian MacMillan." The premier hired two prominent Calgary lawyers to represent him - and then left for Ottawa to work on the Royal Commission on Banking and Currency. With his private life in turmoil, Brownlee spent his time drafting the structure of the nation's new central bank, the Bank of Canada. It was the sort of businesslike response Albertans had come to expect from a man still regarded as one of the best leaders the province has ever had.

MacMillan was the daughter of the mayor of Edson, Alberta, and had met the premier on a

couple of occasions before moving to Edmonton in the summer of 1930 to enrol in a secretarial course. According to testimony at the trial, Brownlee befriended her and eventually secured her a job with the provincial government. MacMillan claimed that was the beginning of a torrid three-year affair in which she had been a reluctant participant. In his instructions to the jury, Acting Chief Justice William Ives (known in legal circles as "Cowboy Billy") noted the circumstantial nature of the case against Brownlee: "The story of the female plaintiff is wholly and entirely unsupported by any other evidence..." But after five hours of sometimes heated deliberation the jury decided it believed her more than it did Brownlee. It found that the premier had indeed seduced MacMillan, and awarded her damages of $10,000 and her father (also a plaintiff) $5,000. Judge Ives refused to accept the verdict, on the grounds it was unsupported by evidence, and dismissed the case, awarding costs to the premier. Appeals and counter-appeals would continue until 1940, with the $10,000 judgement against Brownlee finally being upheld, but by that time there were no winners in a case that had enthralled Canadians for months. The trial effectively ruined both Brownlee and MacMillan, and utterly destroyed a party that had governed Alberta competently for 14 years.

The Depression proved to be the downfall of many governments across Canada, and eventually might also have seen off the Brownlee administration. But the MacMillan scandal triggered one of those momentous political shifts which have marked Alberta's history. In sweltering heat at the provincial election of August 22, 1935, not a single UFA candidate came close to being elected. Yet the government was replaced not by the opposition Liberals, but by a radical new political movement led by William Aberhart, a school principal and founder of the Calgary Prophetic Bible Institute. Armed with a radical economic theory devised by British military engineer Major Clifford H. Douglas, Aberhart's movement promised adult Albertans a "social credit" of $25-a-month to pay for essentials such as food and shelter. In the midst of the Great Depression it was the straw many people were looking for, and Aberhart's Social Credit party took 56 of 63 seats in the 1935 election.

The province had elected the most controversial government in Canada's history.

There was, however, a significant problem with the Social Credit plan: money. Provincial government revenues were small, and actually providing adult Albertans with a $25-a-month handout would cost the province $170 million a year - six times total government income. There was not enough money in the provincial treasury to meet the civil service payroll, and $15 million in government bonds were due by the following spring. The Aberhart government fired civil servants and raised taxes, but it was not enough. On April 1, 1936 Alberta became the only province ever to default on a bond issue. Other Alberta securities were promptly delisted by major stock exchanges and borrowing money became a near impossibility. The province retaliated by arbitrarily cutting in half the interest paid on all Alberta bonds, debentures and other securities. Politically, Aberhart and the Socreds were promoted as champions of the suffering West in a great struggle with "moneyed interests" in the East. Yet lost in the rhetoric was the fact the province was welching on investments made in good faith by many ordinary folk - Albertans among them.

Undaunted, the Aberhart government launched it's most famous, or infamous, fiscal policy. It issued $500,000 in "prosperity certificates", or scrip. After two years and the purchase of appropriate government stamps, these would allegedly be redeemed for regular $1 or $5 bills. To get the scrip into circulation it was issued as pay to provincial and municipal employees. This way the government was effectively borrowing $500,000 at no interest. The problem was only Ottawa could issue legal tender - and in any event those accepting the scrip had to believe that a bankrupt government which had just defaulted on its other financial obligations would at some point redeem the certificates with real money. When it was revealed that the province itself would not accept scrip in payment of taxes or at government liquor stores, the plan was doomed. It eventually offered to redeem any scrip

Enjoying the swimming pool (below) at Chateau Lake Louise, Alberta, in the midst of the Depression. For those with jobs and a stable income, the 1930s would often be remembered as an era of affordable luxuries when a dollar stretched a very long way.

National Archives of Canada

A train guard (above) selling goggles to passengers in an open observation car, to protect their eyes against dust and smoke. The railways were hard hit by the loss of goods traffic during the Depression, but reduced costs meant they were successful in expanding the market for tourism.

National Archives of Canada

in circulation. That turned out to be only $12,000, and much of that was kept by people as a memento of strange times. Ironically, Alberta's "funny money" became more popular, and valuable, as a tourist curiosity than it ever had been as currency. (By the end of the 20th century, Alberta scrip in good condition could fetch $450.)

The Aberhart government also passed legislation to control banks, and opened its own - called Treasury Branches. It sought to censor newspapers, regulated wages, and imposed price controls on just about everything. Laws were passed to prevent foreclosure on farms. Reporters from as far away as New York and London arrived to cover this strange experiment in interventionist politics and Alberta's Social Credit revolution became an international story - and rarely a positive one. There wasn't much the Socreds could do about out-of-province reporting, but the Accurate News and Information Act tried to put Alberta newspapers under government control and ignited an all-out war between the Aberhart government and the press. "The newspapers who are the mouthpiece of the financiers persist in publishing falsities that are entirely unfair and untrue," argued the premier. "They are determined to confuse all whom they can beguile into reading their spurious articles and they want to give Alberta a black eye in the sight of the world."

Four years of chaotic, confrontational government polarised Albertans as never before, and the pundits confidently predicted that a looming provincial election would bring an end to the Social Credit experiment. The province's debt stood at $129 million, with $12 million in unpaid interest, and Alberta's reputation as a place to invest had been ruined. Almost all of the government's important legislation - including its attempt to control the press - had been thrown out by the courts. As for Premier Aberhart, he admitted in a radio broadcast "I'm dead, but I won't lie down." Perhaps Albertans appreciated that stubborn streak. Many certainly appreciated that the Socreds had at least attempted to protect ordinary folk from the Depression - even if their policies were unconventional and unsuccessful. Whatever the reason, in the provincial election of 1940 the Socreds held on to 36 of the Legislature's 57 seats. The party eventually moderated its policies, and under new leadership continued to govern Alberta for another three decades.

The populist politics of the 1930s and the erosion of traditional limits on government involvement in the lives of Canadians would have a profound impact on the future social development of the country. And nowhere was this more apparent than in changing attitudes towards medical treatment, which prior to the Depression had depended entirely on the means of the individual and the ethical responsibility of doctors to provide medical care for those who couldn't afford it. During the Depression the number of people who were able to pay their doctor little or nothing grew exponentially, particularly in rural areas where a doctor was very often paid in kind - eggs, meat, potatoes, or wood - by farmers who had no cash. On the Prairies many doctors struggled to make a living in farming communities no longer able to support them.

Originally the relief system didn't cover medical costs, and unsurprisingly many medical associations argued that it should. In 1933 Winnipeg doctors actually went on strike to support their demand for relief payments. If the state provided groceries, rent, and even clothing for families on relief, why not cover their medical expenses, argued the doctors. The idea grudgingly caught on, with some doctors negotiating contracts to provide limited medical services to patients on relief. Steadily the revolutionary idea of socialized medicine began to gain a following, even within medical associations. If a person couldn't afford medical treatment for themselves or their family, was it not the

John David and Lady Eaton (left) opening a new Toronto home furnishing store in 1930. Canada's most trusted retailer, Eaton's made headlines when a federal commission probed its labour practices. Seamstress Annie Wells told MPs she was paid nine and a half cents for a dress the company then sold for $1.69. John David remembered the era as "a good time for everybody." The latest in women's wear during the Depression (opposite page). Magazines and movies continued to popularize fashion trends, as they had during the 1920s, and for many women dressing as smartly as you could afford was one way of thumbing your nose at an era of hardship and poverty.

Left: City of Toronto Archives
Right: National Archives of Canada

duty of government to step in and pick up the cost? The response of governments was an emphatic "no" - but even the thought of the monumental cost of a public health system failed to kill the notion entirely. The idea of socialized medicine would long outlive the hard times that created it, although in the 1930s it's unlikely even its most ardent proponents would have predicted its expansive future.

The Depression was also a watershed era for federal-provincial relations in Canada. During the 1920s the provinces had been consistently supported by the courts in their defence of traditional provincial jurisdiction. The Judicial Committee of the Privy Council (precursor of the Supreme Court) had consistently favoured the provinces in its decisions. Resources, energy, automobiles, social services - in all these areas provincial jurisdiction had been upheld and expanded. But the financial realities of the Depression ended all that, highlighting the great weakness in the provincial position: Ottawa had most of the money. Without financial assistance from the federal government the provinces could not fulfill their responsibility for unemployment relief, let alone expand other services. Clearly the Depression was also national crisis, and so logically needed the mobilization of national resources.

Nor was unemployment the only issue requiring a national approach. Aviation and radio broadcasting clearly called out for national regulation. And if Ottawa was being called upon to support expanded social services, should it not have some say in how its money was being used? The federal government would henceforth have a say in education, health, and other areas of provincial jurisdiction, and the division of responsibilities that had been the foundation of the Canadian federation since 1867 began to break down. The tensions that have ever since underwritten federal-provincial relations arguably got their start here, undermining traditional federalism and prompting a never-ending debate over the division of power and money.

Despite the growth of federal influence in provincial areas and the establishment of new federal institutions (most notably the Bank of Canada, and the Canadian Radio Broadcasting Commission - Canada's first broadcast regulator and also the forerunner of the CBC), new leaders, new doctrines, and new policies kept appearing at the provincial level, leaving the Bennett government looking sleepy by contrast. No one had actually found an antidote to the Depression, but at least some provincial politicians appeared to be still actively searching for one. By contrast, Bennett's most surprising foray into government

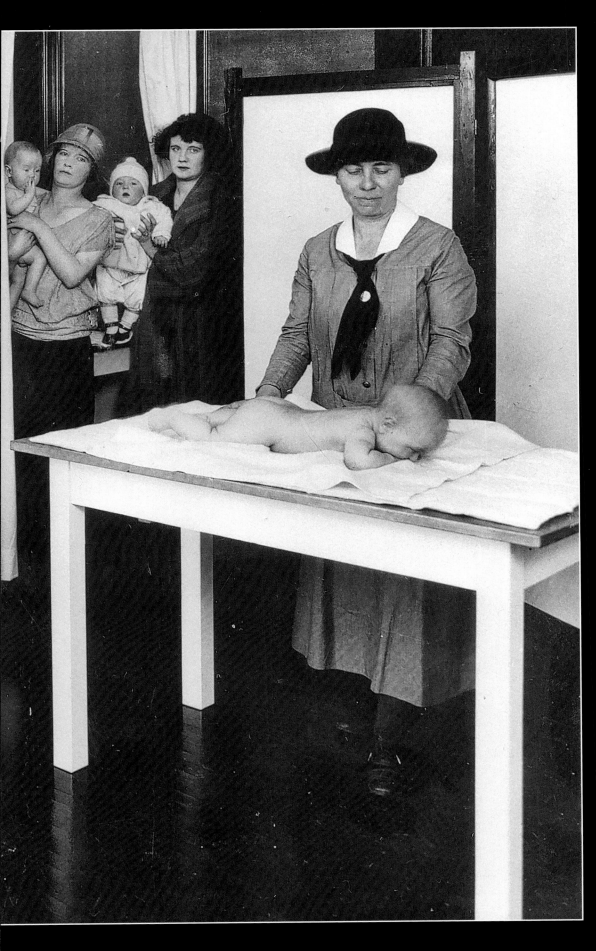

A Victorian Order of Nurses baby clinic in Calgary, Alberta. Before the Depression huge strides were taken in improving public health, but in the 1930s cash-strapped local and provincial governments were often unable to afford such programs. For many Canadian families even basic nutrition became a challenge

Glenbow Archives

activism came about almost by accident, with the establishment of the Select Committee on Price Spreads and Mass Buying. It was a cumbersome name for a cheeky probe led by Minister of Trade and Commerce Harry Stevens, which began by examining the executive salaries of the T. Eaton Company compared to those of its retail clerks. It went on to compare the profits being made by Canada Packers compared to the pitiful prices paid to farmers. "The law has holes big enough for millionaires to crawl through," thundered Stevens, "and company laws that permit the fleecing of the public on one hand and sweatshops on the other." Seamstress Annie Wells told the committee that she was paid less than 10 cents for making a dress that Eaton's sold for $1.69. "You were badgered, harassed, and worried," she told the MPs. "You had no time to get up and have a drink of water, or powder your nose, or even look at anybody." The committee hearings became a sensation, but the prime minister had second thoughts about this activist experiment and attempted to suppress any further excavation of Canadian business practices. A furious Stevens resigned from cabinet and promptly founded the Reconstruction Party, with the goal of "re-establishing Canada's industrial, economic and social life for the benefit of the great majority". Stevens' investigations had proved immensely popular with the public (less so with the country's business leaders), and might have been just the tonic for the Bennett government's flagging image.

But if the prime minister didn't learn much from the Stevens experiment, Eaton's certainly did. The company quickly improved its labour practices and improved pay, eventually developing an enviable reputation as a progressive employer. However, testimony before the committee had highlighted the vast gulf that still existed between Canada's poorest and wealthiest citizens. The Depression years were undoubtedly challenging for Canada's retail industry, but not noticeably so for mercantile aristocracy such as the Eaton family. Lady Flora Eaton, a former nurse, had taken over the company in 1922 after the death of her husband, John Craig Eaton. She is reputed to have scheduled board meetings for Tuesdays because she preferred to spend Mondays in bed. Long European vacations were a staple for Flora, who declared that Italy under fascist dictator Benito Mussolini was "the brightest and happiest of lands". Her son, John David - who would become president of the company in 1942 - had a similar view of Canada during the Depression. "You could take your girl to a supper dance at the hotel for $10, and that included the bottle and a room for you and your friends to drink in," he later reminisced. "I'm glad I grew up then. It was a good time for everybody. People learned what it was like to work." For those learning to work for Eaton's, $10 represented a week's pay rather than a night out.

As the Depression had struck, Eaton's had sold a piece of land at the corner of Carlton and Church streets in Toronto to Maple Leafs' hockey club owner Conn Smythe, who planned to build a new arena that would attract the city's affluent - "a place where people can go in evening clothes, if they want to come there for a party or dinner." But by the time his new Maple Leaf Gardens opened in 1931 the hard times had reached the NHL, with player salaries frozen and the Ottawa Senators on the verge of bankruptcy. Yet a new arena and a new coach, Dick Irvin, paid off for Smythe, with the Leafs winning their first Stanley Cup in 1932. Smythe also introduced radio broadcasts of Leafs games, despite the concerns of some that it would cut into gate receipts. Far from creating a problem, Foster Hewitt's Saturday night CBC broadcasts from Maple Leaf Gardens became a Canadian institution and created a nationwide following for the team. Radio helped work the same miracle for the Montreal Canadiens, but it came too late to save the Depression-battered Ottawa team.

Making Tracks

The Desperate And Destitute Ride The Rails

During the first three decades of the 20th century a network of new railways had become the backbone of the economy and Canada's first national transportation system. With the onset of the Great Depression, this great rail system was rapidly co-opted by an army of the unemployed and impoverished who rode the rails in search of work, a handout, or a meal. Railway police patrolled yards to prevent people from stowing away aboard empty freight cars, but there were too few police and far too many people - mostly single men - willing to take substantial risks to get a ride. And the risks were real. At Red Deer, Alberta three men fell asleep on the tracks waiting for a train, and all were decapitated by the wheels of a locomotive. The oldest was just 19. Finn Dahl was just 17 when he fell while trying to swing aboard a freight train near Medicine Hat. He lost both feet. Frank Reiner, 25, a recent Dutch immigrant, lost his balance while trying to get off a train, which severed his legs. Winnipeg police found Mary Donik and her 17-month-old baby freezing in an empty grain car. She had already travelled almost 1500 kilometres from Sudbury, Ontario, and it's doubtful she would have survived to reach her final destination - relatives in Vegreville, Alberta.

Under pressure from the railway companies and in an effort to control the situation, on September 30, 1932, the government of R.B. Bennett made riding the rails a crime and ordered the RCMP to assist railway police in cracking down on the practice. Hundreds were arrested, including almost 150 in one day at Calgary. Courts handed down fines - usually $1 - or imposed short jail sentences on those who couldn't pay. Many transients simply ignored the new law - there still weren't enough police to search all empty boxcars - while thousands of others just stayed where they were, creating new problems for already overtaxed municipalities. "Don't Give Money To Panhandlers On The Street," warned a headline in the *Lethbridge Herald.* "Nine chances out of 10 he's a panhandler who would rather beg than go to a relief camp." Some cities reluctantly fed the transients. Edmonton provided half a million bowls of porridge, while Medicine Hat and Calgary said they would feed men who were willing to work in return for aid. Many did.

The newspapers were predictably fascinated with the rail-riding phenomenon, devoting much space to public discussion of the issue and detailed coverage of arrests and transgressions. The *Edmonton Journal* went so far as to assign reporter R.F. MacLean to the city's Calder railyards to interview its transient population. Not all found their reception in the Alberta capital to be praiseworthy. "I've drifted from New Brunswick down to Agua Caliente, but Edmonton is the lousiest place for handouts I ever did strike," one hobo told MacLean. "The Dicks (police) are on your tail from the time you drop off until you book out again, and the relief system here is lousy, too." No doubt Edmontonians were glad to hear it. Despite the best efforts of the authorities to limit rail-riding, and the transfer of 3,000 unemployed single men to relief camps by the end of 1933, it would continue until the end of the decade and the onset of a new world war. ■

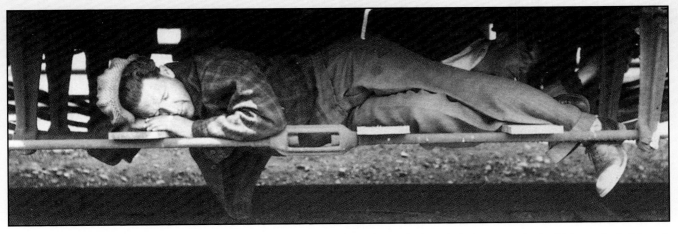

Riding the rails could be dangerous and sometimes even fatal, but desperation drove thousands of mostly single men to take the risk in search of a job or at least a meal. The railway authorities and police discouraged the practice, but the sheer number of transients simply overwhelmed attempts at security.

National Archives of Canada

The 1931 "air pageant" in Edmonton, Alberta. Air mail service across the Prairies had just begun, two years after similar services began in Central Canada, but it would be another decade before aircraft were capable of crossing the Rockies or the vast distances of the Canadian Shield and providing a truly national transportation link.

Provincial Archives of Alberta

A Temperamental Patriot

Richard Bedford Bennett

Perhaps no Canadian prime minister has been less admired and more misunderstood than Richard Bedford Bennett. Amid all the social, economic, and political wreckage left by the Great Depression lies the reputation of one of the most confident and energetic leaders the country has ever produced. Armed with substantial business and political experience, and brimming with no-nonsense determination, in 1930 the dynamic Bennett appeared to be the right man to tackle the looming economic crisis. He certainly believed so. People had underestimated him his entire life, so when he became prime minister he saw it as vindication and an opportunity to show the doubters that he could achieve great things.

Born July 3, 1870, at Hopewell Hill, New Brunswick, Bennett came from an old-established family of modest financial means. Tall, skinny, and quick-tempered, he was regarded as arrogant and something of a mother's boy. Raised as a strict Methodist, he taught Sunday school in his teens and avoided alcohol, cigarettes, and the other temptations teens usually find alluring. He became a school teacher, before leaving to study law at Dalhousie University and becoming a partner in a Chatham law firm (where Max Aitken, the future Lord Beaverbrook, was his junior). At the age of 27 Bennett accepted an offer to become a partner of James Lougheed in Calgary. The raw, bustling West suited Bennett and he thrived in Calgary. His successful partnership with

Lougheed, already one of the city's leading lights, made him wealthy enough to finance a political career. Bennett was always temperamental and not much of a team-player, but after a successful foray into territorial and provincial politics (he was the first leader of the Conservative Party in Alberta) he was elected to Parliament in 1911 as the Conservative MP for Calgary West. James Lougheed saw in Bennett leadership potential that many others did not. "He can solve any problem he puts his mind to. No man is quicker to strip a problem of unnecessary verbiage and translate it into a simple and understandable language," Lougheed wrote. "Some day Bennett will be called upon to solve the greatest problems in Canada. Some day Canada will turn to him to get the country out of its difficulties." It was an accurate prediction. Bennett served as finance minister in the short-lived Conservative government in 1926, and a year later became the first Conservative leader elected by a convention, held in Winnipeg. He took centre stage in Canadian politics just in time to face the worst economic crisis of the 20th century. In winning the 1930 federal election Bennett promised swift action to defeat what he assumed was nothing more than a temporary economic downturn. "I propose that any government of which I am the head will at the first session of Parliament initiate whatever action is necessary to that end, or perish in the attempt."

In Ottawa, Bennett's self-confident directness was not as

Prime Minister R.B. Bennett (above) at work in his 17-room suite at Ottawa's Chateau Laurier Hotel, his home in the capital during his time in office. Most evenings he spent alone, answering the letters that came to him by the thousands.

R.B. Bennett's funeral in Mickleham, England, in June 1947. He had spent the final years of his life in self-imposed exile in Britain, and is the only former prime minister not buried in Canada.

Glenbow Archives

admired as it had been in Calgary. Liberal politician "Chubby" Power quipped that the new prime minister "exhibits the manners of a Chicago policeman and the temperament of a Hollywood actor." In a letter home British diplomat Sir Allan Lacelles attempted to explain the temperament of the new Canadian leader, who soon after taking office travelled to London to represent the country at an Imperial Conference. "Aggression is the only method of negotiation he knows...," wrote Lacelles. "He was pitchforked into the law courts of the West, where abusing the plaintiff's attorney and beating the table in one's shirt sleeves are the recognized and only forensic methods. Western politics are equally crude. Great wealth came to him early and unexpectedly; he has never had a wife or child to dragoon him, as only wives and children can; he has never even had a close and candid friend; and his only home, since he grew up, has been a series of hotels, so that he has not even had the valuable social training that a man gets from dealing with his own cook."

Despite not having his own cook, Bennett was confident the economy would quickly right itself, as it had done several times in the previous decade. In fact the depression got worse and his efforts on behalf of improved trade within the British Empire foundered. Behind the confident façade, Bennett was deeply shocked by the increasing hardship he saw across the country. His personal generosity was well-known, although Bennett himself rarely spoke about it. It's estimated he gave $25,000 a year to charitable organizations (a large sum in the 1930s). And it is also thought he spent around $1,000,000 of his own money in replying to personal requests for help from desperate Canadians. He could certainly afford it. As controlling owner of the E.B. Eddy match company, the country's largest safety match manufacturer, Bennett was one of the richest

men in Canada. Sadly for his public image, his wealth was more widely recognized than his generosity.

The gradual realization that this was a depression like none that had gone before eventually prompted Bennett to rethink his opposition to increased government regulation of the economy and massive public spending on relief. But the realization came too late. Bennett had vowed to overcome the depression and unemployment, or perish in the attempt. In the 1935 federal election he perished. Bennett remained leader of the opposition until 1938, but despondent over his rejection by voters and conflicts within the Conservative party he eventually emigrated to Britain - where in 1941 he was made Viscount Bennett of Mickleham, Calgary and Hopewell and sat in the British House of Lords. Just before leaving Canada, he had told *The Star Weekly* that "England is home to me." But his true feelings were likely to be found in another interview several years later, when he told another reporter, "It may not be a good thing to tear up one's roots as I have done. I've spent the happiest summers of my boyhood in New Brunswick. I love it with all my soul."

Despite Bennett's shattered political reputation, many of his initiatives live on, including the CBC, the Bank of Canada, minimum wage legislation, maximum hours of work, pension legislation, unemployment insurance, and national marketing boards for farm products. (Although some of these were not successfully enacted until long after Bennett left politics.) It is a surprisingly liberal legacy for a very conservative politician. Bennett died of a heart attack while taking a bath on June 26, 1947. The only prime minister not buried in Canada, his grave lies in St. Michael's churchyard, at Mickelham, south of London. ∎

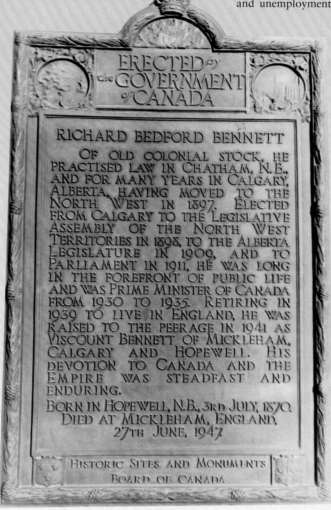

This plaque (above), commemorating the memory of former Calgary MP and prime minister R.B. Bennett, was erected in that city in 1960.

Glenbow Archives

The continuing failure of Bennett's government to make a serious dent in the Depression leaves the impression that there were no public policy successes in that dark decade, but there were a few. Among them the extraordinary reclamation of almost 200,000 square kilometres of drought-ravaged land, stretching along the U.S. border from southwest Manitoba to southern Alberta. It began with the establishment of Prairie Farm Rehabilitation Administration (PFRA). Originally planned as a temporary measure, the PFRA was so successful with irrigation projects and the promotion of new dryland farming techniques that it became permanent in 1939 - and went on to become one of the most effective and practical organizations ever created by Ottawa. It took science, political will, and the hard work of thousands of farmers, but the PFRA eventually rescued from desert the entire Palliser Triangle.

Leading the PFRA assault in southern Alberta was the redoubtable Asael E. Palmer, superintendent of the federal experimental farm at Lethbridge. In his book, *When the Winds Came*, Palmer recounted one typical story of the time; the saving of Alex Flanagan's farm at Hutton, southeast of Drumheller. When Palmer offered to reclaim his farm, Flanagan said he'd already given up. "There's nothing to be done. I've tried everything during the last four years and the soil moves with every breath of wind and cuts off any plant growth that may have started." But with much encouragement and the prospect of government help, the farmer agreed to try again. Before planting spring rye, Palmer advised him to prepare the fields - 10 acres at a time, starting on the windward side of his farm - by ploughing up the hard subsoil under the drifting piles of dust. After seeding, he was to spread a scattering of straw or "trash cover" over the ploughed land, which prevented further drifting. With the help of his son and brother, Flanagan did as he was asked. The soil held, and a heavy shower allowed the rye to germinate. While most crops in the district continued to fail, Flanagan's rye stood waist high. When he harvested Flanagan left the

The Mothers' Picnic (below) in Vancouver's Stanley Park, 1935. With no sign of economic improvement the Canadian public was becoming increasingly restless, and police estimated some 20,000 people gathered at this event to show support for the men in relief camps.

Glenbow Archives

stubble high enough to protect the soil, and the following year sowed crested wheatgrass - raising a good crop of hay. Flanagan's farm was on the way back, and as more and more farmers adopted the PFRA techniques, so were the southern Prairies.

The PFRA was, unfortunately, a rare instance of successful government intervention. British economist John Maynard Keynes was one of the very few who had early on argued that the Great Depression was so widespread and disastrous it would only be defeated when governments primed the economic pump by spending money on large public projects. "The voices which tell us that the path of escape is to be found in strict economy... are the voices of madmen and fools," he wrote. "The only way out is for us to discover some object which is admitted even by the deadheads to be a legitimate excuse for largely increasing the expenditure of someone on something." The only other

Strikes by relief workers became common by the mid-1930s, like this one in Edmonton in 1934. Patrols toured the streets to make sure relief recipients were respecting the work stoppage. There was violence when patrols discovered relief workers picking potatoes on the city outskirts.

Glenbow Archives

alternative, he suggested, was to wait for a major war to boost public spending. In that last suggestion he was closer to the truth than even he knew. Keynes' suggestion that governments take direct responsibility for stimulating economic growth was a revolutionary notion in the 1930s, but with no other solution in sight to the deepening economic crisis political leaders eventually began to listen.

In Europe and the United States, governments stopped waiting for the Depression to end and began an expansion of public spending, regulation of the economy, and a safety net of social welfare programs that would come to be a defining feature of the next half century. For the first time nations grappled with the idea of spending huge sums of public money on a crisis other than war, and in the process the old ideals of limited government were swept away. In Germany and Italy the transformation was cataclysmic, eventually replacing democratic government with totalitarian dictatorships that saw no limits to the power of the state. In the U.S. the public demand that politicians do something to battle the ongoing depression led to a less radical but nonetheless dramatic shift in public policy. In 1933 an energetic new president, Franklin D. Roosevelt, launched a raft of ambitious legislation and christened it his "New Deal." Aimed at kick-starting the American economy and mitigating the worst social effects of the Depression, it proved to be popular and - more importantly - showed some signs of working.

In Canada, R.B. Bennett stayed in power as long as possible before calling an election, in the forlorn hope that the economy would suddenly improve and his reputation be redeemed. It has been suggested that the gravity of the Great Depression completely eluded the prime minister, but it seems that by 1935 he understood it would take a different approach to make any dent in the problem. At the very least he could be in no doubt that doing nothing would lead to electoral disaster. South of the border Roosevelt's attempt to spend the U.S. out of depression had not yet proved itself, but it was popular. So the vacillating Bennett used the new medium of radio to appeal directly to the Canadian people in a series of five broadcasts that laid out what many began calling Bennett's New Deal. "In the last five years great changes have taken place in the world. The old order is gone. We are living in conditions that are new and strange to us," the prime minister announced in a radio broadcast. "I am for reform. And in my mind, reform means government intervention. It means government control and regulation."

Bennett did not have Roosevelt's gift for "fireside chat" politics, but with an election looming this most conservative of prime ministers now advocated minimum wages, maximum work hours, and increased holidays, plus unemployment, health and accident insurance for workers, improved old-age pensions, a Wheat Board to market grain, and other marketing regulations.

Payday (below) for relief workers at an army-run camp near Kitchener, B.C., in the summer of 1933.

National Archives of Canada

Relief workers (below) near Halifax, Nova Scotia. The country was beginning to lose patience with the Bennett government's inability to make a dent in the Depression. In an effort to stave off political defeat, the prime minister offered his own version of the American "New Deal" policies.

The Combines Act, Companies Act, and even the Criminal Code would be overhauled and modernized, and a Trade and Industry Commission would be established to ride herd on Canadian capitalism. Eventually most of this legislation was disallowed by the courts because it clearly trespassed into provincial jurisdiction (Roosevelt ran into a similar problem with the U.S. Supreme Court). Nevertheless, it was the most revolutionary set of measures ever proposed by a Canadian prime minister. Unfortunately for Bennett, many Canadians viewed his new policies as too little too late, political opportunism, or simply didn't believe he was serious. It also provoked a further split in his government and party, many of whom did not share Bennett's conversion to greater government involvement in the economy and increased regulation of business.

Bennett's problems were compounded by growing unrest among the unemployed. In the spring of 1935, 4,000 men from the B.C. relief camps went on strike and descended on Vancouver, threatening to occupy the city until they were found "real work". Originally there was considerable support for the strikers among Vancouver's citizens, who donated money to keep the protest going. One picnic attracted 20,000 people and raised thousands of dollars. But after six weeks of marches, traffic disruption, and at least once case of looting (at the Granville Street Hudson's Bay store), the strikers understood that their welcome was wearing thin. The prime minister had refused to get involved in something he argued was a provincial matter, so the strike leaders decided to take their protest to Ottawa. With much media sympathy and the active support of train crews, 1,000 strikers set off from Vancouver on June 3. When they reached Calgary they were joined by hundreds more unemployed, surrounded city hall and demanded food from the besieged mayor. He obliged, and the strikers - now about 2,000 strong - spent a festive evening in Bow River Park being entertained by a band.

By now christened the "On To Ottawa Trek," the next day they piled on to CPR boxcars and continued eastwards. By the time they reached Regina the number had swelled to 3,000, and there were many more unemployed waiting to join them in Brandon and Winnipeg. The trekkers now had the prime minister's attention, and he agreed to meet with a delegation that travelled ahead to Ottawa. The meeting did not go well, with Bennett sternly lecturing the delegation on the perils of fomenting revolution. "There sat Bennett behind his desk, surrounded by officials and guards. There were the press, and in front of Bennett the eight representatives of the trek," Ronald Liversedge wrote in his book *Recollections Of The On to Ottawa Trek* (Toronto, McClelland and Stewart, 1973). "The prime minister wasted no time, but went into his diatribe of abuse, condemnation, and threats, his face crimson with hatred. He then singled out Slim Evans, and roared, 'We know you down here, Evans! You are a criminal and a thief.' [Evans had indeed been convicted of misappropriating union funds.] At this Slim calmly rose to his feet, and

The On To Ottawa Trek reaches Kamloops. B.C., in June 1935. As the protest rolled eastwards it picked up more and more support, finally getting the attention of the Bennett government.

looking the prime minister in the eye, he said, loudly and distinctly, 'And you're a liar Bennett, and what is more you are not fit to run a Hottentot village, let alone a great country like Canada.' The delegation was then hustled out, and that was our negotiation." A biased account, no doubt, but it did capture the confrontational nature of the meeting.

Most of the strikers had stayed in Regina, and during a gathering on July 1 in the city's Market Square they were confronted by police who had been ordered to arrest some of their leaders. The strikers set up barricades and peppered the police with rocks, and in the ensuing melee 40 police plus 60 trekkers and Regina residents were injured. One police officer, Regina detective Charles Millar, was clubbed to death. No one was ever convicted of the killing, and a Saskatchewan public inquiry and decades of research have failed to reconcile the widely differing accounts of what actually happened during the Regina Riot. What does seem clear is that Ottawa spurned an offer by the Saskatchewan government to facilitate the peaceful disbanding of the trek, and against the advice of the senior RCMP officer in Regina (who couldn't see what laws had been broken) insisted on apprehending its leaders.

As had happened in the Winnipeg General Strike of 1919, the violence effectively ended the trek and the men dispersed, many back to relief camps. More than 1,000 trekkers eventually went on to fight for the Spanish Republic during the Spanish Civil War in a volunteer Canadian force - the Mackenzie-Papineau Battalion - partly named

A soldier of the Mackenzie-Papineau Batallion (below) in a trench in central Spain in 1937. Most of the 50,000 international volunteers fighting for the Republican side in the civil war were students and intellectuals, but the Mac-Paps were mostly working men who'd been radicalized by their time in the relief camps.

National Archives of Canada

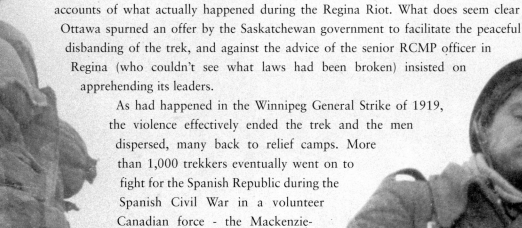

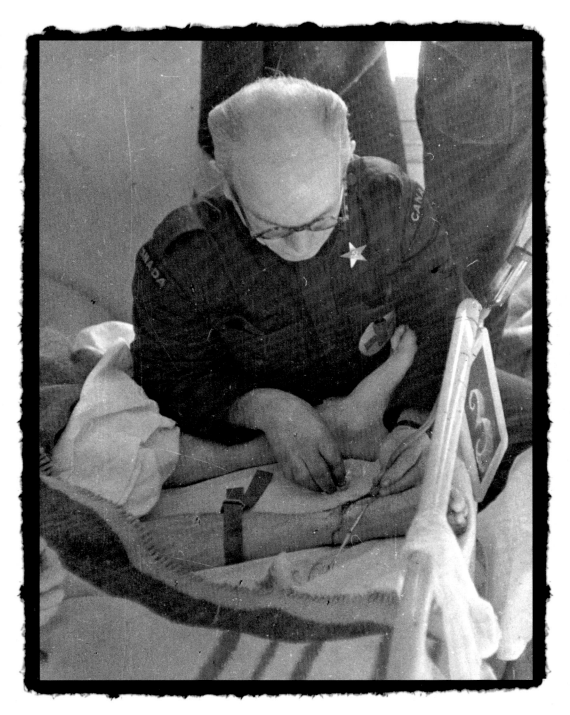

Canadian Dr. Norman Bethune (right) operating on a wounded patient in Spain. An icon of the international left, Bethune was also a pioneer in battlefield medicine, introducing innovations - including blood transfusions - that would later save many lives in World War Two.

National Archives of Canada

after the grandfather of Liberal leader Mackenzie King. Four of the On to Ottawa trek leaders who met with the prime minister - Paddy O'Neill, Tony Martin, Peter Neilson and Red Walsh - went to Spain, and Neilson and O'Neill died there. (Many of the Spanish Civil War veterans eventually returned to Canada and saw service with the Canadian forces during World War Two.) On the surface at least it appeared that the government had won the On To Ottawa confrontation. Yet Bennett's reputation suffered mightily as a result of the Regina violence, which had horrified many Canadians, and in a general election the following October the voters passed judgment on his five-year-old government.

The federal election of 1935 was one of the strangest in Canadian history. The parties of the right (the Conservatives and Harry Stevens' Reconstructionists), and of the left (the CCF and

Idealists In Action

The Mackenzie-Papineau Battalion

In 1937 communist and socialist activists fanned out across Europe and North America, holding mass meetings to raise money and recruit volunteers for the year-old civil war in Spain. That country's Republican government - a coalition of leftist and centrist politicians - was facing a revolt by the nationalist military supported by Germany and Italy. In most countries recruits to the Republican cause were overwhelmingly students and intellectuals, but in Canada they included many of the unemployed working men who had taken part in the failed "On To Ottawa Trek" in 1935. They were among 50,000 volunteers from 53 countries who served in the Republican International Brigades. At first, Canadian volunteers served with either American or British units, but by the summer of 1937 a Canadian unit, the Mackenzie-Papineau Battalion, was formed at Albacete under the command of Edward Cecil-Smith, a journalist from Toronto.

The Mac-Paps, as they became known, fought in five major campaigns. Half-trained, barely equipped and lacking medical and logistics support, they suffered appallingly high casualty rates. By September 1938, when they were withdrawn from action, only 35 of the unit's 1,200 Canadians were still on their feet. The Mac-Paps enjoyed considerable popular support in Canada, but getting them home was no easy matter since participation in the Spanish war was illegal under Canada's Foreign Enlistment Act. And the government of Prime Minister Mackenzie King (after whose grandfather the Canadian battalion was partly named) actively considered charging them. That didn't happen, and finally their journey home was paid for by private donations. In February 1939 the first shipload of repatriated volunteers arrived in Halifax: 272 men, including 55 in need of immediate medical attention. Cheering crowds met the trains taking Mac-Pap veterans home to cities across Canada, but no official reception was ever held. Records relating to Canadians in the Spanish Civil War are sketchy, but it is thought 1,448 served the losing Republican cause, including 721 who lost their lives. Many of the survivors later fought in World War Two, which they saw as an extension of the Spanish conflict.

Although the Mac-Paps and the Spanish Civil War are now largely forgotten in Canada, a monument to the battalion can be found in Victoria, B.C. One of the few Canadians to attain widespread recognition after service in Spain was Dr. Norman Bethune, who developed the first mobile army medical (MASH) units while fighting on the Republican side. ■

Members of the Mac-Paps returning to Canada in 1939. Of the 1,200 Canadians who served with the battalion, only 35 came through the Spanish Civil War unscathed, and 721 were killed.

National Archives of Canada

federal Social Credit), all offered platforms to tackle the Depression - whether Canadians believed they could deliver or not. The Liberals, by contrast, offered no economic solutions and ran instead on a simple promise to end social and political unrest - "King or Chaos" as the Liberal slogan put it. Less than half of voters were inclined to view the situation in such simplistic terms, but with 45% of the popular vote the Liberals were able to take 171 seats - with the disunited Bennett Tories reduced to 40. It would take the Conservatives years to rebuild, and to come to terms with the new era of interventionist politics. By contrast, future generations of Liberal politicians would argue that they created the modern Canadian welfare state, and thus were the only party that could be trusted with maintaining it. Yet as historian Donald Creighton later observed, in 1935 "political victory came to the party that had the least to offer - the party that, so far as the central issue of the welfare state was concerned, had no proposals at all." (*Canada's First Century*, 1970, Macmillan, Toronto).

Relief workers (below) near Long Branch, Ontario, loading stone for sidewalk repairs. When Prime Minister Bennett acknowledged in 1935 "we are living in conditions that are new and strange to us" it wasn't news to men such as these.

National Archives of Canada

A Troubled Prince

Edward VIII's abdication shocks the Empire

The Prince of Wales (left) at his ranch, near High River, Alberta. A regular visitor to Canada, the prince had declared himself "a Canadian in mind and spirit," and a great many Canadians looked forward with anticipation to his reign as Edward VIII. It was not to be. The 42-year-old shocked the Empire when he announced his intention to marry twice-divorced American Wallis Simpson. It was not seen as an acceptable match for a king and head of the Anglican Church, and Edward was forced to choose between Simpson and the monarchy.

He chose "the woman I love," renounced the monarchy, and went into exile. As the Duke of Windsor (the courtesy title given him by his younger brother, George VI) he would return to the 1,600 acre Alberta spread even after his abdication - the last time in 1950. George Webster, mayor of Calgary and later a member of the provincial legislature, is pictured below with Edward while he was still Prince of Wales. The future king seemed particularly fond of Calgary and developed a close friendship with the English-born Webster.

Photos: Glenbow Archives

Relief workers with snowshoes (opposite left), near Upper Brockway, New Brunswick, in the winter of 1934. And the midway at the Canadian National Exhibition in Toronto (below), in 1935. Despite the hardships of the Depression, Canadian endured and life went on - and by mid-decade there were even signs of a slow economic recovery.

National Archives of Canada Photos

The government that Mackenzie King led into office in 1935 had some new faces, but many more old ones. Perhaps not surprisingly then, the Liberals still held to its traditional belief that the solution to economic depression lay in the greater liberalization of trade - which in this instance no government had been able to achieve. The party also believed, as it had done since the founding of the country, in loose federalism and a limited role for the national government. It had traditionally resisted Conservative attempts to use the power of the state for broad national goals. A national economic policy, the creation of a Bank of Canada, the nationalization of the railways, the Canadian Radio Broadcasting Commission, and the expanded social benefits and regulations of Bennett's "New Deal" - these were all Conservative innovations.

In 1935 King was no closer to having an answer to Canada's economic malaise than he had been five years earlier, but unlike Bennett he knew enough to realize he didn't have an answer and didn't promise one. As an economist King understood that no one had a quick fix for the Great Depression, and as a shrewd politician he was not about to suggest solutions to a problem he was now convinced would only be solved in increments. And his timing was good, because things were starting to get a little better. Unemployment began to fall, slowly. It seemed as if Canada and the rest of the industrialized world had settled into a long, slow period of economic recovery. Ottawa's tax revenues were also increasing slowly, which provided a reasonable excuse for avoiding big expenditures and major expansions of government.

Archibald Belaney (right) perpetrated one of the 20th century's most convincing and long-running hoaxes. Known to the world as Grey Owl, he convinced everyone he was a Canadian-born aboriginal conservationist. As such, he became one of Canada's most popular and famous personalities, writing a number of best-selling books and lecturing in North America and Europe. Born in Hastings, England in 1888, he immigrated to Canada in 1906. Belaney served with distinction in the Canadian Army during the Great War, being wounded and gassed (which may have eventually hastened his death). After the war he worked as a trapper and guide, and eventually joined the Canadian Parks Branch, working briefly at Riding Mountain National Park in Manitoba, and then at Saskatchewan's Prince Albert National Park from 1931-38. Along the way he adopted the persona of Grey Owl, masquerading as an Ojibwa (his first of three marriages was to an Ojibwa woman). The fact that he was actually an Englishman with a boyhood fascination with the outdoors was not uncovered until after his death in 1938. The unmasking of his real identity destroyed his reputation and undermined his achievements (he is credited with helping preserve the Canadian beaver from extinction). In recent decades Belaney's reputation has been revived, and his life was the subject of a popular 1999 movie staring Pierce Brosnan. His epitaph at Prince Albert reads: "Say a silent thank you for the preservation of wilderness areas, for the lives of the creatures who live there and for the people with the foresight to realize this heritage, no matter how."

National Archives of Canada

That appeared to suit the always-cautious King, who busied himself with minor government reorganization. He did support the creation of a national air carrier, Trans-Canada Airlines, since it was clear government alone was prepared to take on the task of inaugurating coast-to-coast services. Besides, there was no real public opposition to the idea. As a result of the Depression Canadians had become understandably sceptical about relying too much on the initiative of private enterprise. Public opinion was now more inclined to support state involvement in the economy.

As for "King or Chaos", there was still labour unrest, with tension between government and business on the one hand, and the unemployed and unions on the other. Demonstrations and protests continued. In 1937 the radical U.S.-based Congress of Industrial Organizations (CIO) backed a strike of workers at the General Motors plant in Oshawa, Ontario. The government of Premier Mitch Hepburn waded into the fray on the side of GM, hiring special police (popularly

Bathing in Lake Couchiching, near Orillia, Ontario. Curiously, in tandem with memories of poverty and deprivation, many of the youngsters who grew up in the 1930s also fondly recall it as a time of freedom and simplicity - before the onset of our noisy, stressful consumer society.

National Archives of Canada

known as Hepburn's Hussars) to guard the plant and break up demonstrations. Hepburn's fiery anti-radical rhetoric and tough line with the strikers helped him win an election the same year, but the noisy confrontation in Oshawa overshadowed what was clearly the more important development. There were now jobs to be fought over.

If you looked closely enough you could see the beginning of an economic recovery. Farm machinery giant Massey-Harris had been Canada's manufacturing star in the 1920s, its products exported worldwide, but with the onset of the Depression it found itself operating at 10% capacity and laid off most of its workforce. Ironically, the champion of Canadian capitalism began its revival with a huge order from an unlikely source: the Soviet Union. The Soviets' centrally-planned economy could not build tractors quickly enough to satisfy the demands of its collectivized farms and fulfill Stalin's dream of making the country a major exporter of grain. So Moscow placed a $6 million order with Massey-Harris, and the company was very glad indeed to take the communists' money.

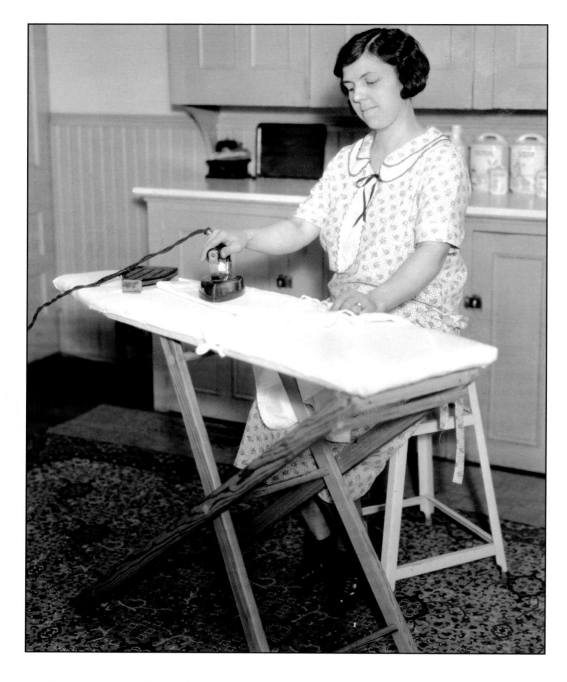

The reputation of capitalism and conservatism had suffered mightily as a result of the Depression, but the really big political losers were the provinces. In British Columbia, a delegation of leading businessmen appeared before a royal commission and actually argued for the abolition of their "wasteful and useless" provincial government. An extreme point of view, to be sure, but there is no doubt that the inability of the cash-strapped provinces to meet the social challenges of the Great Depression had encouraged many people to conclude that only a strong central government could best defend their welfare and prosperity. For a country founded on a careful division of political power, this was a significant shift. Canadians had traditionally identified more closely with their provincial governments than with the far-off Dominion government in Ottawa. The Great Depression had, however, created a definite hierarchy among Canadian governments, with the provinces now several rungs lower than at the beginning of the decade.

Immigration slowed to a trickle during the 1930s, but that didn't mean an end to pioneering. Areas such as Alberta's Peace River farming country and Quebec's mineral-rich Val d'Or region were the new frontier. This photo (above) shows a group at a shower for a new bride at Val d'Or.

National Archives of Canada

Spirits Of The Departed

William Lyon Mackenzie King

William Lyon Mackenzie King, Canada's longest-serving prime minister.

National Archives of Canada

As Canada's longest-serving prime minister (almost 22 years in total), during his lifetime most Canadians thought they knew all there was to know about William Lyon Mackenzie King. Intelligent, careful, and shrewd, King provided Canadians with competent if unspectacular leadership. Few people would have guessed that their staid, serious, and rather dull prime minister - Canada's dominant political figure for a quarter of the 20th century - held regular séances during which he sought guidance from the spirits of his mother, Leonardo da Vinci, and a pet Irish terrier, among many others.

William Lyon Mackenzie King was born in Berlin (now Kitchener), Ontario in 1874. His grandfather was William Lyon Mackenzie, leader of the 1837 Rebellion in Upper Canada. King studied economics and law at the University of Toronto and the University of Chicago, and also later at Harvard University. In 1900 he entered the federal civil service and became deputy minister of the newly-created Department of Labour. King eventually joined the Liberal party and won a seat in the 1908 election. The following year he was appointed minister of labour in Prime Minister Wilfrid Laurier's cabinet. Those early years in government, and his admiration of Laurier, influenced King's entire political life, but they proved to be a relatively brief introduction to politics. He lost his seat in the 1911 election and went to work as a labour consultant for the Rockefeller Foundation in the United States. King ran and lost again in the 1917 federal election. Unlike most English-speaking Liberals, he had stood by Laurier in opposition to conscription, which was an unpopular position outside Quebec. Two years later he was elected Liberal

leader in the first leadership convention held in Canada. His party was still bitterly divided over conscription, but King's skills as a conciliator had been well honed by his work in the U.S., and he put them to good use. The reinvigorated and reunited Liberals won the 1921 election.

Like his great hero, Laurier, King never lost sight of the "great issue" of unity between English and French Canada. But unlike Laurier he never established lofty goals for the country or rallied the nation with great oratory and soaring political vision. He is remembered for competent administration and the careful avoidance of what he called "entanglements" rather than for great achievements. Yet he led Canada through half the Great Depression and all of World War Two, and like all successful political leaders he had ambition, stamina and determination. King introduced unemployment insurance (originally proposed by the Bennett Conservatives) and the family allowance. But he was, above all, a practical leader who tailored his policies to prevailing opinions and avoided rocking the boat. "It is what we prevent, rather than what we do that counts most in government," he said - and that pretty much sums up his style of leadership.

Privately though, King is surely Canada's most eccentric prime minister. For most of his adult life he regularly sought advice from the spirits of his mother (to whom he was devoted), his grandfather, Laurier, William Gladstone (the nineteenth-century British Liberal prime minister), saints Luke and John - and even his beloved dog, Pat! But it was all done in typical King fashion - very discreetly. After his death one of the mediums he consulted said that she had not even realized he was a politician,

Prime Minister King and U.S. President Franklin D. Roosevelt, at Quebec City in 1936. Despite their differences, the two men had a long and amicable relationship.

National Archives of Canada

Prime Minister King (above) and his beloved dog, Pat, in a 1947 photograph. This was actually King's third dog of the same name, and it survived its owner by several years.

Prime Minister King and President Roosevelt (above) at the official opening of the Thousand Islands Bridge, at Collins Landing, New York, in the summer of 1938. The bridge across the St. Lawrence River connects northern New York State with south-eastern Ontario, and is jointly administered by the U.S. and Canada through the Thousand Island Bridge Authority.

let alone the prime minister. After a 1932 séance he wrote: "There can be no doubt whatever that the persons I have been talking with were the loved ones and others I have known and who have passed away. It was the spirits of the departed." King's occult leanings were known to few people during his term in office, and only became public knowledge after his death, from his extensive diaries.

The King diaries - 50,000 pages long - provide a fascinating (and often astonishing) record of the best-educated and longest-serving prime minister of Canada. He kept a daily journal from 1893, when he was an 18-year-old student at the University of Toronto, until just a few days before he died in 1950. During his years in office the diaries represent a unique political and social history of Canada. In his will he asked that the diaries be destroyed, except for the parts that he had indicated should be published or used. Except that he never indicated which parts of the diaries he wanted made public. By 1980 all of them had been made available for research.

King never married, but had a close female friend, Joan Patterson, a married woman, with whom he spent much of his leisure time. Patterson was one of the few close confidantes of the mostly friendless prime minister. (He once wrote that "I've always found, that you can control people much better if you don't see much of them.") King died in 1950 and is buried in Mount Pleasant Cemetery in Toronto. He is pictured on the Canadian $50 bill. After the Great War, King's formidable political ability reunited a shattered Liberal party under his leadership, and over the next three decades he succeeded in creating one of the most durable governing dynasties in the world. Through sheer political longevity, the unprepossessing King set a tone for Canadian government that in many ways seems the antithesis of dynamic leadership. Yet he led the country to economic recovery and played a leading role in World War Two. His legacy was a united Canada well positioned to become one of the most prosperous societies on earth. ∎

Not everyone was comfortable with this shift of political power, particularly in western Canada, which during the Depression had gone from booming frontier to basket-case and where many people remained sceptical that far-off Ottawa grasped the fundamentals of geography and economics they faced on a daily basis. Towards the end of 1937 an exchange of letters between George Ross, son of a pioneer rancher in the Milk River country of Alberta, and federal Agriculture Minister James Gardiner, former premier of Saskatchewan, encapsulates a concern that was already central to western politics and relations with Ottawa. "Our family have been raising cattle in Alberta since 1885," wrote Ross. "We have a ranch in Alberta and one in Montana. Physically the Alberta ranch is far superior to the Montana ranch. On the Montana ranch we have to produce ten cows to buy a car; on the Alberta ranch we have to produce 22 cows of the same quality to buy the same car, and it is true of practically everything we buy, saddles, harness, ropes, boots, everything. I have three boys growing up. Which ranch do you suppose they are going to work? If they are one half as intelligent as I hope, it will take some flag-waving to keep them in Canada."

Gardiner's partisan response echoes that of Liberal politicians from Laurier, to Trudeau, to Chretien. "We will only get what's coming to us in Western Canada when Alberta returns 15 Liberals, instead of 15 nameless individuals, to the House of Commons, to back up the 16 or 17 who come down continuously from the province of Saskatchewan, and from a half dozen to 13 who come down from Manitoba... If every man in Alberta who has the ability which you have and holds the point of view which you hold, would get into the Liberal organization and work it to the limit, we would get the results desired and you would be surprised at the support you

would get from Eastern Canada to put them over." Throughout the remainder of the century many westerners would be stubbornly resistant to this argument. (The Ross boys would, with equal stubbornness, remain in Canada, and their children were still ranching in southern Alberta at the end of the 20th century.)

More generally, the hardships faced by Canadians during the Depression can be read in the demographic changes that occurred in the 1930s. Although the country's population increased from 10.5 to 11.5 million, that was the slowest rate of growth since the global recession of the 1880s. In 1929 almost 170,000 immigrants had arrived in Canada, but that number fell to 12,000 by 1935, and never rose above 17,000 for the remainder of the decade. Indeed, the Immigration Act provided for the deportation of immigrants who were forced to apply for social assistance, and from 1930 to 1935 a total of 30,000 were sent packing. Young people were generally forced to postpone marriage and starting a family until they could afford it, and consequently the country's birthrate declined by 25%.

The country would never quite regain the surging confidence and optimism it had exhibited through the early years of the 20th century. Canadians were, on average, poorer in 1939 than they had

The 1930s had been particularly hard for the newly-settled areas of the West, where families such as this one in Alberta (below) struggled to eke out a living. But most persevered, and by the end of the decade things were slowly improving.

Glenbow Archives

been a decade earlier. In the cities they were more likely to be unemployed, or underemployed, and across rural Canada farming families had become inured to poverty and poor markets. The 1930s had a profound impact on the lives of all who struggled through those dismal years, and nowhere was the impact felt more heavily than on the Prairies. Population statistics tell the tale. Across the West's broad farmlands and bustling new towns and cities, which until 1929 had been filling up at a truly phenomenal rate, thousands gave up the struggle. Some 66,000 people left Saskatchewan, 24,000 abandoned Manitoba, and another 21,000 quit Alberta, their dreams of a new life in tatters. Some returned to Eastern Canada, others moved on to British Columbia or the U.S., and a few made the sad journey back to the homelands they had recently left with such purpose and optimism.

With Canada's enhanced international stature after the Great War, and the passing of the Statute of Westminster giving Ottawa complete control over international relations, the country might well have been more active in global affairs during the 1930s - but the economic emergency at home overshadowed all else. Ottawa actually retreated from the active participation in international affairs championed by former prime minister Robert Borden. When Japan invaded Chinese Manchuria in 1931, Canada refused to condemn the Japanese aggression and avoided taking sides in a conflict that would eventually embroil the entire Pacific in war. When Mussolini's Italy attempted to create an African empire by invading Ethiopia in 1935, Canada's representative at the League of Nations led a call for economic sanctions - but fearing a backlash in Quebec (where sympathy for Catholic Italy was strong) the newly-elected King government quickly repudiated the move. Italy's brutal campaign in Ethiopia continued, and the league's credibility was crushed. *Winnipeg Free Press* editor John W. Dafoe was among the few who understood the consequences, and placed the blame squarely on the Canadian government's shoulders: "With assurances of the most distinguished consideration, (the League of Nations) was ushered into darkness by Mr. Mackenzie King." Most seriously of all, Canada strongly supported international appeasement of Adolf Hitler and Nazi Germany as a way of avoiding conflict. "Behind the great Atlantic moat, millions of Canadians still practiced mass hypnosis," wrote author Ralph Allen. "Day by day in every way the world was getting better and better, and would get better if enough people kept saying so and believing it." Preoccupied with the Depression, and with the awful memory of the bloodletting of the Great War still so recent, Canadian insularity was perhaps understandable. It would, however, have tragic repercussions.

For a young and developing country, the 1930s were, in most respects, the worst decade of the 20th century. Politically, the country seemed more fractured and argumentative than it had ever been, with its federal and provincial governments haggling over the distribution of a much diminished economic pie. The blurring of constitutional rights and responsibilities created tensions between Ottawa and the provinces that would bedevil their relations for many decades to come. The country as a whole had been injured by the Dirty Thirties, and the lives of millions of individual Canadians had been forever changed. The devastated Prairies would eventually recover, Alberta spectacularly so, but for many the dream of the Last Best West had been blown away like so much desiccated topsoil. Impoverished Newfoundland had been returned to colonial status, and would shortly endure a bruising public debate on its future. Arguably, no nation suffered more from the impact of the Depression - economically, socially, and politically - than did Canada. Ironically the cure for the economic malaise lay not in the quiet resumption of world trade and improved demand for exports, but rather in another international cataclysm that would call Canadians back to the battlefields of Europe and require the battered country to muster its depleted resources in defence of its most basic beliefs. ∎

'Canada Made Us'

A Royal Tour Revives The Monarchy

When King George V died on January 20, 1936, a great many Canadians looked forward to the forthcoming rule of his eldest son, Edward, the Prince of Wales. Edward loved the country, owned land in Alberta, and had pronounced himself "a Canadian in mind and spirit." Yet this most Canadian of royals was never to reign as Edward VIII. The 42-year-old announced his intention to marry an American woman, Wallis Simpson, whom he had known since 1931. He sought the approval of his family, the Church of England, and the political establishment to marry her. But Simpson had already been married twice (her second divorce was still pending), and Edward found enormous opposition to the match. And not only in Britain. The reaction of former prime minister Robert Borden was typical of the response of Canada's establishment. "The King's insensate folly in determining to marry a woman twice divorced created a scandal which has been exploited to the fullest extent by lewd newspapers of the baser sort in the United States," wrote Borden. "Apparently, the King places before all obligation of duty, and above all concern for the welfare of the Empire his silly infatuation for this woman, and his desire to make her his queen.

It would be difficult to exaggerate the intense concern that

Queen Elizabeth accepting flowers from a child during a stop at Beavermouth, B.C., in July 1939. The royal train is in the background.

National Archives of Canada

empire, which, as Prince of Wales and lately as King, I have for twenty-five years tried to serve. But you must believe me when I tell you that I have found it impossible to carry the heavy burden of responsibility and to discharge my duties as King as I would wish to do without the help and support of the woman I love." His younger brother, David, took the throne as King George VI and immediately made Edward the Duke of Windsor before he left for lifelong exile. The Duke and Simpson were married in France on June 3, 1937 and afterwards lived mostly in Paris. During World War Two, Edward served as governor of the Bahamas. (He died in Paris in 1972. His wife died there in 1986.) In later years his reputation was further eroded by revelations of the couple's apparent regard for Hitler and his regime.

The negative impact of the abdication on the monarchy, not to mention Prime Minister Mackenzie King's public ambivalence towards Canadian involvement in any new European war, persuaded British leaders of the need to cement its historic links with the senior dominion. By the fall of 1938 many in the British government were convinced that war was likely, and with the Americans stubbornly on the sidelines the idea of fighting it without Canada alarmed British Prime Minister Neville Chamberlain. In October it was announced that the new King and Queen would visit Canada the following spring, with a side trip to the United States. The trip would provide an opportunity to influence public opinion and cement ties with both countries. For his part, the Canadian prime minister saw the trip as a way to distract a country seriously battered by a decade of economic hardship. And if it came to war, the unifying aspects of a royal visit wouldn't come amiss.

The royal couple arrived in Canada on May 17, 1939, aboard the Canadian liner *Empress of Australia*, and the trip was more successful than anyone could have predicted. From coast to coast Canadians turned out in their millions to greet the frail George VI, the first reigning monarch to set foot in the largest country under the British crown. Quebec Premier Maurice Duplessis failed to show up for a welcome lunch in Quebec City, but it didn't seem to matter. French Canada was as wild over the royal couple as everywhere else in the country. It surprised many Quebecers that the King spoke excellent French, and that Queen Elizabeth (better known to later generations as the Queen Mother) was fluent. He praised the way "English and French have shown in Canada that they can keep their pride and distinctive culture." The Queen visited the Dionne quintuplets, and chatted with innumerable school children who presented her with flowers. This did not please one nationalist writer at *Le Devoir*, who complained that "by the smile of a Queen and the French words of a King, the English have conquered once more the cradle of New France."

But ordinary Quebecers seemed to love it. "Over a 25 mile route, draped in gala colours and lined with militiamen and blue-bereted veterans, one million people or so were stretched along the street curbs and crowded on stands and verandas, on roofs and garages, cheering the sovereigns," *Canadian Geographical Journal*

King George and Queen Elizabeth arriving in Hope. B.C. The royal tour proved to be a greater public relations success than even its most enthusiastic promoters had imagined.

National Archives of Canada

disturbs our people. Last week, during a temporary indisposition which confined me to my room, I spent two sleepless nights in grieving over this deplorable incident and in endeavouring to forecast the future. For I was fully conscious that the issue of the present crisis might be so grave as eventually to disturb the Empire's unity. All this because of the absurd infatuation of a middle-aged man for a twice-divorced woman. Physicians of this city are convinced that the King is suffering from a certain type of psychosis."

On December 10, 1936, Edward submitted his abdication and it was endorsed by the British Parliament the next day. In one of the most famous broadcasts of the decade, Edward went on radio to announce his decision. "You all know the reasons which have impelled me to renounce the throne. But I want you to understand that in making up my mind I did not forget the country or the writer Gustave Lanctot wrote of their arrival in Montreal. "The feature of the day was the Stadium with 35,000 schoolchildren massed in the circular stands, one thousand of whom formed with red, white and blue dresses, a huge Union Jack, while the whole multitude chanted, between cheers, "Vive le roi, Vive la reine!" On the route between Montreal and Ottawa, a million well-wishers turned out to cheer and wave at the royal train.

It was the same across the country. The prime minister had not been wrong in thinking Canadians were ready for something other than drought and economic depression. Alberta's Medicine Hat, for example, had stagnated through the 1930s. Yet the one event that everyone remembered from the end of that dreadful decade was the visit in May 1939 of King George VI and Queen Elizabeth. Visitors from neighbouring Saskatchewan and Montana, as well as thousands of Albertans, flocked to the city. Cheering crowds lined the railway tracks for three miles outside the city as the royal train

arrived. On the platform the royal couple were greeted by 4,000 schoolchildren and another 2,000 Cubs, Scouts, Brownies and Girl Guides. One lifelong resident of the city, Ethel Davies, remembered the day as "one of the greatest there ever was... not even one person missed it."

The royal visit was more than public relations success. It helped revive a monarchy badly shaken by Edward's abdication, and cemented relations with the Canadian people. It also proved to be an important morale-booster for a reluctant king, his wife and children, who had been thrust so suddenly into the limelight. As the Queen herself later remarked to Prime Minister King, "Canada made us." And not a moment too soon. Within a matter of months Britain would be faced with its most serious military threat in nine centuries. Invasion seemed imminent, and the trans-Atlantic lifeline to Canada would be crucial to survival. ■

The royal couple riding through Ottawa in an open carriage. King George was the first reigning monarch to set foot in the largest country of the Empire, and his fluency in French (Queen Elizabeth was even more fluent) surprised many.

National Archives of Canada

Prime Minister Mackenzie King and Queen Elizabeth during a stop in Banff, Alberta. Despite his sometimes uncomfortable relationship with the British government, King was an enthusiastic monarchist - and this was also a public relations opportunity he was not about to miss.

National Archives of Canada

PART TWO

1939-1946

A Canadian infantry platoon advancing near Gruchy, France, in July 1944. Two decades after the end of the Great War, the "war to end all wars," Canadians were once again caught in the maelstrom of a global conflict. This new war would require sacrifices on the battlefield, but it would also make enormous demands on the home front and transform the Canadian economy in the process. Ironically its first victim was the Great Depression.

National Archives of Canada

King thought that Hitler was nice?

Into The Maelstrom

Battered By The Great Depression
A Reluctant Nation Goes To War

'*The forces of evil have been loosed in a struggle between the pagan conception of a social order which ignores the individual and is based upon the doctrine of might, and a civilization based upon the Christian conception of the brotherhood of man, with its regard for the sanctity of contractual relations and the sacredness of human personality.*'

Wiilliam Lyon Mackenzie King

Prime Minister King (opposite left) receiving a warm welcome in Berlin in 1937. Privately, King came away convinced that Adolf Hitler "is really one who truly loves his fellow man." Luckily for King, his profoundly mistaken appraisal of the German leader would not become public until decades after the war.

National Archives of Canada

*I*n the summer of 1937 Prime Minister Mackenzie King set off to Berlin for a face-to-face chat with German leader Adolf Hitler. King was apparently convinced that his powers of persuasion could do more to avert war in Europe than rapid re-armament or threats of economic sanctions by the League of Nations. At their meeting Hitler impressed the Canadian prime minister, who wrote that he found him "a man of deep sincerity and a genuine patriot". As for those who suggested Hitler was preparing for aggressive war against his neighbours, King wrote with certainty that "the Germans are not contemplating the possibility of war".

The prime minister's diaries, not published until long after his death, show how profoundly mistaken he was in his assessment of Hitler. "He smiled very pleasantly, and indeed had a sort of appealing and affectionate look in his eyes," he wrote of his encounter the Fuhrer. "His eyes impressed me most of all. There was a liquid quality about them which indicated keen perception and profound sympathy (calm, composed) - and one could see how particularly humble folk would come to have profound love for the man... I believe the world will yet come to see a very great man - mystic - in Hitler." King's apparent inability to link the man to the increasingly ominous policies followed by his regime is shocking in its naivety, but in his discussions with Hitler he found the comfort he had been seeking. Appeasement was clearly the way to deal with German ambitions. When British Prime Minister Neville Chamberlain announced that he would follow King to Berlin for his own chat with Hitler, King was ecstatic. "I am sure the Canadian people will warmly approve this farseeing and truly noble action," he told reporters. "I believe it will be found that Chamberlain has saved the day." After the agreement between Chamberlain and Hitler in Munich in the fall of 1938 (which Chamberlain claimed had secured "peace in our time") King believed war had truly been averted. "The heart of Canada is rejoicing tonight at the success which has crowned your unremitting efforts for peace," he wrote to the British PM. "Reason has found a way out of conflict." It was wishful thinking par excellence.

Chamberlain's deluded efforts to appease Hitler would soon destroy his political career and reputation. Among his countrymen Chamberlain's name has become a byword for self-delusion and moral cowardice in the face of evil and aggression. Perhaps unfairly so, because the reality of Hitler's ambitions did eventually hit home with the British leader and he abandoned his policy of appeasement and prepared for war. Not so Chamberlain's Canadian cheerleader. Future prime minister Lester Pearson (then a diplomat) wrote that "King prefers Chamberlain the appeaser to Chamberlain the avenger." In March 1939, barely six months before the outbreak of war, King told Parliament that he would not provide Britain with public assurances of Canadian support in any conflict with Germany. "We have tremendous things to do at home, in housing the people, in caring for the aged and helpless, in meeting our heavy burden of debt, in making provisions for Canada's defence, and in bringing our standard of living and civilization to the level our knowledge now makes possible." King wondered why Canada should be called upon "to save periodically a continent that cannot run itself, and to this end, risk the lives of its people, risk bankruptcy, and political disunion?"

He was far from being alone in wondering this. Always the consummate politician, King understood and correctly interpreted the mood of many Canadians - particularly in Quebec. After the experience of 1914-18, the country did not want another war. The isolationism that gripped the United States was reflected in Canada, at least superficially. But the widespread hope that Germany might be appeased was based upon the belief that, a mere two decades after the Great War, no one could actually be mad or evil enough to plunge Europe, and the world, into another bloodbath. Not even the strange, ranting Adolf Hitler. When it eventually became apparent that armed aggression was indeed central to Hitler's plan, there was little question that Canada would once again put its people, its treasury, and its fragile unity at risk to stand beside Britain.

German leaders giving the Nazi-salute (above) at the opening of the All-German Games in Berlin's Olympic Stadium, June 27, 1937. Prime Minister King can be seen on the far left. A strong supporter of appeasing Hitler's Germany, King came home convinced that war could be avoided.

National Archives of Canada

As literary icon Stephen Leacock wrote in the *Atlantic Monthly* in the summer of 1939: "If you were to ask any Canadian, 'Do you have to go to war if England does?' he'd answer at once, 'oh no.' If you then said, 'Would you go to war if England does?' he'd answer, 'oh, yes.' And if you asked, 'Why?' he would say reflectively, 'Well, you see, we'd have to.' " Such was the country's conflicted view of the global struggle as it unfolded.

The newsreels of Japan's invasion of Manchuria, the Italian attack on Ethiopia, civil war in Spain, and German rearmament and the Nazis expansion into Austria and Czechoslovakia, left most Canadians in no doubt that the "war to end all wars" and the efforts of the League of Nations had not rid the world of all conflict, but still the desire for peace - real or imagined - was extremely powerful. "We all longed for peace - everybody," said Great War veteran Angus Macdonald (soon to be Canada's navy minister). "Some longed so deeply that they came to believe that never again would there be war." Even at the 11th hour, most people hoped for the best and many accepted the argument that preparing for war would only serve to hasten it. And nowhere was that public mood so gratefully exploited as in Ottawa.

The Great Depression had given federal governments a valid excuse for trimming military spending, which happily coincided with Prime Minister King's personal distaste for such expenditures. The result was that by the late 1930s Canada was spending less on defence than any other industrialized country - $1.46 per citizen (0.5% of national income), compared with Britain's $23, the United States' $6.50, and Australia's $3.30. A report on Canada's war-readiness made dismal reading. There were but 25 obsolete aircraft, without a single bomb, and the country possessed no anti-aircraft guns. The navy had six destroyers and five minesweepers, but much of the ammunition and equipment at both Halifax and Esquimalt naval depots was so old it was deemed to be useless. The army consisted of just 4,000 regular troops, with 16 light tanks (purchased from Britain in 1938), 23 anti-tank guns, and five mortars. "About the only article of which stocks are held is harness," reported the Chief of the Defence Staff, Maj. Gen. Andrew McNaughton. And in a modern, mechanized war there would likely be little need of horses or cavalry, noted the general. The good news was that there were 46,000 at least partially-trained members of the militia. The bad news was that number compared to 55,000 in 1913, when the Canadian army had been woefully unprepared for its entry into the Great War.

King's distrust of the military and his opposition to defence spending was well established, but that didn't mean he was opposed to defensive alliances - just in case of trouble. He managed to get a commitment from U.S President Franklin Roosevelt that if Canada were attacked the U.S. "would not stand idly by if domination of Canadian soil is threatened." King's response was a commitment to make Canada "as immune from attack or possible invasion as we can reasonably be expected to make it." So spending on the army was cut, while the emphasis turned to the air force and navy for home defence. Naval manpower was boosted, and several destroyers and four new minesweepers were added to the fleet. The badly neglected RCAF's budget increased almost tenfold to $30 million by 1939, with the establishment of a five-squadron reserve and the purchase of some new aircraft. It was still small potatoes compared with the re-armament going on in Europe, but it was a start.

Later generations of Canadians would be united in the belief that World War Two was that rarest of conflicts, a just war, and with the benefit of hindsight the righteousness of fighting against Nazism is crystal clear. There has rarely been a more ruthless or determined manifestation of evil than Hitler's Third Reich. Yet with the memories of the Great War still raw this was not so clear to Canadians in the 1930s, and it took most people some time to accept that Japan, Italy, and especially Hitler's Germany, were on an unalterable collision course with their country's international interests and domestic values. At the 1936 Berlin Olympic Games the 100-strong

Canadian team had actually given Hitler the Nazi salute as they marched past his box - the only Commonwealth team to do so. It was meant as a "gesture of respect," officials hastily explained.

Canada's response to the mass exodus of Jews from Germany and neighbouring countries was to stiffen immigration controls beyond the barriers erected during the Depression. The amount of capital an immigrant needed to enter the country was raised from $5,000 to $15,000, and only farmers were admitted. Cairine Wilson, Canada's first female senator, was among the most outspoken critics of the government's policy. "We must be big enough and courageous enough to admit to Canada a fair share of the unfortunate persons involved," she told the Senate. Frederick Blair, the deputy minister of immigration, responded that if Jews "would divest themselves of certain of their habits I am sure they could be just as popular in Canada as our Scandinavians." Wilson made numerous attempts to get Jewish refugees admitted to Canada, but with little success. Of 100 Jewish orphans she sponsored for immigration, all but two were rejected. In marked contrast to the country's later reputation, of the 800,000 Jews who fled Europe between 1933 and the outbreak of war, barely 4,000 found refuge in Canada.

Germany's annexation of Austria in the spring of 1938 shocked many Canadians, but not so much as the news that the Third Reich was using a Dutch-based dummy company to buy the St. Lawrence River island of Anticosti from the Consolidated Paper Company. That was getting much too close to home. The public was outraged, and the King government blocked the sale and ordered the RCMP to keep an eye on German government activities in Canada. The sudden increase in public and media concern over German intentions sent anti-war commentators to

British children evacuated to Canada (below). Widespread bombing of Britain seemed imminent, and a German invasion a very real possibility, so in the summer and fall of 1940 about 7,000 British children were evacuated to Canada (and another 3,000 to the U.S.). Some went to relatives, but most were taken in by strangers, and almost all spent the entire war with their new families.

National Archives of Canada

their typewriters. F.R. Scott, the Montreal poet, and son of a Great War veteran, wrote that "elderly sadists of the last war are emerging from their obscurity to join the war dance again, their eyes glistening and their mouths watering as they think of the young men whom they will send to the slaughter." A significant number of Canadians were inclined to agree, and publicly at least the prime minister maintained his accustomed position astride the political fence. It was not always easy. The Canadian contribution to the air war in 1914-18 was still a source of national pride, and a steady stream of Canadians - some with flying experience, but many without - sailed to Britain to join the RAF. But when Britain proposed an official aircrew training program based in Canada, King recoiled. Barely 12 months before the outbreak of war, the idea of Canada aiding and abetting British re-armament remained politically unappealing.

Yet as with so much about this contradictory leader, what King said was not always a sure guide to what he would actually do. His reluctance to get the country involved in another European conflict was real, as was the threat to national unity and the solidarity of King's government. But he clearly understood that, although a majority of Canadians of British origin wished to avoid war, there was no question that in the event of hostilities they would expect the country to support Britain. Among French Canadians, however, there were many who would oppose involvement in any war that didn't directly threaten Canada. At one point in 1938 the looming prospect of having to deal with this divisive issue sent a frazzled King to his bed for two weeks. The prime minister's solution to the dilemma, in typical King fashion, was to downplay the

Prime Minister King (above) with a portrait of his late mother, in the library of his home. Only a handful of people knew that the prime minister used séances to commune with his mother, father, grandfather and others. Thankfully, disagreement among the spirits regarding Hitler's intentions persuaded King their advice was of limited value in wartime.

National Archives of Canada

possibility of Canadian forces becoming directly involved in another European conflict, while at the same time preparing the public for the eventuality of war. And first and foremost, to promise absolutely no conscription! "The days of great expeditionary forces crossing the oceans are not likely to recur," he told Parliament soothingly. "Conscription of men for overseas service would not be a necessary or effective step. Let me say that so long as this government may be in power, no such measure will be enacted." The promise to avoid conscription seemed to settle French Canadian public opinion, and was acceptable to Conservative leader Robert Manion. The rank and file of the CCF now also rebelled against socialist intellectuals like F.R. Scott and "their continuous attempt to force upon the CCF an isolationist policy". Gradually Canada's cautious prime minister was leading public opinion towards the inevitable.

When Hitler threatened Poland, Chamberlain assured the Poles that if there were a German invasion Britain would not allow their country to become another Czechoslovakia. Canada was not consulted, but after years of refusing to give guarantees of support for Britain that was hardly something King could complain about. Privately he now admitted that if it came to war he could not "consider being neutral in this situation for a minute". Despite the clear misgivings of many Canadians, support for Britain had never really been in doubt. "If a great and clear call of duty comes, Canada will respond," confirmed King. That call came on September 1, 1939, when nine armoured divisions of German troops attacked across the Polish border. Britain declared war two days later, and King George called for the support of "our peoples across the seas, who will make our cause their own". The news reached the Canadian prime minister as he conducted one of his regular séances. His deceased father apparently informed him that Hitler had already been killed by a Polish agent, while his grandfather insisted that the German leader was alive and could not be trusted. The apparent confusion unsettled King and for the duration of the war the prime minister would mostly avoid resorting to séances for guidance - which would no doubt have been of some comfort to Canadians, had they known about King's regular consultations with the spirit world.

Newfoundland declared war on Germany immediately. In the first act of hostility in North America a German ship had been seized in St. John's and the crew confined to the city's YMCA. But Prime Minister King took his time in bringing the issue to the Canadian Parliament. At the end of the first week of September the prime minister kicked off a ritual debate on the declaration of war. Bruce Hutchison, King's biographer, calls his speech "bumbling and lamentable," full of references to obscure documents and a "recital of details that no one cared to hear". It was hardly a ringing call to arms, but the response was almost unanimous, with only CCF leader J.S. Woodsworth and three other MPs speaking against participation in this "foreign conflict". Without the necessity of a recorded vote, on September 10 Canada entered the most destructive war in history. The CBC interrupted an NBC broadcast of band music from Philadelphia to make the official announcement - then returned to the Kenneth Martin band playing *Inka Dinka Doo*. In most newspapers the declaration of war took second place to stirring accounts of Polish forces beating back the Germans on three fronts. Six days later, Poland surrendered.

An Arctic Odyssey

The Epic Voyage Of The St. Roch

The outbreak of World War Two ignited one of Ottawa's infrequent bursts of interest in affirming Canadian sovereignty in the Arctic. The task was given to the RCMP, which determined the best way to show the flag was to send the force's 32-metre, schooner-rigged ship *St. Roch* through the Northwest Passage. Only one person had ever sailed a ship through the famed Passage, Norwegian Roald Amundsen, who in 1903-06 had successfully navigated the Arctic waters from east to west. Ironically the skipper of the *St. Roch* was a Norwegian-born Canadian, Sergeant Henry Larsen, who had idolized Amundsen from his youth and who nurtured a burning desire to replicate his hero's achievement. Fascinated with tales of the Arctic, Larsen moved to Canada's West Coast and served as navigator for two voyages on one of the few trading vessels plying Arctic waters. He gained valuable experience dealing with the variable conditions of the Arctic seas and became well acquainted with the Inuit, mastering the skills necessary to survive in the harshest of environments.

In 1927, Larsen had learned that the RCMP was having a small patrol vessel built in Vancouver for service in the Arctic. He was determined to sail on her. He became a Canadian citizen that year, applied for service in the RCMP and was accepted. When it came time to name a captain for the *St. Roch*, Larsen's sailing skills made him the obvious choice. Larsen spent the next dozen years

patrolling western Arctic waters. The ship had been sturdily built of Douglas fir and Australian eucalyptus "iron bark" to resist the crushing pressures of sea ice. She was equipped with a small 150 horse power diesel engine, but her sails gave the *St. Roch* the ability to undertake long voyages without the necessity of refuelling. The ship supplied isolated RCMP posts in the western Arctic, carried out regular police activities, and responded to emergencies. A floating RCMP detachment, it was mostly crewed by non-seamen, but Larsen had become a master of the Arctic waters.

In 1940 the *St. Roch* was ordered to sail from Vancouver to Halifax. It was the challenge Larsen had been preparing for his entire life. Leaving port on June 21 and rounding Alaska, the ship entered the Passage from the west. Blasted by gale-force winds, and constantly hemmed in by fog and ice floes, it managed to cover 8,400 km by September 25. With winter closing in, Larsen anchored in Walker Bay, Victoria Island. The summer of 1941 was particularly short in the Arctic, with only six weeks suitable for sailing, and the little ship was forced to spend a second winter frozen in ice, this time in Pasley Bay on the Boothia Peninsula. Larsen and most of his men survived the grim ordeal, except for crewman Albert Chartrand, who died of a heart attack.

The men of the *St. Roch* were not idle during the long months in the Arctic. They gathered census information, and as representatives of the Canadian government they acted as game wardens,

RCMP Sergeant Henry Larsen (above), captain of the St. Roch. The Norwegian-born Larsen was determined to follow in the footsteps of earlier Arctic explorers.

National Archives of Canada

postal handlers, custom and tax officials, registrars of shipping, and general welfare officers. Larsen conducted the earliest salinity readings of the western Arctic Ocean, and collected Inuit artifacts and specimens of marine life. He was also the first to make a colour movie of Arctic life. That film and the large archive of still photos Larsen and his crew collected provide a priceless historical record.

The final segment of the voyage proved to be the most daunting, as the ship fought its way eastwards. One cylinder on the engine broke, and the storms and ice were the worst the expedition had encountered. At one point Larsen wondered "if we had come this far only to be crushed like a nut on a shoal and then buried by the ice?" However, the *St. Roch* managed to reach Baffin Bay, and eventually the North Atlantic. On October 11, 1942 it sailed triumphant into Halifax Harbour. After a season patrolling the eastern Arctic, in 1944 Larsen received orders to take his ship home to Vancouver. As before, most of the crew had little or no prior marine training, and success depended to a very large extent on the captain's skill, resourcefulness, and leadership abilities. This time Larsen decided to use the more northerly Parry Channel Route through the Passage, via Lancaster Sound, Barrow Strait and Viscount Melville Sound. Although the route still presented formidable difficulties, they were far less life-threatening than the ones encountered on the more southerly route.

On board for the return journey was William Cashin, a 17-year-old dock worker in Halifax who had been hired by Larsen as a deckhand. "All we had to eat was dry goods, powdered milk, canned meat, bully beef, and Spam," Cashin recalled years later. In contrast to the earlier voyage, it took the *St. Roch* only 86 days to sail from Halifax to Vancouver. Larsen and his ship became the first to navigate the Northwest Passage west to east, the only ship to sail through the Passage in both directions, and the first to make a one-way journey in a single sailing season. In 1950 Larsen took the *St. Roch* from Vancouver to Halifax via the Panama Canal, becoming the first vessel to circumnavigate North America. Retired by the RCMP in 1954, the ship was declared a National Historic Site and sits in dry-dock, open to visitors, at the Vancouver Maritime Museum. ■

The RCMP's marine patrol vessel St. Roch in the ice near Point Barrow. The summer of 1941 was particularly short, with a mere six weeks of sailing weather for the shop to complete its traverse of the Northwest Passage.

National Archives of Canada

nlike 1914, at the outbreak of World War Two there was no great public display of patriotic enthusiasm. Just about everyone knew someone - a father, an uncle, a neighbour - who had served overseas in the horror that was still known as the Great War. There were disabled veterans in most communities, their minds or bodies shattered by the experience of industrialized warfare. "In August 1914 the Canadian people had gone to war in high fighting spirit. In September 1939 they accepted the blow fate had dealt them," wrote historian A.R. M. Lower. "Ten years of depression and 20 years crumbling of old institutions and beliefs did not provide the soil in which buoyant, fighting spirits flourish. There was little jingoism: neither jubilation nor active protest. Canadians reluctantly prepared to accept their fate." This time, there were few illusions about the looming conflict. B.C. artist Emily Carr noted in her diary that the public mood was grim. "Nobody was smiling. Everybody spending Labour Day guiltily, in a melancholy peace."

Still, there remained close to a million Canadians on relief and for many unemployed young men the lure of $1.30 a day and three square meals was enough of an incentive to volunteer. So many men appeared at recruitment centres that only near-perfect physical specimens were accepted. Rev. Morris Zeidman of the Scott Mission in Toronto reported an additional 100 hungry men in his soup kitchen line-up. "They left their jobs and homes to join up, and they weren't wanted." As John Dougan, of Claresholm, Alberta, explained, the motivation of many Western farm boys was simple: a steady job, steady pay, "and an opportunity to get out of the terrible trap in which they found themselves". There was a steady flow of the youthful and adventurous to recruiting centres across the country, and initially medical officers had the luxury of turning down more recruits than they accepted. In Quebec, where support for aiding Britain was allegedly least enthusiastic, Montreal's French-speaking regiments were among the first to report a full muster of volunteers. In New Westminster. B.C., neighbours John Mahony, a newspaper reporter, and Ernest "Smoky" Smith, an unemployed construction worker, both enlisted early on. They didn't know each other, but before the war ended they would be among 16 Canadians who would win the Victoria Cross.

King was determined that this time Canadian blood would not be shed in a futile European trench war, and that there be no repetition of the awful conscription crisis that had split the country and the Liberal party in 1917. If Canada had to fight, it would be a limited war. The country would send a single volunteer army division to Britain, and another would be trained and held in reserve in Canada. There would be no wartime expansion of the navy, but the RCAF would be beefed up for the purpose of home defence. King also reversed himself on the aircrew-training proposal he had so recently turned down. Canada would now take the leading role in a $600 million Commonwealth Air Training Plan (50% funded by Ottawa), providing the organization and airfields to train 20,000 aircrew a year for the Royal Air Force. There would be no need for conscription, and most of the money spent would stay in Canada. It was a modest plan for a modest war, and apparently precisely what most Canadians wanted to hear.

Not Quebec Premier Maurice Duplessis, who called a provincial election in the clear hope of taking advantage of French opposition to the war. It was close, but with the active intervention of Ernest Lapointe and other federal ministers from Quebec, Duplessis's strategy failed and he was defeated. Ontario Liberal Premier Mitch Hepburn also opposed King's policy of limited war,

Montreal Mayor Camillien Houde (above) addressing an anti-war rally in 1939. Quebec Premier Maurice Duplessis called a snap election weeks after war was declared, arguing that Ottawa was using the conflict as a pretext for extending its power in the province. He was defeated by the provincial Liberals.

Montreal Gazette/National Archives of Canada

but for the opposite reason. "When the real fury of this thing strikes us, the people of Canada will realize they have made a tremendous mistake in endorsing King and his half-hearted war effort," he warned. When the Ontario government passed a resolution condemning King's management of the war effort, the prime minister saw it as a threat to his authority and called a snap election early in 1940. King was rewarded with a whopping majority (181 of 245 seats) from a country that clearly thought the Liberal plan for limited involvement in the war to be an appropriate response. The national self-delusion was complete.

Hitler, however, was not contemplating a modest war, and most certainly not a re-run of the previous one - in which he had served as an enlisted man. In April, 1940, his troops invaded Norway. A month later German armoured columns stormed through Holland and Belgium, bypassing the huge French Maginot Line defences. By the beginning of June the French were in full retreat and British troops sent to support them were bottled up around the North Sea port of Dunkirk, from whose beaches many were miraculously plucked by a fleet of mostly civilian vessels of all types and sizes. The evacuation quickly became a rallying cry for the beleaguered British and their pugnacious new prime minister, Winston Churchill. The 20,000 troops of the First Canadian Division had been dispatched to Britain the previous winter, and the 1st Brigade actually landed in central France after the Dunkirk evacuation as part of a half-hearted effort to form a new Allied line of defence in Brittany. Fortunately the hopelessness of such a plan was quickly recognized and the train delivering the untested and half-trained soldiers to the front was reversed and the Canadians withdrawn before they could be overwhelmed. Much of the brigade's new equipment was abandoned in the French port of Brest, but only one Canadian died and five more were taken prisoner. By June 12 the French had capitulated, and among the European nations Britain stood alone in its opposition to the Nazis.

An anti-war rally (below) staged by University of Montreal students on March 23, 1939. The looming war, in particular the possibility of conscription, was unpopular among many French Canadian politicians, media, and intellectuals.

Montreal Gazette/National Archives of Canada

5th (WESTMOUNT) FIELD BATTERY
ROYAL CANADIAN ARTILLERY
RECRUITS WANTED
RADIO OPERATORS - MECHANICS - SURVEYORS
APPLY THIS TRUCK OR THE CRAIG ST. DRILL HALL

Recruiters on the street in Montreal (above) after the outbreak of war in September 1939. Recruitment was brisk among anglophone and francophone Quebecers, despite the opposition of the Duplessis government and much of the French Canadian establishment.

National Archives of Canada

In Ottawa the reality of Hitler's intentions and Britain's precarious situation finally sank in. In a rare display of oratory, the prime minister told parliament: "The forces of evil have been loosed in a struggle between the pagan conception of a social order which ignores the individual and is based upon the doctrine of might, and a civilization based upon the Christian conception of the brotherhood of man, with its regard for the sanctity of contractual relations and the sacredness of human personality." The situation was indeed dire. With German troops and aircraft just a short hop from the southern coast of England, an invasion seemed likely and defeat a very real possibility. If that happened, Canada was likely to become the centre of British resistance. Churchill said as much in a speech in London. "Even if... this island or a large part of it were subjugated and starving, then our Empire beyond the seas, armed and guarded by the British fleet, would carry on the struggle - until in God's good time the New World, with all its power and might, steps forth to the rescue and liberation of the Old."

The U.S. remained reluctant to become directly involved in the war but had already pledged to defend Canada in the event of an attack by Germany, and President Roosevelt called the prime minister to suggest a meeting. The result was the creation of the Permanent Joint Board on Defence, which would co-ordinate Canadian and U.S. war plans. It was America's first direct response to the German threat, but privately Roosevelt told King that Britain might have to surrender to the Nazis. The idea appalled the Canadian leader, who at long last had fully absorbed the threat posed by Hitler. "It seems that the U.S. was seeking to save itself at the expense of Britain, that the British might have to go down," he wrote. "My reaction was that I would rather die than do aught to save ourselves or any part of this continent at the expense of Britain." Churchill rightly feared the Canada/U.S. agreement meant King and Roosevelt would place the defence of North America ahead of any aid to Britain, but in fact it left Canada free to devote all its efforts to the defence of Britain, safe in the knowledge that the U.S. would backstop its neighbour if things went badly wrong.

King's appreciation of the Nazi threat and the potential scale of Hitler's ambitions may have been slow to form, but he was above all a practical man and faced with the reality of a new war with Germany he did what he did best. He organized. Historians are lavish in their praise for King's efforts to put together what has been called the most powerful and talented cabinet in Canadian history. Ernest Lapointe continued as King's deputy and right-hand man, former finance minister J.L. Ralston (a decorated veteran of the Great War) was appointed Minister of Defence, workaholic Nova-Scotian James Ilsley replaced Ralston in finance, Charles "Chubby" Power was given the task of creating a Canadian air force, and Angus Macdonald became the minister responsible for the navy. But perhaps the most influential of King's appointments was American-born Clarence Decatur Howe, who was made Minister of Munitions and Supply. The no-nonsense Howe recognized few limits to his authority, and with the odd exception (he was not allowed to demolish the historic East Block of Parliament and replace it with a modern office building) King let him follow his instincts. With near dictatorial powers, and the ability to let huge government contracts, Howe revolutionized Canadian industrial production. With the aid of top business executives such as Argus Corp founder E.P. Taylor and future CN Rail president Donald Gordon - who worked for a dollar a year - the formidable Howe set about turning Canada into the arsenal of democracy.

Troops of the Regiment de la Chaudiere parade for Prime Minister King (below) during a visit to England early in the war. King's support of appeasement was by this time forgotten, and he vowed he "would rather die" than leave Britain to face the Nazi peril alone.

National Archives of Canada

Men of the 2nd Canadian Division aboard an unidentified troop ship leaving Halifax in the late summer, 1939. Sailing orders for the ships that transported Canada's army across the Atlantic were top secret, for obvious reasons. A troop ship would have been a prime target for German U-boats.

National Archives of Canada

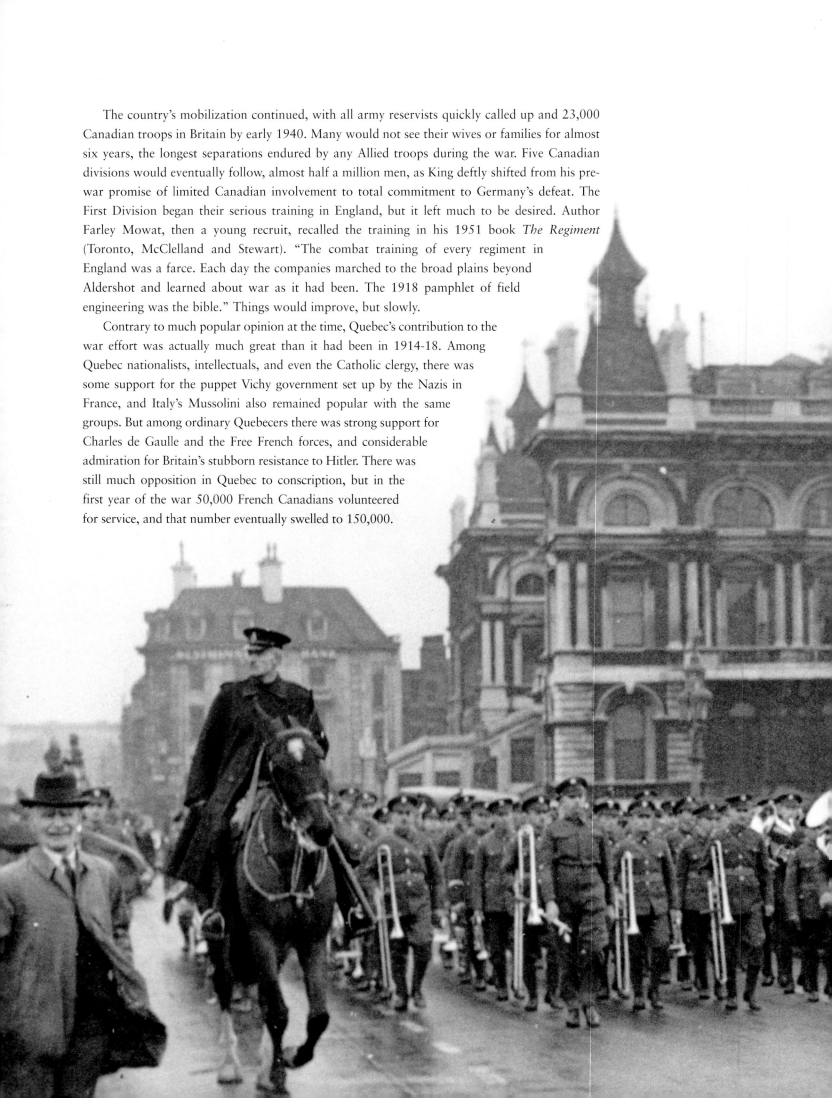

The country's mobilization continued, with all army reservists quickly called up and 23,000 Canadian troops in Britain by early 1940. Many would not see their wives or families for almost six years, the longest separations endured by any Allied troops during the war. Five Canadian divisions would eventually follow, almost half a million men, as King deftly shifted from his pre-war promise of limited Canadian involvement to total commitment to Germany's defeat. The First Division began their serious training in England, but it left much to be desired. Author Farley Mowat, then a young recruit, recalled the training in his 1951 book *The Regiment* (Toronto, McClelland and Stewart). "The combat training of every regiment in England was a farce. Each day the companies marched to the broad plains beyond Aldershot and learned about war as it had been. The 1918 pamphlet of field engineering was the bible." Things would improve, but slowly.

Contrary to much popular opinion at the time, Quebec's contribution to the war effort was actually much great than it had been in 1914-18. Among Quebec nationalists, intellectuals, and even the Catholic clergy, there was some support for the puppet Vichy government set up by the Nazis in France, and Italy's Mussolini also remained popular with the same groups. But among ordinary Quebecers there was strong support for Charles de Gaulle and the Free French forces, and considerable admiration for Britain's stubborn resistance to Hitler. There was still much opposition in Quebec to conscription, but in the first year of the war 50,000 French Canadians volunteered for service, and that number eventually swelled to 150,000.

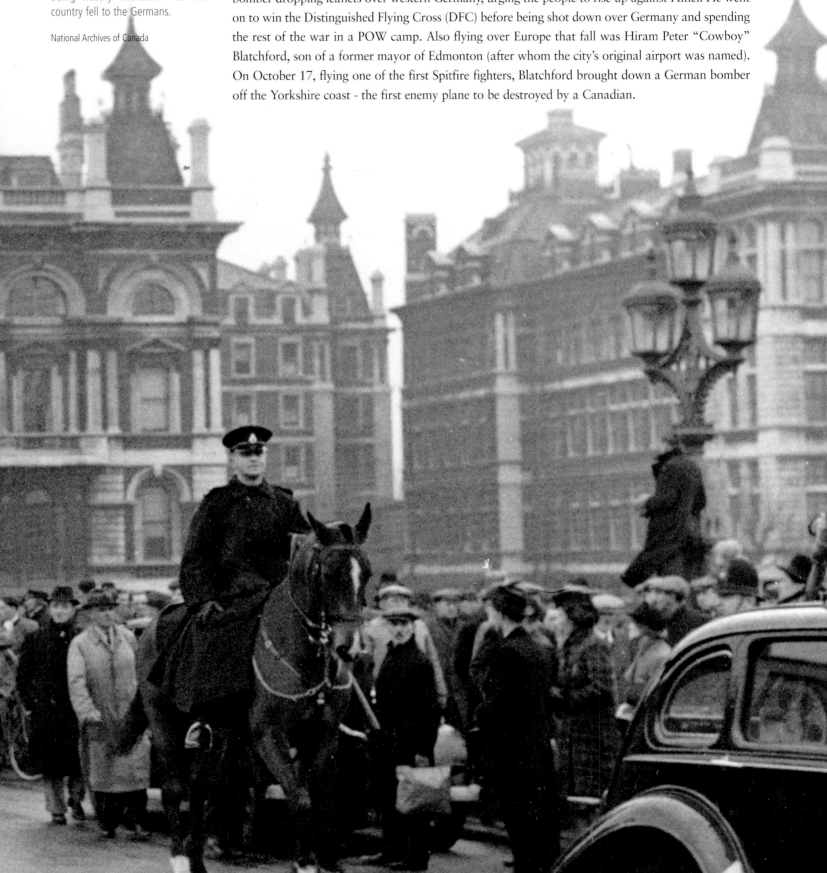

The first Canadian troops - 20,000 men of the 1st Canadian Division - march through Liverpool, England (below), after arriving in Britain in 1939. Some would briefly see action in France the following year, before being hastily withdrawn as the country fell to the Germans.

National Archives of Canada

In contrast to the Great War, this time the government took more care to recognize the contribution of Quebec volunteers and created French-speaking infantry and artillery units.

For some Canadians, the war began early and in the air. At the outbreak of outbreak of hostilities a number of Canadians were already flying with the British air force, among them George Walker of Gleichen, Alberta, who had joined the RAF in 1937. In September 1939 he was co-pilot of a Whitley bomber dropping leaflets over western Germany, urging the people to rise up against Hitler. He went on to win the Distinguished Flying Cross (DFC) before being shot down over Germany and spending the rest of the war in a POW camp. Also flying over Europe that fall was Hiram Peter "Cowboy" Blatchford, son of a former mayor of Edmonton (after whom the city's original airport was named). On October 17, flying one of the first Spitfire fighters, Blatchford brought down a German bomber off the Yorkshire coast - the first enemy plane to be destroyed by a Canadian.

The RAF's 242 Fighter Squadron, made up of Canadian pilots, destroyed 30 German aircraft in the skies over France in the spring of 1940, before being evacuated with their Hurricane aircraft ahead of the seemingly unstoppable German invasion. Calgary's Willie McKnight and Toronto's Stan Turner had already shot down five German planes. "Although the squadron had done well... we had also been badly mauled," Turner later recalled. "Seven pilots had been killed, two wounded, one had a breakdown, and our CO was missing." When France surrendered French troops set up machine guns along the runway of the airfield at Nantes, where 242 Squadron was based, threatening to destroy any aircraft that attempted to leave. There was a tense stand-off between the French and British troops before the Canadians were allowed to fly away. "As we headed for England we felt not so much relief as anger," remembered Turner. "We wanted to hit something, and there was nothing to hit... But we knew the real war had only just begun."

As the four-month Battle of Britain began, about 80 Canadians were already flying with the RAF fighter force, many with 242 Squadron (another 200 were flying with RAF Bomber Command). The 242 was now commanded by the legendary British pilot Douglas Bader, who had fought his way back to active duty despite losing both legs in a plane crash. The no-nonsense,

Canadian Defence Minister Layton Ralston (below), visiting troops in Britain. The highly regarded Ralston eventually became convinced that Canadian losses in Europe meant conscription was inevitable - which was not the view of Prime Minister King, who fired him.

National Archives of Canada

Link trainers (right) - early flight simulators - at the Virden Flight Training School in Manitoba, and pilot trainees (below) with Curtiss P-36 aircraft at the Little Norway training centre on Toronto Island. Both facilities were part of the massive Commonwealth Air Training Plan, arguably Canada's largest single contribution to the war effort (and at almost $1 billion the most expensive). Between 1940 and 1945 a total of 131,000 aircrew (including 50,000 pilots) graduated from 231 training sites across Canada. More than half of the fliers were Canadian, but they also included many from Britain, the Commonwealth, the U.S., and occupied Europe. Winston Churchill credited the plan with turning the tide in the air war, and U.S. President Franklin D. Roosevelt called Canada "the Aerodrome (airfield) of Democracy." The air training plan used more than 10,000 aircraft to train fliers from a dozen allied nations. It was a display or organization and manpower the Germans could not hope to match.

National Archives of Canada Photos

upper crust Bader initially didn't think much of these scruffy looking colonials with a reputation for wildness, but after he discovered they'd lost all their spare clothing in the evacuation from France he handed out his own shirts and opened an account for the boys with a local tailor. In one famous action on August 30, 1940, the 242nd took on a force of German bombers and about 30 escorting fighters, destroying a dozen enemy aircraft, damaging others, and forcing the retreat of the rest. Bader and his wingman, McKnight, accounted for five of the downed planes.

The first Canadian air force unit to see action in Europe, the RCAF's No. 1 Fighter Squadron, was committed to the Battle of Britain on August 24, and in its first attack tragically mistook three RAF aircraft for German bombers - destroying one before realizing the error. Two days later over southern England the squadron broke up a German bombing raid, destroyed three enemy aircraft. They also lost one pilot, R.L. Edwards, who became the RCAF's first fatality of the war. Twenty Canadian pilots were killed during the Battle of Britain. In the famous words of Winston Churchill, "never in the field of human conflict was so much owed by so many to so few". Willie McKnight survived and is credited with destroying 21 enemy aircraft (twice winning the DFC), before being shot down over the English Channel in January 1941. After the war Bader visited Calgary to honour his young comrade, and the city's McKnight Boulevard is named after him. Cowboy Blatchford survived until May 3rd, 1943. Leading an attack on a power plant in occupied Holland, his fighter was badly damaged and he was forced to ditch in the North Sea. His body was never recovered. As it had been a generation earlier, the part played by Canadians

December 1939. A worker does a final check (below) on a shell before it's filled with explosive. The sudden demand for war supplies ignited Canadian industry after a decade in the doldrums.

National Archives of Canada

in the air war would be a massive contribution to the Allied cause, with 25,000 Canadian pilots serving in every theatre of the conflict.

Perhaps Canada's single greatest contribution to the war effort, and certainly the most expensive, was the British Commonwealth Air Training Plan, founded at the end of 1939 to train aircrew for the Allied forces. At airfields across the Prairies, pilots, navigators, gunners, wireless operators, and other aircrew - more than 131,000 in all - were trained for combat. They came from every corner of the empire (Britain, Australia, New Zealand, South Africa, Fiji, India), from occupied Europe (Poland, France, Belgium, Norway), and prior to Pearl Harbor included almost 1,000 volunteers from the U.S. But by far the largest contingent was from Canada itself: an incredible 72,835. By 1945 fully one quarter of the aircrew strength of the British and Commonwealth air forces would be Canadian. The cost of training all these men would eventually top $2 billion, with Canada footing almost three-quarters of the total bill - an enormous contribution from a country of just 11 million people.

In the early months of the war German bombing took a heavy toll among the RAF's female air controllers (26 were killed in London during a single raid), and Canadian women trained as operations room staff were in high demand. Phyllis Patterson joined the RCAF in Edmonton and was among an early group of Canadian women to travel to Britain. She sailed aboard the luxury liner *Queen Mary*, which instead of its usual compliment of 2,100 passengers was loaded with 14,000 troops. The great ship was much faster than most other vessels and travelled alone across

A machinist (below) works on part of the firing mechanism of a naval gun at a plant in Sorel, Quebec. The poster behind him is typical of wartime exhortations to workers - optimistic, even in the dark days of 1940-41.

National Archives of Canada

'The Falcon Of Malta'

Canadian Fighter Ace Buzz Beurling

George "Buzz" Beurling, the top Canadian fighter ace of World War Two, is far less well known than his counterpart in the war of 1914-18, Billy Bishop, but the two were in many ways similar characters: mavericks who had a problem with authority. Beurling was born in 1921 in Verdun, Quebec. A disinterested student and a loner, one enthusiasm became the focus of his life: a love of planes and flying. He was a fixture at the nearby Cartierville airport, and sold model airplanes to raise money for flying lessons. By the time he was 16 he quit school and got a job in Northern Ontario as a co-pilot and navigator, hauling mining supplies into the bush.

After getting his pilot's license he travelled to the U.S. and tried to volunteer for service in China flying against the Japanese invading Manchuria. The 18-year-old was promptly deported back to Canada, where he made an unsuccessful attempt to join the Royal Canadian Air Force (which rejected him because he hadn't completed high school). When war broke out in Europe, Beurling made yet another attempt to enlist, this time in the air force of Finland. However, the Finnish consulate in Montreal insisted he get written permission from his father, which papa Beurling refused. In the spring of 1940 he heard that the Royal Air Force was recruiting experienced pilots in Britain, and he travelled to Glasgow aboard a munitions ship. Beurling presented himself at the nearest RAF recruiting station and was ecstatic to learn that he had qualified. All he needed was a birth certificate - which he had failed to bring with him! It took four months and a trans-Atlantic round-trip to retrieve the document, but by the fall of 1940 Buerling was finally in uniform.

After training, Beurling's obvious ability led the RAF to offer him a commission as an officer, which he turned down. He was

Canadian fighter ace Buzz Beurling, with 32 "kills" to his credit he was Canada's top World War Two fighter pilot.

National Archives of Canada

transferred to an active fighter squadron and on only his third mission over France shot down his first enemy aircraft. Two days later he did the same thing. Unfortunately Buerling's ability in the air was matched with an obstinate refusal to obey orders that put him in constant conflict with authority. By the summer of 1942 his superiors had had enough of the maverick Canadian, and he'd had enough of them. He volunteered for relocation to the Mediterranean island of Malta, a strategic British base being pounded to rubble by German and Italian air raids. On Malta there was little time for formality, just round-the-clock flying and almost daily combat. It suited Beurling perfectly.

His commander was Flight Lieutenant P.B. "Laddie" Lucas. "I felt I was in the presence of a very unusual young man," Lucas later wrote. "He didn't give a damn for me. A youngster really, who was champing at the bit to get to it, to get an airplane and have a go." And have a go he did. By the fall Beurling had destroyed 27 enemy aircraft and become a legend for his shooting ability and his recklessness (he'd also picked up a new nickname, "Screwball"). On October 14 the Germans launched a massive raid on the island and in the melee Beurling shot down three more aircraft, but his Spitfire was heavily damaged. Wounded in the chest, leg and foot he was forced to bail out over the sea. It was the fourth time he'd been shot down, and after two weeks in hospital and being awarded the Distinguished Service Order (his second medal), he was ordered back to Canada to help sell war bonds. Not, however, before surviving yet another crash, when the bomber transporting him back to Britain went down in a storm near Gibraltar. Only Beurling and one other passenger survived.

The prospect of being a media star had not appealed to Beurling, but once back in Canada he found himself revelling in the

Buzz Buerling signs an autograph for Helen Fowler (above) during a visit to the Aluminum Company of Canada (Alcan) offices in Kingston, Ontario. A notorious loner, Beurling was at first wary of public and media attention, but he later came to revel in it.

National Archives of Canada

public attention. Dubbed "The Falcon of Malta" by the newspapers, he also became a favourite of Prime Minister Mackenzie King. Unfortunately, Beurling tended to get carried away in describing death in air combat, often in graphic, bloody detail. During one appearance in Vancouver most of his horrified audience simply got up and left. His career as a war bond promoter was mercifully short. Beurling was sent back to England and became an instructor, but he was desperate to go back to flying and constantly requested a posting to an operational squadron. Finally, in September 1943 he was transferred to the RCAF and 403 Squadron. His main job was to teach young pilots how to shoot, but he also flew missions and pushed his tally of enemy aircraft to 32. He even accepted a promotion to Flight-Lieutenant because it gave him more opportunity to fly, but he continued to be rebellious and obstinate with his superiors. Only days before D-Day, Beurling was granted an honourable discharge from the RCAF and returned to Canada.

After-the-war Beurling couldn't settle, and his reputation for insubordination meant he couldn't find a regular flying job with one of the new airlines. There are even reports that he resorted to begging on Montreal street corners. Finally, in 1948 he volunteered to fly for the newly-independent state of Israel. He was killed a few months later when a transport plane he was flying in crashed in Italy. Sabotage was suspected but never proven. Beurling was given a grand funeral and lay in Rome's Verano Cemetery for two years before being reburied in Israel, where he is honoured as a hero. In Canada he remains virtually unknown. ∎

the submarine-infested North Atlantic, speed its only protection. "One day the captain informed us that the Germans had announced the sinking of the Queen Mary, so we laughed heartily and felt brave," recalled Patterson. "On the following day the ship lurched sharply, and for a few hours took a zigzag course to lose a submarine that was tracking us. Suddenly we all recognized our vulnerability." The ship travelled far off course to lose its pursuer, and by the time it docked in Britain had nothing but chocolate bars to feed its passengers. "When we docked in Scotland on a dull, rainy afternoon, we heard a thrilling sound, someone singing, lovely and clear, from the dockside," Patterson remembered years later. "It was Vera Lynn, a tiny figure in a trench coat and beret, standing on the dock in the pouring rain, singing her heart out for us."

Early in the war the Royal Canadian Navy (RCN) took responsibility for convoy security in the western sector of the North Atlantic, with the destroyers *St. Laurent* and *Saguenay* escorting 18 merchant ships out of Halifax harbour on September 16, 1939. They were the first of 25,000 vessels shepherded across the ocean by the Canadian navy during the war. It was a role for which the RCN was poorly equipped and barely trained. About the only thing the navy did not lack was enthusiasm. At the outbreak of war the RCN had six destroyers, four minesweepers and a motley collection of small craft. For more than a year destroyers such as the *Saguenay* conducted Canada's naval war almost alone. At first they fought beside British warships against German submarines prowling the approaches to the British Isles. When the U-boats moved west into the North Atlantic, the RCN vessels went after them. Their task was to protect merchant ships. In the early morning of December 1, 1940, *Saguenay* was shadowing a convoy some 450 km west

HMCS Edmunston (opposite left), a corvette, launching at Victoria, B.C. Mrs. Martin Malti (top right), a member of the Mi'kmaq First Nation, at work in a Pictou, Nova Scotia shipyard. And the christening ceremony for the S.S. Fort Esperance (right), at Montreal's United Shipyards. During the war Canada was launching as many as a dozen new ships each day to replace the staggering number being sunk by German U-boats and aircraft. In 1940 alone the Allies (not then including the U.S.) lost 1,000 ships to enemy action. Before 1939 the Canadian ship building industry had employed about 3,500 people, but within two years had expanded to a workforce of 80,000.

National Archives of Canada Photos

of Ireland when she was torpedoed by a U-boat. On fire, with 23 sailors dead, and missing a large section of her bow, the ship's guns nevertheless kept firing and forced the submarine to retreat - saving the convoy. *Saguenay* limped to port in northwest England (sustaining more damage when she hit a German mine), and eight weeks later was back in the thick of the Battle of the Atlantic.

In 1940 Ottawa ordered the building of a fleet of corvettes, originally designed as coastal patrol vessels. Weighing less than 1,000 tons and armed with depth charges and four-inch guns, these sturdy little ships would become the backbone of RCN operations against German U-boats during the Battle of the Atlantic. German submarines hunted in what came to be known as wolf packs, lining up across the path of a convoy. "Wolf pack was right," recalled Calgary sailor Ossie Hodges. In October, 1941, he was part of a convoy escort led by the destroyer HMCS *Columbia*. "There were so many of them. We were lucky to stay afloat. We'd go to move to the left, and there would be, not one, but a line of subs pointing right for us. We'd try the other side - same thing. We managed to run through, I don't know how." Six merchant ships and the Royal Navy corvette *Gladiolus* were not so lucky.

The RCN would eventually boast almost 100,000 sailors, and after a few weeks training many found themselves battling German U-boats. They learned on the job, often at terrible cost, but played a critical role in preserving Britain's lifeline across the North Atlantic. A typical Allied convoy, assembled off Halifax or St John's, was a floating city up to six miles wide, composed of all manner of ships from various nations. Canadian escort commander James Lamb, author of *The Corvette Navy* (Toronto, Macmillan of Canada, 1977) called the convoy "a living thing" and a "miracle of organi-

zation". A single convoy in July, 1940, carried a million tons of cargo, including 85,000 tons of grain, 85,000 tons of sugar, 88,000 tons of other food, 35,000 tons of lumber, 37,000 tons of iron and steel, 310,000 tons of oil, 80,000 tons of tanks and other armoured vehicles, and 250,000 tons of munitions. Without the hundreds of such convoys that braved the North Atlantic and the German U-boats, Britain could not have resisted Hitler. Churchill later confessed the destruction of this North Atlantic lifeline was the only threat that might have brought Britain to its knees. And with good reason. In 1940 alone the Allies lost 1,000 ships to attacks by German submarines and aircraft.

Women working on the interior of a tank (above) at the Montreal Locomotive Works. Munitions and Supply Minister C.D. Howe brushed aside concerns about the growing cost of the war effort. "If we win the war, no will care," argued Howe. "If we lose it, it won't matter."

National Archives of Canada

Despite Prime Minister Mackenzie King's early determination to limit the involvement of Canadian troops in Europe, in 1941 he was persuaded to send two largely-untrained battalions for the defence of Hong Kong. It proved to be one of the most tragic and foolhardy decisions of the war. The recently retired commander-in-chief of Britain's Hong Kong Garrison, Major General A.E. Grasett, was a Canadian and he managed to convince both Canadian and British governments that if the Japanese entered the war and threatened Hong Kong, they could be deterred by a reinforcement of forces in the colony. Churchill originally thought Hong Kong couldn't be defended and Grasett's idea "the height of foolishness", but he was eventually persuaded otherwise - a change of mind he later "regretted deeply". London requested that Canada send "one or two" battalions to Hong Kong, and the decision was taken in Ottawa to send two. King would later suggest he had opposed the decision, but there is no objective evidence that he had.

The Winnipeg Grenadiers and the Royal Rifles of Canada, 1,975 soldiers in all, sailed from Vancouver on October 27. Most were raw recruits, and to make matters worse their ship, the *Awatea*, couldn't accommodate their 212 vehicles. A plan was belatedly devised to cram 20 "priority vehicles" aboard the ship, but they arrived the day after it sailed. Japan had not yet entered the war, but with the Tokyo government now led by the bellicose Hideki Tojo that seemed just a matter of time. The *Awatea* arrived in Hong Kong on November 16 and the Canadians began to settle into their exotic surroundings, where even a private soldier's pay went a very long way indeed. Beer was 10 cents a bottle, and a local servant could be hired for 30 cents a week. "What a time," wrote Bill Allister, a signalman with the Royal Rifles. The downside was the knowledge that 30 miles way on the Chinese mainland was an invasion force of 50,000 experienced Japanese troops.

A gas decontamination drill in downtown Edmonton (below). With hindsight the likelihood of a gas attack on Canada was remote, but radio and newsreel coverage made the war seem very close - and in any case preparedness was a civic duty.

Glenbow Archives

Female munitions workers (bottom left) having their hair styled, in a still from a 1941 National Film Board documentary. The message was clear: Women may be involved in war work, but the femininity of the nation's wives, mothers, and daughters is secure. Collection bins (above), sponsored by Canada Packers. The collection of material for the war - everything from metals to bones and fat - produced a mammoth national recycling effort that would make later "blue box" programs look trifling by comparison.

(Main) Glenbow Archives
(inset) National Archives of Canada

On December 8, the day after the attack on the U.S. Pacific fleet at Pearl Harbor, Japanese aircraft began bombing Hong Kong. Within a week Japanese forces had overrun the Kowloon peninsula, the portion of the colony attached to mainland China, and laid siege to Hong Kong Island. With no possibility of outside help, the outcome was never in doubt. The soldiers of the Canadian, British, and Indian garrison fought bravely, but they were no match for the much larger force of battle-hardened Japanese. The Canadians lacked training and combat experience (in one instance lobbing grenades at their attackers without realizing they had first to remove the pin), but in the defence of Hong Kong they proved to be stubborn and determined. On December 18 the Japanese launched a successful night attack from the mainland and gained a foothold on the island. The following day enemy troops overran the Canadian headquarters of Brigadier J.K. Lawson. Refusing to surrender, they were killed to a man. Worse, much worse, was yet to come. When Hong Kong fell on Christmas Day, half the Canadians had been killed or captured. For those taken prisoner, particularly the wounded, it was the beginning of a dreadful nightmare. At the hospital at Stanley on Hong Kong Island, rampaging Japanese troops bayoneted to death 70 Allied wounded and raped the hospital's nurses - some of whom died of their injuries.

Ralph MacLean was a lance-corporal with the Royal Rifles and was taken prisoner near Stanley that day. He recounted his experience in a 1983 anthology of Canadian POW stories (*In Enemy Hands*, Daniel Dancocks, Hurtig Publishers, Edmonton). "Through a loudspeaker across the valley, a Japanese officer speaking perfect English told us if we came across with a white flag we'd be given safe conduct. So we decided to surrender. Most of the fellas had their hands tied behind their backs, and we marched back behind the lines. We went by different groups of our fellas that had been bayoneted. They were tied up in groups of six to 10 and butchered.

We figured we'd end up the same way." Similar scenes were played out all across the colony. Japan had not signed the 1929 Geneva Convention on the treatment of prisoners of war, and Allied soldiers who surrendered were accorded no protection at all until they reached a POW camp. Once there, prisoners were treated with contempt and faced appalling conditions. Don Geraghty of Hamilton was a 17-year-old rifleman with the Royal Rifles, and was eventually housed in the former Sham Shui Po colonial barracks, which had been turned into a Japanese POW camp. "They were burying fellas six a day, "he later recalled. "Originally they were supplied with wooden boxes, but a lot of the guys were bloated from beriberi (dysentery), and they would have to fit them in the best they could."

The battle for Hong Kong lasted 17 days, leaving 290 Canadian dead and almost 500 wounded. For those taken prisoner, "We were to find that this was merely the first act in a long and terrible crucifixion," wrote Bill Allister. For the next three years and eight months the survivors would endure brutality and starvation. "We were truly a legion of the condemned," recalled Allister. In 1943 some 1,200 of the Canadians would be shipped to Japan as slave labour. Many did not survive the brutal conditions. Ken Gaudin of St. Lambert, Quebec, remembered a father and son from the Royal Rifles, Elmer and Bliss Cole of Lac St. Jean, Quebec. "Bliss - he'd only be 18 or 19 at that time - woke up to find his Dad dead beside him. That hurt all of us, because we thought the world of the two of them." Of the 1,975 Canadians who served in Hong Kong, 555 would not return to Canada - nearly half of those dying as prisoners of the Japanese. "We watched our comrades die or go mad, watched pride and manhood ground in the dust," Allister later wrote.

The surprise attack on the U.S. Pacific fleet at Pearl Harbor and the bloody fall of Hong Kong, along with reports of Japanese atrocities elsewhere in southeast Asia, were to have tragic consequences for Japanese Canadians. Particularly in British Columbia, where paranoia about Asian immigration already ran deep. As recently as 1935 a pledge to oppose voting rights for B.C.'s Asian residents had

A naval officer questioning Japanese-Canadian fisherman (below) while confiscating their boat, in Esquimalt, B.C., just two days after the Japanese attack on Pearl Harbour. Antipathy towards Asian immigrants was widespread and politically acceptable even before the war, but reached new heights after the fall of Hong Kong.

National Archives of Canada

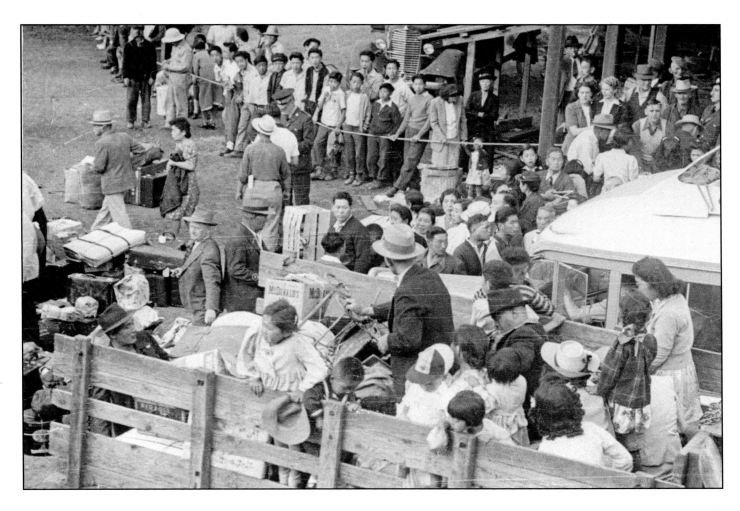

Early in 1942 the federal government began moving Japanese-Canadians from the B.C. coast (above), seizing their property, and dividing families. The fear of a Japanese attack was real, but it never materialized - and there was scant evidence of any threat posed by members of the Japanese community in Canada.

National Archives of Canada

been a prominent part of the provincial Liberals' election platform. The prospect of a Japanese attack on B.C., which was a military impossibility but seemed real to many people, added fuel to widespread existing prejudice. Some politicians and many newspapers were quick to brand Japanese Canadians (many of whom had been born in Canada) as a potential "fifth column" of pro-Japanese sentiment and support. (Lieutenant-governor W.C. Woodward predicted the province would be subject to Japanese bombing raids within six months.) When Japanese forces invaded Alaska's Aleutian Islands, and a Japanese submarine shelled a lighthouse on Vancouver Island, the threat seemed very real - although that proved to be the extent of the war on Canada's Pacific coast.

The King government originally planned on ordering the removal of only Japanese-born immigrants from the Pacific coast, but the upsurge of anti-Japanese public sentiment convinced it otherwise. Beginning in the spring of 1942 with the removal of 1,200 men of military age to work camps in the B.C. interior, some 23,000 Japanese Canadians in B.C. would eventually be relocated and their property confiscated and sold. The government in Ottawa knew the threat from a Japanese attack was, at best, improbable, but made no serious effort to calm the very real public anxiety. Ernest Trueman, a federal Department of Labour manager, was in no doubt of the government's motivation. "The reason for the mass evacuation is not because of the Japanese, but because of the whites," he later wrote. "The problem was one of mass hysteria and racial prejudice."

The Japanese relocation camp at Slocan, B.C., in the winter of 1942. The war was a disaster for the Japanese community in B.C., which was dispersed across the West. News of the treatment of Canadian prisoners of war did not help matters, and it would take many years for wartime scars to heal.

National Archives of Canada

The Friendly Invasion

The Building Of The Alaska Highway

An all-weather highway through Canada linking Alaska with the lower 48 states had been talked about since the early 1930s, but during the Depression years the cost was considered prohibitive and it was not until the Japanese attack on Pearl Harbour and the belated U.S. entry into World War Two that the project was taken seriously. The road itself was part of an overall plan that also called for the construction of an oil pipeline running from Norman Wells in the Northwest Territories to Whitehorse in the Yukon, and a series of airfields that would be able to support military aircraft flying to Alaska (and later Russia). The Americans paid for the construction and agreed to turn over the Canadian portion of the highway and other facilities to the Canadian government after the war. Canada provided the right of way, waved all taxes, import duties and immigration regulations, and provided construction materials along the route.

The chain of airfields, known as the Northwest Staging Route, was used to ferry war planes from Great Falls, Montana to Ladd Air Base in Fairbanks. Existing Canadian airfields were expanded (particularly Blatchford Field in Edmonton), and new airports were built in Grande Prairie, Alberta, Fort Nelson, B.C., and Watson Lake and Whitehorse in the Yukon. The first group of aircraft to try and use the route, 13 B-26 bombers and 25 P-40 fighters, actually left Edmonton for Fairbanks in January 1942, before construction of the highway began. It was not an auspicious beginning, with only 11 planes reaching Fairbanks, the rest crashing or forced to make emergency landings. After repairs, eight bombers and 13 fighters eventually completed the trip, but the dreadful toll added impetus to calls for a highway with navigational markers that planes could follow. Eventually some 8,000 aircraft would make the trip along the staging route.

Construction of the highway officially began at Dawson Creek on March 8, 1942, but was actually delayed a month because of bitterly cold weather. By June more than 10,000 American troops had poured into the Canadian north. The general route of the highway was along a line of existing airfields from Edmonton, to Fairbanks, Alaska. It supposedly followed existing winter roads and old Indian trails, where any existed, but in reality it ran almost 2,500 km through a rugged, mostly unmapped wilderness of "mountains, muskeg, and mosquitoes". When the ground wasn't frozen, the 11,000 pieces of heavy equipment hauled in by the U.S. Army Corps of Engineers often reduced it to a clinging mud that swallowed vehicles and men and made all work extremely hazardous. River crossings were particularly dangerous. In the early days a dozen American servicemen drowned when a pontoon bridge collapsed near Fort St. John, B.C.

Almost a third of the U.S. servicemen who laboured on the highway were black troops, originally prohibited from active service or northern deployment. Often poorly treated, inadequately trained, and last in line for equipment, the black regiments nevertheless were among the most successful in battling the Canadian wilderness. In one famous incident on the Sikanni Chief River, a black unit bet their paycheques they could break records for building a river crossing. Their bridge was complete in an astonishing 84 hours - half the usual time. When the last portion of the road was roughed in at the end of October 1942, the work was officially completed by a unit led by Corporal Refines Sims Jr., a black serviceman from Philadelphia. (Many of the black soldiers who worked on the Alaska Highway went on to see active service in Europe and the Pacific, and their courage and professionalism played a major role in the desegregation of the U.S. Army by the time of the Korean War - the first branch of U.S. government to officially embrace racial equality.)

The building of the highway had taken eight months, at a cost of just under $20 million - although it was hardly finished. It was, at that point, a rough and ready road with 133 temporary bridges. The first recorded journey from Edmonton to Whitehorse was completed in late October, a few days after completion of the route, by U.S. Army Air Corps officer Lt. Robert Gill. It took him five days, during which his Jeep flipped over once and got stuck several times. The highway was eventually finished by civilian contractors during 1943, doubling the width to about four metres, straightening curves, reducing hazardous grades, and building permanent bridges. The final cost was $147 million.

By far the most poorly conceived of the northern projects proposed after Pearl Harbour was the Canol pipeline. Short for Canadian American Norman Oil Line, the goal was to provide a safe alternative to shipping oil by sea from Alaska to British Columbia and the lower 48 states. The answer was a 12 centimetre pipeline running almost 1,000 km from Norman Wells in the Northwest Territories to Whitehorse in the Yukon. Construction of the pipeline was relatively easy (although it ran over passes as high as 2,400 metres). Crews simply laid the welded pipe on top of cleared ground. As with the Alaska Highway, it was the associated road that proved to be the greatest challenge.

With much controversy, the Canol project was finally completed in February 1944, and officially opened three months later. Less than a week after that the Americans withdrew from further oil exploration in the Canadian north. In its final hearing on the project, the U.S. Senate declared "the money, transportation, materials, and manpower would have been better employed elsewhere. Most of them have been wasted." Less than a year later the U.S. military decided to abandon the $134 million project, and without a market for Canol's oil Ottawa waived its option to purchase the pipeline. By November 1945, the entire development was abandoned, "inert, like a dead snake stretched out... along the ground."

Dozens of communities were profoundly impacted by the various Alaska projects, but none more so than Edmonton, which became the administrative centre and jumping off point for much of the construction activity. As many as 50,000 soldiers and civilian employees passed through the city between 1942 and the end of the war, and the Alberta capital's population during those years jumped from 95,000 to 120,000. Edmonton relief payments - almost $1 million in 1939 - were reduced to zero by 1943 as people found well-paying construction work and administrative jobs. (The big problem was housing, with the Edmonton Emergency Accommodation Bureau reporting in 1943 that it was short some 1,200 housing units. There was a boom in basement conversions, but still one realtor claimed to have 150 clients for houses he couldn't find.) The U.S. Army expanded Edmonton's airport, leased 59 office buildings, and built a $2 million hospital (the Charles Camsell, still in use until 1996). After the awful Depression years, U.S. investment and the employment that came with it was much appreciated by the local population. So much so that after a visit to the city the British ambassador to Canada, Malcolm MacDonald, felt obliged to warn Prime Minister Mackenzie King that "This state of affairs tends to play into the hands of those western Canadians who are inclined to assert that the West receives little sympathy and help from Eastern Canada, and that its destiny lies in incorporation with the United States of America."

On a more everyday level, perhaps one of the most lasting innovations associated with the Alaska Highway project had little to do with engineering or road construction. It was the popularization of the winter parka, a modern variation of Inuit clothing which had to that point only been worn outside the Arctic by a few intrepid skiers. It was quickly adopted by military and civilian workers to fend off the severe weather and by 1943 was recognized by the *Edmonton Bulletin* newspaper as the "new thing" in winter clothing. With the post-war development of manmade materials, it would eventually become a staple of the Canadian winter wardrobe. ■

A convoy of construction machinery heads north from Edmonton in November 1942. U.S. Congressman A.J. Dimond called it "the most controversial construction project of World War Two."

Provincial Archives of Alberta

Canada's entry into the war accomplished something the nation's leaders had not been able to do in almost a decade: it stopped the Great Depression in its tracks and eliminated unemployment. At the outbreak of war the official number of unemployed had stood at 330,000, but the actual number unable to find work was likely significantly higher. By 1941 there was a chronic labour shortage. The change was swift and dramatic. All debate about government's role in stimulating economic growth stopped and Canadian industry was revved up to a wartime footing (thus fulfilling economist John Maynard Keynes prediction years earlier). Canada's shipyards, devastated by the depression, serve as a good barometer of the rapid change in circumstances. Early in 1939 the industry employed a mere 3,500 people across the country. Two years later there were 80,000 shipyard jobs, for both men and women, and a shortage of people to fill them. In one of the great ironies of Canada's story in the 20th century, hand in hand with the most destructive war in history came renewed prosperity. As young men left for service overseas, at home the dreary 1930s were consigned to bitter memory as ordinary Canadians suddenly had jobs and money to spend.

In fact the spectre of a post-depression buying spree and rampant inflation greatly concerned the King government and spurred it to an unprecedented regulation of the economy. The all-encompassing agenda of rent, wage and price controls, tax increases, rationing, and control of industrial production could only have been justified by a wartime emergency - but Ottawa was thoroughly convinced the alternative was economic anarchy. "If it doesn't work, the whole economy is going to go down the drain," fretted Wartime Prices and Trade Board chairman Donald Gordon. For politicians and business leaders who clung to the traditional belief of limited government, such deep involvement in the economy was troublesome, but they contented themselves with thought that it could all be quickly reversed when the war over. It would not. The wartime increase in Ottawa's income and spending is breath-taking (and foreshadowed the enormous growth in government to come). Two years before the war Canada's defence budget had been a piddling $5 million but by the time the conflict was over it would have grown to $5 billion! Leading the remodelling of Canadian industry was King's single-minded "minister of everything", C.D. Howe, who used the power and finance available to him to turn out the

The "Little Happy Gang" (below), a group of girls from Moose Jaw, Saskatchewan, sewing socks for Canadian troops as part of a Red Cross program. The war effort involved Canadians of all ages, from all walks of life, in an unprecedented national undertaking. It was a triumph of organization and involvement.

National Archives of Canada

Quebec City munitions workers (left to right) Laurette Maurice, Roberta Perry, and Celine Perry, relaxing in a National Film Board photo. Among some sections of Canadian society - particularly in Quebec - employing women in the industrial workforce was viewed as a controversial move. The government went to some lengths to provide images of happy, and above all feminine munitions workers "doing their bit" for the war effort.

National Archives of Canada

ammunition, tanks, aircraft, and ships that would help beleaguered Britain stand against the Nazi onslaught. Howe countered the concerns of those who worried about government debt with a forthright and irrefutable argument: "If we win the war no one will care. If we lose it, it won't matter." Canadian Max Aitken (Lord Beaverbrook), who served as Winston Churchill's wartime supply minister in Britain, called C.D. Howe "one of a handful of men of whom it can be said 'But for him the war would have been lost.' The same, of course, could be said of Aitken - R.B. Bennett's former junior partner in law - whose energy and single-mindedness won for him in Britain the same enviable reputation Howe had in Canada.

Tens of thousands of rural Canadians left their farms and small communities for war work in the cities. Those jobs deemed "non-essential" to the war effort were swiftly eliminated, and non-essential industries were obliged to switch to production of war materiel. Tip Top Tailors switched production from sports coats to army uniforms at the rate of 25,000 a week. To change your job or move to another city for employment required a permit. Ottawa simply told business and labour what to do. Canadians mostly accepted the situation as necessary to produce victory in a war widely viewed as unfortunate but undeniably just. And the pay was good. Wartime salaries rose to an average of $25 a week, and in the war industries there was usually as much overtime as you wanted. Luxury goods and things like gasoline and automobile tires were in short supply for the average Canadian (although there was a thriving

A De Havilland Mosquito (below) under construction at a plant in Downsview, Ontario. The powerful, lightweight Canadian-built fighter bomber was one of the most versatile planes of the war - and one of the most feared. Originally rejected by the military, the twin-engine, wood-framed aircraft was developed by De Havilland as a private project. Twice as fast as any other bomber, the Mosquito could carry the same load as the much larger and heavier Flying Fortress. It was also a ferocious night fighter. Known as the "Timber Terror," some 7,700 were eventually built in Canada, Britain, and Australia.

MEN of VALOR
They fight for you

"When last seen he was collecting Bren and Tommy Guns and preparing a defensive position which successfully covered the withdrawal from the beach." — Excerpt from citation awarding

Victoria Cross to Lt.-Col. Merritt, South Saskatchewan Regt., Dieppe, Aug. 19, 1942

The scope of the national effort summoned up by Canada during World War Two still boggles the mind. Support for the troops, commitment to the war industries, and absolutely no thought of defeat were the order of the day. Posters like this one were part of a sustained government propaganda program to maintain public support for Canada's volunteer army.

black market), but despite the rationing many people ate better food during the war than they had been able to afford during the depression.

Among the army of Canadians finding new and lucrative employment in the war industries were some 50,000 women. Among them Montrealer Olive Villeneuve Renaud, who quit her low-paying job as a domestic servant and got a better one at the same factory where her father worked. "I must tell you, my father was not very happy - he didn't even want me to ride with him and his friends to the plant the following Monday," she recalled in a 2001 anthology for the Department of Defence. "After all, I was just a girl. But I told him it was too bad, I was going with them anyway. Then somehow the local priest, Father Odias Valois, got wind of my plan to go to work at the plant. He came to my parents' house and told me he had found me a job at yet another private home...I told him I wouldn't go; that life was over, and I was going to work at the plant. He said I could not do that - I would be 'lost' if I went to work there. He was afraid that I would learn bad things, I would be debauched, and that my reputation would be ruined." But her new job paid $3 a day, compared to $5 a week for domestic work. For Olive, as for the thousands of other young women entering the industrial workforce for the first time, it was simply no contest.

A wartime Victory Bond march (below) in Toronto. The campaign was enormously successful, raising a staggering $12 billion by the end of the war. It helped convince Ottawa of the revenue-raising potential of such schemes, and after the war Canada Savings Bonds became an investment staple.

City of Toronto Archives

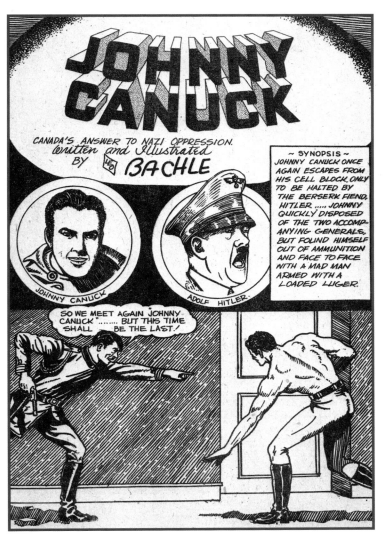

Paper was in short supply during the war, and comic books were a very low priority. However publishers stayed in business by producing "Canadian whites" - uncoloured comic books on recycled paper. The subjects were invariably patriotic, such as this one (above) with Johnny Canuck battling the evil Nazis.

National Library of Canada

In addition to the women who joined the army, navy and air force, thousands more volunteered to work in munitions, manufacturing and chemical plants, producing everything from shells to aircraft to tanks. Faced with a critical shortage of labour, in 1942 Ottawa organized the cross-Canada registration of unmarried women in their 20s, to be assigned to war work across the country. Tens of thousands more women went to work to replace the men who were in uniform - and not just in munitions plants. The packing industry employed thousands. As did the dairy industry, which in addition to butter and cheese was converted to the production of huge quantities of powdered egg for Britain. At Edmonton's Great Western Garment Company, the largest manufacturer of military uniforms in the country, almost 90% of the workforce was now female. It was the beginning of a trend. Edmonton hired its first policewoman at the end of 1942, and Calgary soon did likewise. In the fall of the following year the first group of 20 female ticket collectors began work on Edmonton streetcars. As the Alberta capital's first and only female "milkman", 24-year-old Isabel York from Camrose even got the same pay as the men she worked with. But for most women such equality would take another three decades, or longer.

The new competition for female labour made it difficult for schools, which relied heavily on women teachers, and where the pay was low and the hours long. Many teachers - men and women - joined the forces, while others found more lucrative employment outside education. By the middle of the war schools across the country were seriously understaffed. But the shortage of labour was most acute on farms, where there was no end to the heavy workload women had taken on during the depression years. As their menfolk joined the forces or went looking for paying jobs, women increasingly took responsibility for keeping family farms going. When Lethbridge dairy farmer Alan Hamilton joined the army in 1942, his 19-year-old daughter, Elaine, took over management of the operation with the help of two younger sisters. The Hamiltons were typical of many Canadian farm families during the war years.

The Great War had for the first time united Canadians in a great national undertaking, and 25 years later the response was, if anything, more prodigious. In the words of historian Desmond Morton (*A Military History of Canada*, Hurtig Publishers, Edmonton, 1985), the entire country was "directed, regulated, rationed and exhorted" to a degree unimaginable in the pre-war years. There were programs to round up metal, rubber, fat, and bones (to make explosives and glue). It was the greatest recycling effort in Canadian history. Everything from Great War souvenir helmets and shell casings, to surplus cooking pots and wrought iron railings were collected for the war effort. By the end of 1943, Alberta's grain elevator agents alone had collected from farmers nearly 60,000 tons of scrap metal - everything from tractors to woodstoves (not to mention a great many Bennett Buggies). But what Ottawa needed most was money, and it came up with some remarkably successful ways to raise it. The 25-cent War Savings Stamps were affordable for almost everyone, and a huge hit. Children were encouraged to buy them with their allowances, adults gave them as Christmas stocking stuffers, and they were popular door prizes at a host of community events. The more expensive Victory Bonds could be bought in denominations of $50, $100 or $1,000, and raised a gargantuan $12 billion by war's end. When they were offered for sale, in many communities they were oversubscribed on the first day. There were also all manner of campaigns to support the beleaguered mother country: Seeds for Britain, Milk for Britain, Jam for Britain, and even an Overseas Cigarette Fund - all financed from donations, bake sales, whist drives, raffles, dances and concerts.

Canadians were much better and more quickly informed about the progress of this war than they had been in 1914-18. For the first time radio, and in particular newsreels at the movie theatres, brought the sounds and sights of warfare to the home front. BBC radio news reports were regularly rebroadcast to Canadians, including the defiant and pulse-quickening speeches of Winston Churchill: "We shall fight on the beaches... we shall fight in the fields and in the streets. We shall never surrender." Churchill became as popular a figure in Canada as he was in Britain. In the early years of the war, when the news was invariably bad, CBC announcer Lorne Greene (later of *Bonanza* television fame) earned the nickname "The Voice of Doom". War

The "Voice of Doom" - CBC news announcer Lorne Greene (above) at the microphone in December 1942. Greene would survive his reputation for delivering bad news, and go on to become a much loved international television icon of the 1960s.

National Archives of Canada

correspondents like the CBC's Matthew Halton became household names with their reports from Europe. And perhaps more than any conflict before or since, this one became synonymous with popular music. Whether it was Vera Lynn's *We'll Meet Again*, Bing Crosby's *White Christmas*, or Glenn Miller's *In the Mood*, music permeated the war years - recorded, broadcast, or played on the tens of thousands of pianos that were still fixtures in many homes. Between the outbreak of war in 1939 and August 1940, sheet music and record sales doubled. Like the movies, music provided a welcome distraction from depressing war news, casualty lists, and for those with loved ones in the forces the ever-present fear of a telegram and a visit from a military chaplain or local minister.

It was also a time of shortages. Some were entirely predictable. Metal, rubber, and cloth were all diverted for military use, as was silk (used for parachutes) and gasoline. But some shortages needed explanation. Dentists became hard to find (so many were in uniform), and even if you could find one treatment might be limited because most dentist's drills came from Britain - which had virtually stopped exporting them. Teacups without handles suddenly appeared in the stores. There was a shortage of manpower and these cups were much quicker to manufacture. The same was true of bakeries, which had plenty of flour but few experienced bakers. The huge variety of pre-war bread was dropped in favour of basic, white loaves (a trend that would outlast the conflict).

The rationing of gasoline was a particular irritant for an increasingly mobile society with money to spend. In the spring of 1942 a nationwide 40-mile-an-hour speed limit came into effect as a method of reducing gas consumption, and within a matter of weeks it had reduced traffic accidents by 50%. That same year, with gas and tires increasingly difficult to obtain, a Calgary doctor came up with a novel idea for saving fuel. Rather than driving to house calls - the pre-war norm - he hired a secretary and allowed patients to make an appointment to see him at an office. It was an idea which would catch on.

At the beginning of 1942 the defeat of Germany seemed at best uncertain, and Japan's entry into the war increased the pressure on the King government to provide additional military support to the Allies. That once again raised the spectre of compulsory overseas service and conscription, a move supported by the opposition Conservatives and a growing number of Liberal ministers. At the outbreak of war the prime minister had, however, promised that he would not impose conscription. That was a promise taken very seriously in Quebec, where there was still opposition to the war among many opinion-leaders. King's announcement that he would hold a national referendum on the issue united Quebecers opposed to the war, who formed a new organization called La Ligue pour la defense du Canada to campaign against conscription. Led by journalist Andre Laurendeau and strongly supported by *Le Devoir* newspaper, the Ligue attracted the support of old-guard nationalists, elements of the Catholic church, and up and coming politicians including Pierre Trudeau and (future Montreal mayor) Jean Drapeau. The outcome of the referendum in April 1942 was predictable: Quebec voting overwhelmingly against conscription and the rest of the country voting equally massively in favour. King's response was typical of a prime minister for whom national unity was as important as winning the war: "Not necessarily conscription but conscription if necessary." Vague as it was, it became King's most memorable wartime utterance. For all practical

Johnny Wayne and Frank Shuster (below) taking part in a CBC radio broadcast of The Army Show. More than any other medium, radio provided Canadians with a sense of shared experience during wartime, arguably fostering a greater level of national unity that at any time in the country's history.

National Archives of Canada

Edmonton police officers and U.S. military police (left) on the steps of the city's police headquarters. Giving the U.S. military policing powers was a controversial move, but with almost 50,000 American servicemen and contractors passing through the Alberta capital during the war there was simply no way the city force could have coped with the influx.

Glenbow Archives

purposes, what it appeared to mean was that Canada's policy of voluntary overseas service would remain in place, and the armed forces would have to get by.

The fighting still seemed distant to Canadians at home, but it was creeping closer. There were no direct attacks on Canada's east coast, but U-boats roamed offshore, sinking dozens of ships off Nova Scotia and Newfoundland and even penetrating into the Gulf of St. Lawrence. One U-boat actually landed in Labrador and set up an automatic weather station to beam information back to German naval headquarters. It remained undiscovered for 40 years. Ottawa downplayed the threat -which was very real - but the bodies washing up on the shores of Quebec's Gaspe and elsewhere were a grim indication of the fierce battle going on in the North Atlantic.

In the early hours of October 14, 1942, the Sydney to Port aux Basques ferry *Caribou*, was sunk by *U-69* in Cabot Strait. As the U-boat's torpedoes struck home, the ferry's escort, HMCS *Grandmère* rushed in to ram the attacker, and then dropped a pattern of depth charges when the submarine crash dived. The submarine remained submerged while the ferry's 237 passengers fought for their lives above. For 90 minutes, the *Grandmère's* captain, Lieutenant James

Cuthbert, attempted to find and destroy the submarine in accordance with naval orders, all the while tortured by the knowledge that he could be plucking *Caribou* survivors from the sea. He eventually abandoned his search for the U-boat, and later he recalled the painful decision he and those in similar situations had to make: "God, I felt the full complement of things you feel at a time like that. Things you had to live with. You are torn. Demoralized. Terribly alone... I should have gone on looking for the submarine, but I couldn't. Not with women and children out there somewhere. I couldn't do it any more than I could have dropped depth charges among them."

That night the ferry was carrying 46 crew members from the Newfoundland Merchant Navy, 73 civilians and 118 Canadian, British and American military personnel. Only 101 survived. Of the crew, 31 perished, including the captain, Ben Taverner, and his two sons, Harold and Stanley. The crew losses included five other pairs of brothers, and Bride Fitzpatrick, the only female member of the Newfoundland Merchant Navy known to have lost her life to enemy action during the war. The civilian death toll included five mothers and 10 children. Many of the military passengers were Newfoundlanders in the Royal Navy or the Canadian armed forces who were travelling home on leave, including two nurses. Nurse Agnes Wilkie became the only Canadian Nursing Sister to die due to enemy action during the war. The other, Margaret Brooke, was named a Member of the Order of the British Empire for her efforts to save Wilkie as they drifted through the night on a life raft.

A welder at work at an Ontario aircraft plant (below). The Canadian contribution to the air war, in materiel and lives lost, was enormous. More than 17,000 Canadian airmen were killed, a much higher proportion than in any other arm of the military.

National Archives of Canada

A Man Called Intrepid

Manitoban The Real James Bond?

One of the most fascinating and enigmatic characters of World War Two was Canadian William Stephenson, who became Winston Churchill's spymaster in the Americas. Codenamed Intrepid, he was at least partially the inspiration for super-agent James Bond. Many of the details of Stephenson's early life and his role in Allied intelligence remain clouded in secrecy and uncertainty, partly because of the clandestine nature of his work but perhaps also because he preferred it that way. Reputedly the son of a Scottish-born lumber baron, Stephenson was actually the child of Icelandic immigrants. He was born William Samuel Stanger, in 1897 in Winnipeg. His impoverished mother gave him to a friend's family to raise, then promptly disappeared with her remaining two children. Infant Bill Stanger was given his adoptive family's last name - Stephenson.

As an 18-year-old he volunteered for service in the Great War, and in 1915 was among the first Canadian troops to see action in France. Already promoted to sergeant, while recovering from being gassed Stephenson volunteered for pilot training and transferred to the Royal Flying Corps. As a fighter pilot he scored a dozen victories before being shot down and captured in 1918. He ended the war a captain and a much-decorated war hero. Stephenson returned to Winnipeg and started an unsuccessful hardware business. He had more luck after he returned to Europe, developing the first system for the electronic transmission of photographs and becoming a successful and wealthy businessman. Disturbed by the rise of Adolf Hitler and the Nazi party in Germany, Stephenson used his extensive business contacts across Europe to provide

Sir William Stephenson, Churchill's wartime spymaster in the Americas, in a 1954 photo

National Archives of Canada

detailed information to Winston Churchill, then a British opposition MP, on German rearmament in contravention of the restrictions imposed on the country in 1918. After the outbreak of war, now-Prime Minister Churchill sent Stephenson to the U.S. to establish a covert intelligence agency called British Security Coordination, based in New York. His mission was to create a secret British intelligence network throughout the western hemisphere, and to influence American opnion in favour of participation in the war.

Stephenson worked for no salary. He hired hundreds of people (mostly attractive Canadian women) to staff his organization and paid for much of the expense out of his own pocket. Among his employees was secretive communications genius Benjamin (Pat) Bayly. Bayly, a University of Toronto professor from Moose Jaw, Saskatchewan, created a state-of-the-art secure comunications system for Stephenson - which was eventually adopted by all the Allies. Not least in Stephenson's contributions to the war effort was the establishment of Camp X, in Whitby, Ontario - the first training school for spies and special forces in North America. Around 2,000 British, Canadian, and American agents were trained there, among them five future directors of the U.S. Central Intelligence Agency. Stephenson's most ardent supporters credit him with a hand in almost every major intelligence coup of the war, and with helping the Americans set up the Office of Strategic Services, predecessor of the CIA.

Graduates of Camp X operated in France, Spain, Portugal, Italy, and the Balkans as well as in Africa, Australia, India, and the Pacific. They included Ian Fleming, later the author of the Bond books. "James Bond is a highly romanticized version of a true spy," Fleming was later quoted as saying. "The real thing is ... William Stephenson." Stephenson was knighted in Britain in 1945, becoming Sir William, and a year later awarded the Presidential Medal for Merit, the highest U.S. civilian award in time of war. He was the first non-US citizen to receive the medal. But it was three decades before Stephenson would be honoured in his homeland, finally receiving the Order of Canada in 1979. He died in Bermuda in 1989 at the age of 92.

The man known as Intrepid was far from being the only Canadian involved in covert operations during the war. Hundreds of Canadians were recruited to serve behind enemy lines in Europe and Asia. Many survived to resume their lives after the war, largely unheralded by their country, but a number paid the ultimate price for volunteering for clandestine work. Among them was Montrealer Gustave Daniel Biéler, who trained 25 French resistance groups that systematically blew up rail lines and destroyed and derailed German troop trains in northern France. Bieler was captured in January 1944 and tortured for four months before eventually being executed by firing squad. John (Giovani) di Lucia was born in Ortona, Italy in 1913 and moved to Canada with his family as a young boy. He volunteered for "special duty" while attending an RCAF officer training course at the University of Western Ontario. Di Lucia parachuted into Italy in early 1944 and assisted resistance units with harassing the retreating Germans and preventing them from destroying bridges and other key installations. He too was eventually captured and executed by the Germans.

Hundreds of Chinese-Canadians volunteered for undercover work in Asia - far more than any other group of Canadians - despite the fact they were denied voting rights in Canada at the time and suffered much discrimination. Many underwent gruelling training in Canada as well as at special training camps in Australia and India. Among them was 19-year-old Henry Fung of Vancouver, who was the first, and the youngest, of several Chinese-Canadians who served in the area around Kuala Lumpur, today the capital of Malaysia. He parachuted in on June 22, 1945 and worked at sabotaging Japanese communications and harassing Japanese road convoys. With the Japanese surrender in September, his team took control of the city of Kajang and maintained order until British troops arrived. Fung returned to Britain suffering from malaria but eventually made it back to Canada.

Like Stephenson, the role of these courageous Canadians is little known and rarely acknowledged by their fellow countrymen. Stephenson himself honoured the role played by other Canadians in the allied intelligence services during the war. "Canadians fought behind the enemy lines, as agents for the Allied undercover organizations that operated escape routes and sabotage networks in occupied countries," he wrote. "I was privileged... to have played a role in helping this force to be generated and brought into play. Those who went forth did so as individuals, knowing they would receive no quarter. Most of those who were captured perished after ghastly tortures. But, remarkably, more and more stepped forward to take their places." ■

The man code-named Intrepid. The Manitoba-born spy became a legend in intelligence circles, and according to author Ian Fleming was the model for his cool, charming and deadly James Bond character.

National Archives of Canada

Arsenal of Democracy

uring World War Two the total value of Canadian war production was almost $10 billion - a staggering figure for a country of just 11 million people. The country became a giant arsenal, and was Britain's chief overseas supplier of war materiel. Canada did not accept aid from the U.S. but ran its own lend-lease program called "Mutual Aid" - supplying its allies with $4 billion dollars worth of war materiel. A further credit of a billion dollars was given to Britain. By 1945 Canada's war production was fourth among the Allied nations, behind only the United States, the Soviet Union, and the United Kingdom. The country produced a staggering 815,729 military vehicles, including 45,710 armoured vehicles. Canadian-made vehicles were crucial in equipping the British Eighth Army in North Africa and Italy. Canada also produced rifles, submachine guns, light machine guns, antitank guns and antiaircraft guns, as well as the multipurpose 25-pounder artillery piece. About 30% of the tanks and armoured vehicles produced in Canada were used by the Canadian Army - an incredible one vehicle for every three soldiers, making it the most mechanized field force of the war. The country also produced 9,000 ships, 16,000 aircraft, radar equipment and other electronics, synthetic rubber, and provided the uranium for the Allied nuclear effort.

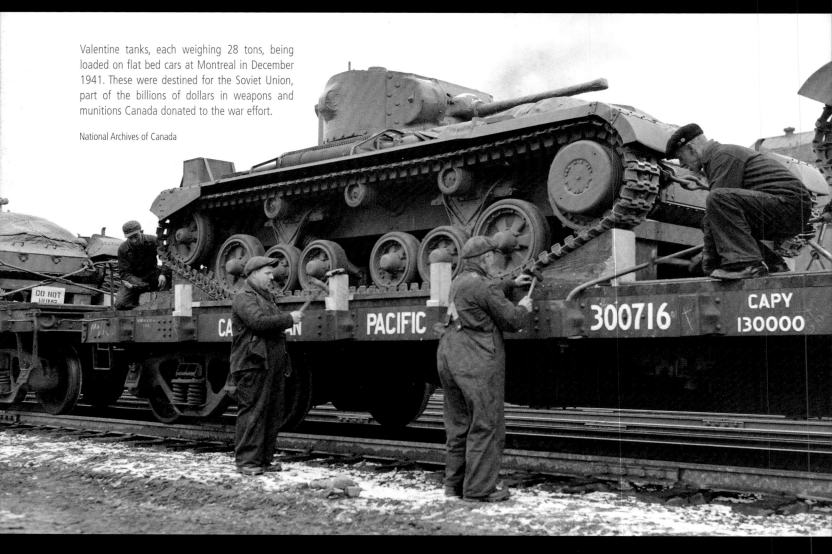

Valentine tanks, each weighing 28 tons, being loaded on flat bed cars at Montreal in December 1941. These were destined for the Soviet Union, part of the billions of dollars in weapons and munitions Canada donated to the war effort.

National Archives of Canada

Defence Minister Layton Ralston (top) shakes hands with the operator of the first Canadian-built tank, the Cruiser, coming off the assembly line at the Angu. Shops of the Montreal Locomotive Works on May 27, 1941. Agnes Wong (above left) of Whitecourt, Alberta, assembles a machine gun at the Small Arm Ltd. Plant in Long Branch, Ontario. Young women from across Canada were often assigned to war work long distances from their homes. And two me (above right) machining a gun barrel at the Sorel Industries plant, Sorel, Quebec. This particular process alone, of finishing the outside of the barrel, took fi hours. It was the sort of highly-skilled work that had been in short supply before the war, but would become a staple of Canadian industry.

Writing messages on bombs and shells (below) wasn't actually encouraged, unless as in this case for a May 1941 National Film Board propaganda film on Canadian war production. At the time Canada stood almost alone as Britain's major ally in the fight against fascism, and its major supplier of water materiel.

National Archives of Canada Photos

C.D. Howe (above), Canada's American-born wartime minister of munitions and supply, speaking at an aircraft plant in Fort William (Thunder Bay), Ontario. The no-nonsense Howe used Ottawa's clout and money to revolutionize Canadian industrial production.

National Archives of Canada

In the air Canada's contribution to the RAF and RCAF had by now expanded greatly to include thousands of pilots, navigators, bombardiers, and other aircrew for the armada of bombers being deployed against Germany and occupied Europe. The major contribution was No. 6 Bomber Group, a mostly-Canadian force of Wellington and Lancaster bombers based in Yorkshire in northeast England. The group eventually won a formidable reputation for its determination and expertise, but at a staggering cost: 17,000 airmen killed. It was a death toll far greater than the prime minister or anyone else in government had anticipated when Canada agreed to a leading role in the air war.

Canada's first experience fighting on the ground in Europe also proved to be costly. At dawn on August 19, 1942, a force of about 5,000 mostly-Canadian troops went ashore at the French port of Dieppe in a major raid that was supposed to rattle the Germans and refine techniques that would be needed for any full-scale invasion later on. Just about everything that could go wrong did. The element of surprise was lost in an unexpected night encounter with German ships, and the men of the 2nd Canadian Infantry Division arrived late and went ashore in daylight rather than darkness. German defences were relatively unscathed by a naval and aerial bombardment, and tanks landed to support the infantry found it difficult or impossible to make headway on the stony beach. Men from southern Saskatchewan, Calgary, Toronto, Windsor, and Montreal were raked by German fire from overlooking cliffs, with little cover and no escape. By mid-morning the decision was taken to abandon the raid and evacuate as many as possible from the beach. Almost a thousand Canadians died that morning at Dieppe, and another 2,000 - many of them wounded - were taken prisoner.

The men captured at Dieppe joined hundreds of Canadians already imprisoned in German camps, most of them airmen. For these POWs the war meant long periods, often years, characterized by short rations, isolation, and maybe the occasional glimpse of the proceeding war. Vancouver's Art Deacon, a fighter pilot with the RAF, was among the first Canadians taken prisoner in Europe, after being shot down during a dogfight over France on May 28, 1940. He crashed a few miles inland from the coast and tried to walk to the Allied lines. After being given civilian clothes he was stopped by two German soldiers, who put him to work digging a grave for one of their comrades - and then let him go without realizing he was a Canadian airman. After being turned away from the American consulate in Antwerp, Belgium, Deacon was ultimately forced to seek medical attention for injuries he'd sustained when his plane crashed - and was promptly arrested. "They patched me up, and just as I was going out the hospital door a civilian said 'Would you step into the office for a minute?' So I stepped in... and here's a German standing there. He said, 'For you the war is over.' " And it was. After time in jail at Nuremberg, Deacon was eventually shipped to a prisoner of war camp at Barth, on Germany's northern Baltic Sea coast.

Pilot Officer Bruce Campbell of Montreal was shot down on the Belgian-Dutch border in July 1941 and after a few days he was befriended by a man who claimed to belong to the Dutch resistance. He introduced Campbell to a local farm wife and her children who gave him shelter for the night, only to be awakened by a German raid. Campbell escaped into a nearby field, but the Dutch woman was not so fortunate. "She was put against the wall and shot, and the children were put into a truck and taken away," he recalled later (*In Enemy Hands*, Daniel Dancocks, Hurtig Publishers, Edmonton, 1983). Campbell was eventually captured, and learned that the resistance fighter who had supposedly helped him had in fact been a German agent working to identify Dutch civilians helping downed Allied airmen. Campbell was the first member of his bomber squadron to be confirmed captured. "I guess I was lucky becoming the first prisoner, because of the group I went over with (Canadians joining the RAF), I think there were about 40 of us, and only about four came home."

Women of the Canadian Women's Army Corps (CWACS) on firefighting duty in London (opposite left). Four companies of CWACS served in Britain during the war, and others served in Italy and Belgium.

National Archives of Canada

Once ensconced in POW camps, the Allied servicemen made continual efforts to escape. The most famous of these, the subject of ex-POW Paul Brickell's 1951 book, *The Great Escape*, and the still-popular 1963 movie of the same name, was a mass escape from prison camp Stalag Luft III on March 24, 1944. The tunnelling was masterminded by a Canadian, Wally Floody, and the escape attempt involved a number of Canadians. "I was in charge of all the tunnelling in the Great Escape," Floody, from Chatham, Ontario, recalled in 1983. " I had been a hard rock miner before the war in Kirkland Lake, and the British figured if I'd been a miner I'd know a lot about tunnelling in sand. But there was absolutely no similarity." Edmontonian Gord King was stocky and athletic, so he was put in charge of pumping air into the tunnel. "We successfully dug a tunnel, [perhaps] the longest ever dug," recalled King in a 1999 interview. It was 40 feet deep and 376 feet long. "It had electricity and lights... There was an air pumper made of kit bags, and it would pump air through a pipe made of coffee tins." Anthony Pengelly, another Toronto airman, helped organize the provision of clothes and documents for the escapees, with the help of a sympathetic German guard. "He was in the Luftwaffe in the First World War, and was a great friend of a lot of us after the war. In fact, at our reunion in 1965 we brought him over here by Air Canada and he was our guest of honour."

The carnage on Dieppe's shingle beach (below) after Operation Jubilee, from among the official German photos taken after the battle. The German propaganda ministry revelled in the stunning defeat of the first Allied landing in France.

National Archives of Canada

King and Calgarian Barry Davidson were among the 124 POWs discovered in the tunnel when a guard saw steam rising from the exit hole and raised the alarm. They were punished by being made to stand naked in the cold for hours, all the while expecting to be shot. But the two survived, while many of the 76 who made it out of the tunnel did not. Only three eventually made their way to safety, 23 were captured and returned to the camp, and 50 were executed by the Gestapo under direct orders from Adolf Hitler. Among the murdered were six Canadians: Henry Birkland, George McGill, Gordon Kidder, Patrick Watson, James Wernham, and George Wiley. Wally Floody was moved to another camp just before the escape, and later worked as a technical adviser on the 1963 movie.

A Disaster Called Jubilee

The Tragic 1942 Raid On Dieppe

Six decades on, it is still not at all clear why the Dieppe raid - code-named Jubilee - was mounted, what it hoped to achieve, and who was primarily responsible for its failure. The British commander in charge, the blue-blooded Vice-Admiral Louis Mountbatten, has traditionally been the target of much criticism by Canadians. It's not even clear that Mountbatten had proper authority to authorize such a large-scale attack. Yet there's no doubt that Canada's senior generals lobbied hard, in Canada and Britain, for a leading role in not just one but a series of raids on occupied territory. The Canadian Corps commander, Gen. Harry Crerar, called the planned operations "trivial" and Ottawa reluctantly gave the go-ahead for "minor raids" involving Canadian troops. The Canadian government was never given, and never asked for, full details of what would rapidly develop into a major operation involving thousands of Canadian troops.

The whole idea of a frontal assault on Dieppe was based on the assumption that it would be preceded by a massive naval and air bombardment to destroy German strong points. The ensuing attack would be a surprise, under the cover of darkness. As Canadian Press war correspondent Ross Munro, later recorded, it was supposed to be "a piece of cake." But the Royal Air Force balked at shifting heavy bombers from attacks on Germany, and the Royal Navy refused to put battleships into the narrow confines of the English Channel, where they might easily be sunk by lurking German U-boats. On that basis, the British commander in southern England, Gen. Bernard Montgomery, withdrew his support from the operation, as did the British naval commander. It continued anyway.

Lt. Col. Dollard Menard, the 29-year-old commanding officer of the Fusiliers Mont-Royal led his 600 men off the landing craft

Canadian troops returning from Dieppe (above). Those who survived the debacle that day and returned to action swore that they had never again faced such terrible fire as on the beach in front of the little French seaport.

National Archives of Canada

and waded towards the beach. "I think that I must have made no more than three steps before I was hit for the first time," he later recalled. "A bullet hits you head-on, like the blow of a hammer... I was hit a second time. It seemed to explode all around me. I was no longer sure I was all in one piece. I had just reached the parapet (separating the beach from the town) when I was hit for the third time." Menard was eventually hit five times, but was pulled to safety aboard one of the evacuating boats and survived. The only Canadian officer to escape unscathed was Capt. Denis Whitaker of the Royal Hamilton Light Infantry, who had led his men up the beach under intense fire, only to have to lead them back when the evacuation was ordered. "The worst part was the dash for the boats amid a hail of bullets and mortar or shellfire. Apart from trying to help the wounded, it was every man for himself. I expected every step to be my last."

The steep beach itself, made up of deep layers of stones, was quite unlike anything the Canadians had trained on and proved a formidable obstacle to the tanks landing in support of the infantry. That 16 tanks made into the town was a minor miracle in itself. The scene on the beach was one of absolute carnage. "Anything I saw in the last war - and I saw plenty - not in the slightest can compare with this," reported medical officer Capt. L.G. Alexander of Calgary. "A combination of fire from every direction, both sides, in front, behind, above - and from every conceivable type of weapon." He was awarded the Military Cross for his bravery in treating the wounded under fire. Cpl. J.A. Gregory of Calgary, another Great War veteran, lost an eye and was wounded in the arm during the fighting. "I was all through the last war, at Vimy and Passchendaele, but I never saw anything to match the terrific fight at Dieppe."

The withdrawal began at 11 a.m. Under intense German fire some of the rescue boats were sunk and others forced to retreat. Almost 2,000 Canadians watched as the last overloaded boat departed. Of the 5,000 troops who had left Dover early that morning, 907 were dead and hundreds more wounded. In the air the RAF and RCAF had lost 119 aircraft, more than on any other day of the war, including during the Battle of Britain. At sea the toll was one destroyer and 30 other vessels lost. Among the lists of dead and missing were more than 100 Albertans, some two dozen from the Stettler area alone. Worst hit were the men of the Calgary Tanks, only three of whom returned to England. All in all, 1,946 Canadians were marched into captivity.

Two Canadians earned the Victoria Cross at Dieppe. Although twice wounded, Lt. Col. (Charles) Cecil Merritt of the South Saskatchewan Regiment took charge of a rearguard action that allowed many troops to escape the disaster. He and the rest of the rearguard became prisoners of war. Reverend John Weir Foote became the first member of the Canadian Chaplain Services to be awarded the VC. Through eight hours of battle, Foote, Chaplain of the Royal Hamilton Light Infantry, continually exposed himself to intense fire to help move the injured to an aid post, saving many lives. Rather than be taken to safety as the Canadian forces withdrew, he walked to the enemy positions to be taken prisoner so

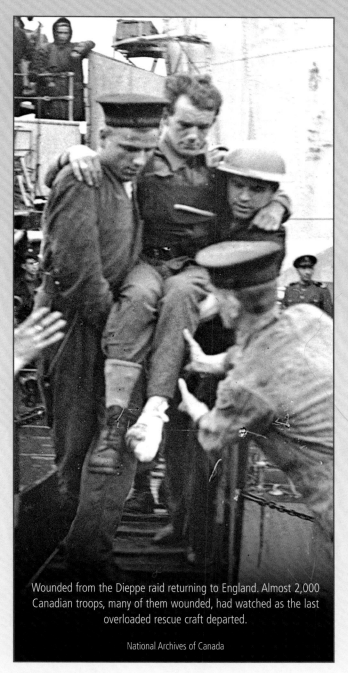

Wounded from the Dieppe raid returning to England. Almost 2,000 Canadian troops, many of them wounded, had watched as the last overloaded rescue craft departed.

National Archives of Canada

that he could accompany the wounded into captivity.

Mountbatten later wrote: "I have no doubt that the battle of Normandy was won on the beaches of Dieppe. For every one man who died at Dieppe in 1942, at least 10 or more must have been spared in Normandy in 1944." A great grandson of Queen Victoria and cousin of Queen Elizabeth II, Mountbatten later served with distinction as Allied commander in Southeast Asia, and as the last British colonial governor in India. A respected public figure in Britain, he was - understandably - less popular in Canada. Mountbatten was killed in an IRA terrorist bombing in 1979. ∎

anada's ground war in Europe began on the morning of July 10, 1943, as the 1st Canadian Division went ashore at Pachino, Sicily as part of the Allied invasion of Italy. Losses were mercifully light, 32 dead and wounded, but it was the beginning of a brutally tough Italian campaign in which Canadians would distinguish themselves over and over again. During the next two months the Canadians were in the forefront of the fighting as the Allies made their way through the rugged Sicilian hills to Messina. The Canadians acquitted themselves well in their first sustained campaign. They fought through 240 kilometres of mountainous country - farther than any other formation in the British 8th Army.

Canadian troops enter the ruined town of Montespertoli, Italy (opposite left). The men of the 1st Canadian Division fought as part of the famed British 8th Army, the Desert Rats, during the Italian campaign and distinguished themselves in the Canadian Army's first sustained action of the war. Pulling a comrade from the rubble (below) after a German artillery barrage. At Ortona the Germans staged what one American correspondent called "a mini Stalingrad." Over Christmas 1943 the Loyal Edmonton Regiment and the Seaforth Highlanders of Canada battled the German 1st Parachute Division for control of Ortona in one of the most hard-fought actions of the war in Italy. It would cost the lives of 1,375 Canadians and 238 other Commonwealth troops.

National Archives of Canada

One result of the Allied invasion of Sicily was the overthrow of the Italian dictator, Mussolini, but although the new Italian government surrendered on September 3, 1943, the Germans immediately seized control of the country and it was German troops that the Allies faced in their advance up the Italian peninsula. Through the fall of 1943 the Canadians fought their way up Italy's mountainous spine. On October 1 at Motta, the Canadians fought their first battle with Germans troops in Italy, and a series of brief but bloody actions followed. The 1st Canadian Division was ordered to take the Moro River and the town of Ortona, which anchored the eastern end of the heavily-defended German line. At the end of December at Ortona the Loyal Edmonton Regiment and the Seaforth Highlanders met the German 1st Parachute Division in one of the most famous and hard-fought battles of the war in Italy. Over Christmas, 1943 the fighting raged through the narrow streets and squares of the medieval town. "For some unknown reason," wrote an Associated Press correspondent, "the Germans are staging a miniature Stalingrad in hapless Ortona." Moving forward house by house, the Canadians eventually pushed the German paratroopers into the town's old castle. "Tired, drenched and mud-covered men blasted and tunnelled their way from one house to the next like demon moles," wrote war artist Charles Comfort, who witnessed the fighting. "Undoubtedly Canadians were joined in the most bitter and costly fighting of the campaign on this

Christmas Eve." During the night of December 27 they once again concentrated their fire on the castle ruins - and the next morning the enemy was gone. In the mini-Stalingrad at Ortona the Canadians suffered 2,339 casualties.

Also in action in Italy were the men of the 1st Special Service Force (SSF), a unique commando brigade made up of Canadian and American elite troops. The unit was made famous after the war in the movie *The Devil's Brigade* (the name given to it by opposing German troops). The film is a colourful but reasonably accurate account of the assault on a mountain

Privates W. H. Rose and R.M. Stuart (above) lead a mule loaded with mortars through the hills around Terreti, Italy in September 1943. The Italian government surrendered at the beginning of that month, but Germany seized control of much of the country and poured in fresh troops.

National Archives of Canada

called La Difenza, one of several fortified high points the brigade captured around Monte Cassino. Among the officers of the brigade was Stan Waters, a University of Alberta undergraduate who left his studies to join the Calgary Tank Regiment. Waters later volunteered for the SSF, and in Italy assumed command of an American brigade after all its senior officers had been killed or wounded (eventually five out of the six SSF battalion commanders were Canadians). After the war Waters stayed in the service and eventually became commander of the Canadian army, retiring in 1975 as a lieutenant-general. In 1987 he became one of the founders

of the Reform Party, and two years later became the only elected senator ever to sit in Canada's upper house. He died of pneumonia in 1991.

In the spring of 1944 the 1st Canadian Armoured Brigade took part in the attack on German lines hinged by the fortress-like monastery of Monte Cassino. On May 11 the regiment attacked in support of the 8th Indian Division, with whom they had trained during the winter. The tanks battered their way across the Gari River and broke through the German lines, but at heavy cost. The Indian troops were relieved by the Loyal Edmonton Regiment and Princess Patricia's Canadian Light Infantry, and in an attack across open fields the Edmonton regiment lost almost as many men as in the entire operation at Ortona. On May 18, Polish troops took the Cassino

Men of the Carleton and York Regiment (above) advancing under sniper fire at Campochiaro, Italy, towards the end of 1943. By now the Canadians were facing German troops who had been ordered to give up no ground without a fight.

National Archives of Canada

Canadian forces crossing the Liri Valley (below) to attack the Hitler Line, in May 1944. The 5th Canadian Armoured Division broke through the German defences to lead the Allied advance northwards. The Canadians would continue fighting in Italy until January 1945, at a cost of 2,119 lives.

mountain and the battered monastery at the summit, and on June 4 the Allies reached Rome. The first troops into the liberated city were the Canadians and Americans of The Devil's Brigade. Less than 48 hours later, the long-awaited D-Day invasion of Northwest Europe began on the Normandy beaches.

The Canadians, by now numbering over 75,000, continued the advance through northern Italy with the British Eighth Army, the Germans resisting with their usual resolve. They were ordered to advance on the Hitler Line straddling the Liri Valley. Under heavy enemy mortar and machine-gun fire, the Canadians breached the defences and the tanks of the 5th Canadian Armoured Division poured through toward the next obstacle. Across a seemingly endless series of river crossings, and the Gothic Line - the new German defensive position - the Canadians would continue to fight their way northward to the Lombardy plain and the Alps beyond. In January 1945 they were ordered to join the rest of the Canadian army in Northwest Europe. In all, 2,119 Canadians gave their lives during the Italian campaign.

In Italy the Canadians perfected the tactics of urban warfare. In this photo, sniper Jack Bailey, of Ontario's Perth Regiment, takes up position inside a ruined house in the town of Ortona.

U.S. President Franklin D. Roosevelt, Prime Minister Mackenzie King, and Winston Churchill (left) at the Quadrant Conference in Quebec City, August 11-24, 1943. The Allied leaders agreed to increase the bombing offensive against Germany and continue the buildup of forces in Britain prior to an invasion of France the following year. They also secretly agreed on a program to build a nuclear weapon, which they feared Germany was already doing.

National Archives of Canada

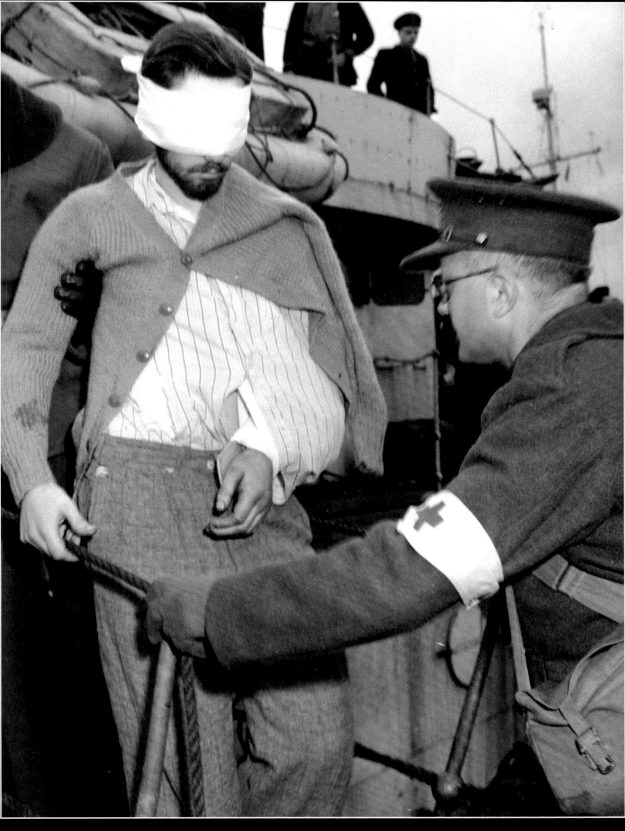

A boarding party from HMCS Chilliwack (opposite left) pulls alongside the German submarine U-744. Winston Churchill later said the Battle of the Atlantic was the one aspect of the war that had troubled him most - its outcome being so uncertain. Wounded crewmen from a German U-boat (above) disembarking from HMCS St. Laurent in Britain during the spring of 1944. New technology, expanded air cover, and the courage of Allied seamen in the North Atlantic were finally turning the tide in the war at sea.

Operation Overlord, the D-Day invasion of France, has become a legendary event, the subject of countless books and movies - and rightly so since it changed the course of history and eventually gave birth to a united and peaceful Europe. But often lost in the telling is the fact that Canada was a major player on the beaches of Normandy. Fifteen thousand Canadians landed on Juno Beach and fully one fifth of the 130,000 troops taking part in the landings were Canadian. Hundreds of Canadian fliers took part in the bombing and reconnaissance missions over France in the weeks preceding D-Day, 16 Canadian minesweepers cleared a path for the invasion fleet, and on the night of June 5, 1944, the 1st Canadian Parachute Battalion was one of three Allied airborne units which dropped into Normandy to seize bridges, cut communications and create as much disruption as possible.

The "Nan White" stretch of Juno Beach at Bernieres-sur-Mer, Normandy on the morning of June 6, 1944 - D-Day. The 9th Canadian Infantry Division can be seen making its away ashore on what was one of the most-heavily defended stretches of beach assaulted by the Allies.

National Archives of Canada

In the dawn light of June 6, troops from the 3rd Canadian Infantry Division, supported by ships of the Royal Canadian and Royal Navies, attacked Nazi strongholds along the stretch of about eight kilometres of French coastline code-named Juno Beach. The lesson of Dieppe had been learned, and Allied cruisers and battleships pounded the German coastal fortifications as the troops went in. Overhead Canadian Spitfire Squadrons of the Second Tactical Air Force provided air cover from dawn until dusk. Paratroopers, including the 1st Canadian Parachute Battalion, assaulted key German defence points behind the coast. They destroyed important enemy installations at Merville, and bridges over the Dives River, while capturing the strategic bridges

over the Orne River and the Caen Canal to prevent Nazi troops from reaching the invasion area. Canada suffered 1,074 casualties including 359 dead on D-Day. Despite those losses, the tactics and bravery of Allied troops on that Longest Day secured the eventual Allied success. They had their foothold in Europe.

Among the Canadians who landed in Normandy after D-Day were nurses of the Royal Canadian Army Medical Corps, hundreds of whom served overseas. Albertan Jessie Morrison later recalled that in the days before the invasion her unit was issued khaki battle dress and given field training - digging trenches, map reading, and route marches - before being shipped to Arromanches in Normandy. "That memorable day we were all caught up with the emotion of the event. Strangely, the first thought for all of us was that we wanted to meet together in prayer." Her unit landed wearing full battle dress, minus weapons, and began treating the wounded in an 800-bed field hospital near the ancient city of Bayeux. A few miles from fierce fighting around Caen, she recalled the night sky blazing with shellfire and the ceaseless roar of the guns. "Everyone worked through the day and night until every patient was cared for, and hundreds passed through our hands in a single night," remembered Morrison. They lived on field rations and slept, when there was time, in ancient Boer War tents. Mobile showers came by occasionally, but the nurses usually gave them a pass. "The boys needed then more than we did."

Soldiers of the Highland Light Infantry of Canada and the North Nova Scotia Highlanders (opposite left) aboard a landing craft en route to the Normandy beaches. Fully one fifth of the 130,000 Allied troops taking part in the D-Day landings were Canadian. German prisoners under guard on Juno Beach (below). During the landings the Canadians suffered 359 dead and twice that number wounded, but they were the only Allied formation to reach all their objectives on June 6.

National Archives of Canada Photos

Nurses of No. 10 Canadian General Hospital, Royal Canadian Army Medical Corps, after landing in Normandy. They, too, had undergone field training - digging trenches, map reading, and route marches - before being shipped to the front. They arrived in full battledress, minus weapons.

National Archives of Canada

The Canadian forces were in the thick of the fighting in the two months after D-Day as the Allies attempted to cut off the German retreat from around Caen. By August 8 they had advanced 30 kilometres, and at Falaise the Canadian, British, and American forces attempted to envelop the German 7th Army. Several hundred thousand German troops fought to escape through a rapidly closing exit at Falaise as the Canadians and a Polish armoured division attempted to tighten the noose. On the edge of the gap 16 Canadian tanks of the South Alberta Regiment, four self-propelled guns and 50 infantry of Canada's Argyll and Sutherland Highlanders moved to block the German retreat. For three days the small Canadian force stalled entire German armoured divisions on the narrow road and single bridge leading into the village of St. Lambert-sur-Dives. When it was over, dozens of tanks and armoured vehicles lay destroyed on the approaches to St. Lambert, 800 enemy troops had been killed or wounded and 2,100 taken prisoner. Overall, the German army in Normandy was effectively destroyed, with the

loss or capture of 300,000 men and most of their equipment. The 12th SS Panzer Division was reduced from 20,000 men and 300 tanks to just 300 men and 10 tanks.

As the British and American armies pushed across France towards the River Rhine and Germany, the Canadians were given the less glamorous but daunting task of sweeping the Germans from northwest France, Belgium and eventually Holland, reducing German-held fortress cities along the way. In liberated communities they came face to face with the reality of what they were fighting for. James Brady, a Metis soldier from St. Paul, Alberta, serving with the 50th Battalion of the Royal Canadian Artillery, kept a daily diary throughout the war. On August 27, 1944 he wrote: "I talked with a French woman.

Canadian medics (below) aid a wounded soldier near Caen, July 1944. After the D-Day landings the battle for Normandy was fierce, with the Canadians in the thick of the fighting around the ancient and strategic city of Caen.

National Archives of Canada

Lance Corporal W.J. Curtis (above), a medic with the Royal Canadian Army Medical Corps, treats a young French casualty while the boy's brother looks on. The battle for Normandy took place among hundreds of thousands of French civilians, many of whom were killed and injured. It was one of the most difficult aspects of combat for the Allied soldiers to deal with.

National Archives of Canada

The SS had whipped her senseless before they left - for no comprehensible reason except a spirit of pure sadism." On September 4th Brady's unit came across the bodies of civilians shot as suspected members of the resistance. "An RAF bomber crew had been captured by these same SS men. They were hung from trees by their thumbs and shot in the head."

Through the fall of 1944 the Canadians advanced through the battlefields of the Great War, across the wide plain of Flanders, past Ypres, St. Julien and Passchendaele. The ultimate goal was the Belgian port of Antwerp and its approaches through the broad, waterlogged delta where the River Scheldt enters the North Sea. Without control of the port and the patchwork of islands and waterways, the final assault on Germany could not be supplied. The battle for the Scheldt would be one of the most decisive and hard-fought of the war, with entire Canadian regiments being consumed in bloody fighting. "It was the worst battleground of the western campaign," war

Canadian soldiers silhouetted against the flash of artillery fire in the early morning of July 25, 1944, at Fleury-sur-Orne, France. In the weeks after D-Day the Allies attempted to surround and cut off the German retreat, which led to bloody fighting around Falaise (birthplace of William the Conqueror) as German forces tried to break out of the closing trap.

National Archives of Canada

correspondent Ross Munro noted. The task of liberating the Scheldt was entrusted to the 1st Canadian Army, under the command of Lieutenant-General Guy Simonds. The unique geography of the area, a maze of channels and islands, made the challenge even more daunting. The south bank of the estuary was covered by open, flat water-meadows enclosed by dykes. Known as "polder country", it was below sea level, well-suited to defence, and a nightmare for the advancing Canadians.

On October 2, the 2nd Canadian Infantry Division began its advance north of Antwerp, while the 3rd Canadian Infantry Division, supported by the 4th Canadian Armoured Division, began an assault over the Leopold Canal. In both areas the fighting was fierce. The well-entrenched German forces made it costly for the Canadian forces to advance. After a month of bitter and

difficult fighting, the island of Walcheren remained as the last obstacle to securing the port of Antwerp. The Germans had fortified their position on the island and the only land approach was along a narrow, raised causeway. To make matters worse, the flats that surrounded the causeway were too saturated with sea water for movement on foot, but held too little water for an assault in boats. The Canadians attacked the causeway on October 31 and, after a bloody struggle, established a foothold. On November 6, the island's capital of Middelburg was captured, and by November 8 all enemy opposition had ended. With the approaches to Antwerp open, the Battle

Canadian armour from the Calgary Tank Regiment assembled for battle along the edge of one of the polders - diked water meadows - that lined the Scheldt estuary. The flooded land, reclaimed from sea and river, was "the worst battle ground of the western campaign" according to one Canadian war correspondent.

of the Scheldt was over and the crucial supply line, essential to fuel the allied advance to liberate Europe, was secured. The Scheldt was cleared of mines and, on November 28, the first convoy entered the port of Antwerp, led by the Canadian-built freighter *Fort Cataraqui*.

The awful losses in the Battle of the Scheldt, and those in Normandy, brought on the conscription crisis that Prime Minister King had been trying desperately to avoid. By October 1944 the five Canadian divisions fighting in Europe were short of 16,000 front line infantry soldiers. Defence minister J.L. Ralston (a soldier himself) visited the troops in Holland and was

shocked after visiting hospitals full of wounded Canadians who had gone into battle with their units at half-strength. According to Ralston's secretary, "His mind was completely made up... He would either force the government to bring in overseas conscription or he would resign". In the event he was forced to resign, and King appointed in his place General Andrew McNaughton, another officer from the Great War. Within weeks McNaughton (originally opposed to conscription) reported that there was no immediate alternative to sending conscripted men overseas. There was much complaining in Quebec, and in the Liberal caucus in Ottawa, some conscripts went absent without leave, and there was even a small mutiny at camps in B.C. - but with the Allies poised for the final assault on Germany there was mostly widespread acceptance (even in Quebec) that the government had no alternative, plus new confidence that the war would be over shortly. It helped that the exhausted Canadian divisions were generally out of action through much of the winter of 1944-45, and made good most of their losses from among the volunteers. As it turned out, few of the conscripts - known dismissively as "Zombies" - ever made it to the front lines. Of the 13,000 sent overseas, only about 2,500 saw action.

The 1st Canadian Army was short 16,000 front line troops when it went into the Battle of the Scheldt, which decimated some units and cost 7,600 dead and wounded. In this photograph (below) Major Bill Ewing salutes during a funeral for 55 men of A Company, the Black Watch (Royal Highland Regiment of Canada).

National Archives of Canada

During the war 40,000 captured German and Italian prisoners were held in camps across Canada - some for as long as seven years. Most were transferred from Europe, but others were U-boat crews captured by the Canadian navy. There were numerous escape attempts, but none were successful. The photo top right shows a group of German POWs arriving at Quebec City in July 1940. Most of the POWs settled into what many called "life in a gilded cage," and after the war a significant number returned as immigrants. Prisoners at the Medicine Hat, Alberta camp even organized their own hockey team (below) - but there was a darker side to their incarceration. In that same Medicine Hat camp two POWs were murdered by fellow prisoners. Five Germans were tried, convicted, and sentenced to death. They were hanged at Lethbridge Provincial Jail in 1946.

National Archives of Canada Photos

German prisoners of war behind the wire at Camp 42, near Sherbrooke, Quebec. In contrast to the treatment of Allied prisoners in Europe, the German and Italian POWs incarcerated in Canada were well-fed and well-treated. Some 40,000 would eventually be held in camps across the country, but their presence was rarely mentioned unless there was an escape attempt.

National Archives of Canada

A young boy outside a black-market restaurant in Amsterdam, Holland, during the winter of 1944-45. The country had been stripped of food by the German forces retreating before the advancing Canadians, resulting in widespread hunger and the starvation of thousands of civilians. Children like this one often carried spoons, just in case there was something to eat.

National Archives of Canada

The final Allied assault to push the Germans back across the Rhine, Operation Veritable, began in February, 1945, with the 1st Canadian Army opening the attack near Nijmegen, Holland. "A great deal of artillery was firing," recalled Frank Holm of the Calgary Highlanders. "We were silent, nervous in anticipation. I believe that after three months of holding positions at the front during the winter, we were genuinely fearful of what was in store for us in this coming offensive. I know I was."

"It took just over a month for the Canadian Army to clear its sector on the west bank [of the Rhine]," wrote correspondent Ross Munro. "This victory at the northern end of the Allied line precipitated the collapse of the entire German front west of the Rhine." The Calgary Highlanders crossed the river on March 29, and the South Alberta tanks followed two days later. There was still fierce resistance in some places, but the war was clearly coming to an end. As British and American forces moved eastwards deeper into Germany, the Canadians were directed north, to liberate the rest of Holland. The fiercest fighting in these final days came in the ancient city of Groningen. With the war all but won, senior commanders decided to avoid further destruction and the city wasn't heavily shelled. The Calgary Highlanders were sent in to dislodge the SS troops defending it, and there was fierce hand-to-hand fighting. When the city at last fell, the Highlanders discovered their immediate task was the protection of German wounded from irate townspeople, enraged after four years of often brutal occupation.

Canadian armour in the Hochwald Forest, Germany (below). The week-long struggle for the Hochwald, bitterly disputed by the First German Army, saw some of the toughest fighting of the campaign in Northwest Europe. With the First Canadian Army were nine British divisions, some Belgian, Dutch, Polish and U.S. units. It was the largest military force under Canadian command during World War Two.

B troop of the 5th Field Regiment, Royal Canadian Artillery, firing a 25-pounder near Malden, Holland, in February 1945, at the beginning of Operation Veritable, the final Allied assault. It took just over a month for the Canadian forces to clear German defenders from the western bank of the great river, and on March 29 the Calgary Highlanders became the first Canadian unit to cross into Germany.

National Archives of Canada

Dutch civilians surrounding Canadian troops (above) after the liberation of the city of Utrecht, May 7, 1945 - the day the war finally came to an end. On April 28 the Canadians had negotiated a truce which permitted relief supplies to enter western Holland and end what is still remembered there as the "Hunger Winter."

National Archives of Canada

The war was finally over, but at an awful cost. In Holland alone, in the two main Canadian war cemeteries, 5,000 young Canadians found their final resting place. On August 27, 1945, gunner James Brady of St. Paul, Alberta, made the final entry in the diary he had kept throughout the war: "Lay in a tulip field and rested for an hour under the stars. What beautiful peace and serenity." Canadians began returning home, with the first troops arriving in June, 1945. Some had been away for fully six years, and almost all had been gone for at least two. Husbands and wives, some of whom had scarcely been married before overseas posting, were reunited. Fathers gazed for the first time on children born after their departure. Older children scanned crowds of soldiers for fathers they scarcely remembered or knew only from photographs. Parents wept in joy for the return of children they feared they would never see again. Staff Sgt. Dave Shepherd of the Ist Canadian Infantry Brigade had been with the first contingent to leave Calgary in 1939, and was eager to get back to the family hardware business. But he told reporters he had no regrets. "If I had to do it all over again, I would."

Wageningen, Holland: In the historic photo below Lieutenant-General Charles Foulkes (left centre), commander of the 1st Canadian Corps, accepting the surrender of German forces in Holland from General Johannes Blaskowitz.

National Archives of Canada

Sailors aboard HMCS Uganda, preparing for the bombardment of Japanese forces on the Pacific island of Truk, in June 1945. The cruiser Uganda (later renamed HMCS Quebec) had been bought from Britain at the end of 1944 and sent to join American and British forces in the Pacific. As volunteers the crew were required to re-enlist for duty in the new theatre of operations, and the majority voted "no." The Uganda was called home to Esquimalt. B.C. - the only ship to effectively vote itself out of the war. Nearly 80,000 Canadians did volunteer for service in the Pacific, and the new Canadian 6th Division was slated to take part in the invasion of Japan. Some 60 Canadian warships were also assembled for the invasion, which was predicted to be an extremely bloody affair. The use of two U.S. atomic weapons against Japan in August 1945 ultimately ended the war and rendered the invasion moot. Ironically when HMCS Uganda was decommissioned in 1956, she was sold for scrap - to the Japanese.

National Archives of Canada

Lieutenant-Commander Fed Day and officers of HMCS Prince Robert with liberated Canadian prisoners at the Sham Shui Po camp in Hong Kong, August 1945. The former British colonial barracks had been converted by the Japanese to house many of the Canadians captured in the fall of Hong Kong in December 1941. In the early months men were dying every day as a result of disease, starvation, and the casual brutality of the guards.

National Archives of Canada

The number of Canadians in uniform had swelled to 1.1 million - fully 10% of the population and a much greater number than in 1914-18. In all, the war had cost 42,000 Canadian lives. This time there was a determination that the end of the wartime economy and the reintegration of 620,000 service personnel into civilian life would be better managed than had been the case in 1918, and in most instances that was the case. There was a broad public consensus that the veterans of this war must receive better treatment than the many soldiers of 1914-18 who lived and died in poverty and distress. The Veterans' Land Act made farmland available to ex-servicemen, loans were provided to start businesses or buy homes, and there were programs to assist veterans in completing or augmenting their education. Access to a university education (one month tuition for every month of active service) launched tens of thousands of successful post-war careers in the professions and business.

Still, the transition to peacetime life - "Civvy Street" as it was popularly known - could be difficult. "Getting used to working again wasn't really hard," Loyal Eddies' veteran J. Bertrand told the *Edmonton Bulletin*. "Everybody was swell to me from the start." He had been seriously wounded in Sicily and on his return home had found work as a streetcar motorman. The hard part, he said, was "getting used to having a home, a place where you are supposed to stay." Such restlessness was common. "I have never been the kind who craved a great deal of excitement, but even I have been restless and found it hard to settle down," reported Harold Gregory, a sergeant with the Seaforth Highlanders. Former air force officer Kenneth Pryor came up with a solution which suited him. He joined the Edmonton police force and walked more than 30 km each shift. "That takes care of your restlessness," he said. The transition back to normal life was particularly hard for the returning Japanese POWs. "As far as Canada was concerned... I left 17 years old and I came back four years later 17 years old," remembered Hamilton's Don Geraghty. "I couldn't cope with the people as they were then. I didn't know the world I was stepping into, and for a few years that was the big problem." But he, too, eventually made the adjustment, becoming manager of an educational book distributor and an active member of Hamilton's Orpheus Male Choir.

The war had obliged Canada to come of age for a second time in less than 30 years, and the effort had been unprecedented. After the United States and Britain, Canada had been the third largest source of Allied war production and manpower, and the country had given away billions of dollars in food and war materiel. As the conflict came to an end the country had the world's third largest navy, fourth largest air force, and a powerful army. Canadian industry had been modernized and expanded, and the poverty and hardship of the Great Depression had been replaced by full employment and prosperity.

The war had also begun to work remarkable change in Canadian society that was all to the good. The early decades of the century had populated the country's farms and cities with many immigrants who were neither English nor French, yet until 1939 there had remained a gulf

Troops returning home (above). The transition to civilian life was difficult for many, particularly for those who had spent the war as POWs of the Germans or Japanese. They returned to a country that had changed significantly, with no sign of the depression that had dogged the country during the 1930s.

National Archives of Canada

Victory celebrations in Montreal (below) on May 8, 1945. For a nation of 11 million people, Canada's contribution to the war had been enormous, with fully 10% of the population serving in uniform and almost the entire economy having been dedicated to the war effort.

National Archives of Canada

between these newcomers and the established population. Relations between the various groups were, for the most part, cordial, but socially many Canadians had remained estranged. The war began the final demolition of those barriers as people from all origins wore the same uniform and faced the same perils, shoulder to shoulder, regardless of whether they or their parents hailed from Kiev or Birmingham, from Kansas or Campania. After 1945, in politics, the arts, and the professions, the unspoken cultural barriers between Canadians gradually began to disappear. There were still the traditional political tensions between French and English Canada, but in a peculiar stroke of irony the most destructive war in human history had left Canadian society more united than ever before. ■

Prime Minister Mackenzie King at Dieppe, France, on August 18, 1945. As part of a visit to Europe to pay homage to the thousands of Canadians who would not be returning home, King laid a wreath on the memorial to Canadians killed in the 1942 raid on the French seaport.

National Archives of Canada

EN
MÉMOIRE DE DEUX
SOLDATS CANADIENS
TOMBÉS ICI LE
19 AOÛT 1942

PART THREE

1946-1953

The Canadian government feared that an economic recession would follow the end of World War Two, as had happened two decades earlier after the Great War. But Canada's modernised industries shifted from military to civilian production with little difficulty, and the country began the most sustained period of economic growth in its history. For Canadians like this young couple visiting Niagara Falls, that meant jobs, prosperity, and the opportunity to attain the Canadian dream.

National Archives of Canada

A Brave New World

The Post-War Baby Boom
And The Age Of Materialism

'As long as mutual confidence does not reign between nations, we will not have true and sustainable peace. Yet, events have shown that this confidence can only be born of a sincere and radical change of attitude on the part of Soviet Russia towards the other countries of the world. Such a change cannot happen overnight, if it is to occur at all during our lifetime.'

Louis St. Laurent

For Canadians, the end of World War Two meant the boys came home, rationing ended, and things started to get back to normal. Except that this turned out to be a completely new normal. No country had been harder hit by the Great Depression, or taken longer to recover, than Canada, and in 1946 the immediate question on everyone's mind was "Will there be work?" After a decade and a half of economic depression, social unrest, and global war, a great many of Canada's political and business leaders were less than optimistic, fearing peace would slow the economy and usher in a recession - just as it had in 1919 after the end of the Great War. This time, however, that didn't happen. For Canada, the five years between the end of World War Two and the beginning of the Korean War proved to be among the most dynamic of the century. The country's expanded and modernized industrial base kept on growing, and the country was launched into the longest and most sustained economic boom of its history. Most dramatic of all, for the first time the vast majority of ordinary citizens found they could aspire to a level of material wealth undreamed of by previous generations. In this boom, the prosperity would prove to be almost universal.

In a world rebuilding from war, Canadian exports continued to be in high demand, and after a generation of austerity pent-up consumer demand sent the population on an unprecedented domestic buying spree - everything from automobiles to household appliances, and the new television sets. Prosperity unleashed an unprecedented new age of materialism, and as tens of thousands

Servicemen waiting for counselling (opposite page) at one of many information centres set up across the country. Ottawa and the provincial governments vowed to help returning veterans reintegrate into society and the workforce, and to a large extent they succeeded. In sharp contrast to the lack of support for Great War veterans, the loans and educational opportunities provided after 1945 helped thousands of servicemen and women towards successful and productive lives.

National Archives of Canada

of young men left the armed forces and married, there was a sudden explosion of births that was rapidly christened a baby boom. Consumerism and the Baby Boom would to a large extent come to define post-war life in Canada. At first it seemed like a reprise of the Golden Decade before the 1914-18 war, but this time the benefits were more widespread and the economy more diversified than ever before. Together with modern communications and transportation, this expansive new age of affluence would complete Canada's transformation from a developing nation into one of the most desirable addresses on the planet - and in the process go a long way towards fulfilling the heady dreams of Macdonald and Laurier.

At the outset, the only fly in the ointment was a shortage of money to pay for Canadian products, particularly in Europe. The European economies had been shattered by the war, and France, Italy, Belgium, Holland, and of course Germany, were effectively bankrupt. Britain was in little better shape. It had borrowed $5 billion from the U.S. and Canada to rebuild, but that money was running out fast. The only country in a position to lend money in large enough amounts was America, and the U.S. Secretary of State, George Marshall, came up with a plan to loan Europe the dollars to buy the materials and goods it needed for reconstruction. Canada didn't need loans, but it did need customers with hard currency, and the Marshall Plan allowed cash-strapped European governments to pay for Canadian imports with American dollars. The plan enabled the nations of Western Europe to rebuild at a far quicker pace than would otherwise have been the case, and nowhere was that more apparent than in the western half of Germany (the east being controlled by the Soviet Union). It became a matter of some bitterness in Britain that the new nation of West Germany was able to recover from the war more quickly than the United Kingdom - the victor in the recent conflict. Yet the stability provided by the Marshall Plan had a second goal that would prove crucial in the coming decades. In 1945 Europe had been divided by what Churchill called an "Iron Curtain" separating the continent between the free nations of the West and the Soviet-dominated East. The Marshall Plan dollars and a new defensive alliance between Europe and North America - the North Atlantic Treaty Organization (NATO) - provided an economic and military bulwark against potential Soviet domination of the entire continent. Together with the creation of a modern, free-market democracy in Japan, it would prove to be the most enlightened and far-reaching act of American foreign policy of the 20th century.

For its part, Canada emerged from World War Two as an important "middle power" and the government of Liberal Prime Minister Mackenzie King had, like the U.S. administration, realized that in an age of long-range bombers and nuclear weapons North America was no longer comfortably removed from potential conflicts an ocean away. Canada could not afford to be a bystander in what was being called a "Cold War" between the Western democracies and Soviet totalitarianism. In the no-nonsense words of External Affairs Minister Louis St. Laurent, Ottawa supported "the creation and preservation by nations of the free world... of an overwhelming preponderance of force" to counter Soviet aggression. The country became a founding member of NATO, to underline Canada's continuing commitment to preserve a free and democratic Western Europe. And it was far from being an empty commitment. During these years defence was the number one item in federal budgets. Canada stationed an army brigade in Germany, an air force division in France, and provided a naval squadron for defence of the North Atlantic. In contrast to Canada's withdrawal from international affairs after the Great War, this time Ottawa actively worked to use the country's new influence - purchased at such a high cost in lives and effort during the global conflict. A prosperous and independent Canada began to develop its own personality in international relations, reflective of the new state of global affairs.

Alex Christie (opposite page) at the pumps of a Supertest gas station in Ottawa, Ontario. The wartime shortages were suddenly gone, and a new age of consumerism was launched that was quite unlike anything that had gone before.

National Archives of Canada

Britain no longer had an overwhelming influence on Canada's role in the world, but through NATO and the Commonwealth relations between the two countries remained close. Indeed, Canada played a leading role in the sometimes difficult modernization of the Commonwealth to include newly-independent British colonies that chose not to retain the British monarch as head of state. Canadian efforts thus helped the old empire morph successfully into a multiracial organization that included new republics such as India and Pakistan. Common British and Commonwealth citizenship was replaced by one based on nationality (even in Canada, where the Citizenship Act of 1947 became the first to define citizens as Canadians

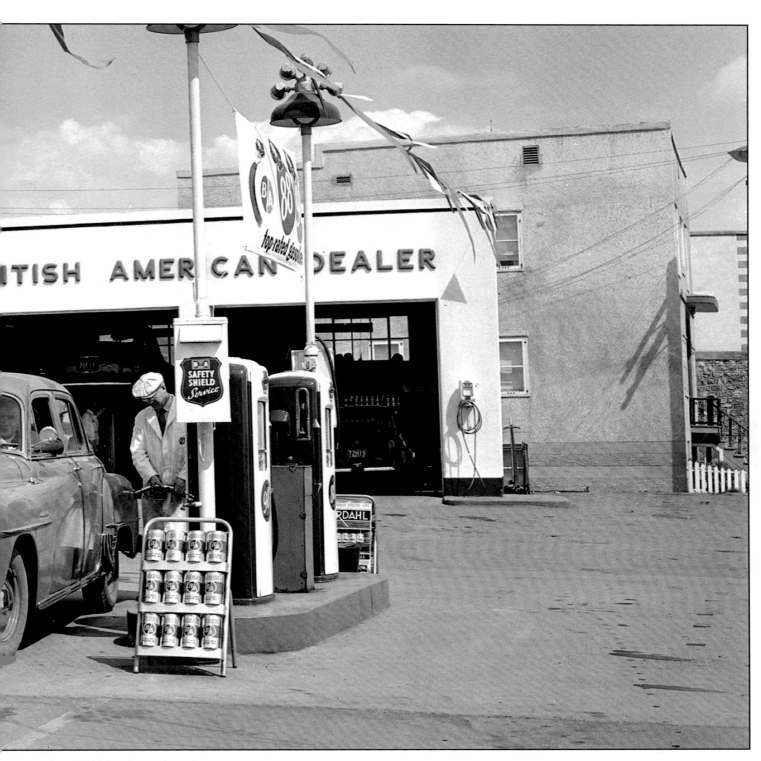

A new British American service station in Calgary (above). Automobiles had been around since early in the century, but it wasn't until after World War Two that they became an indispensable part of everyday life in Canada, changing everything from the way cities were built to the way people consumed. It was the beginning of the age of freeways, drive-ins, and shopping centres.

Glenbow Archives

rather than as British subjects). The United Nations was established in 1945, and although Ottawa was as sceptical of its ability to maintain international peace and security as it had been of the old League of Nations, Canada supported the organization's lofty founding principles and became an enthusiastic supporter of UN actions on food, health, education, and welfare. But the new centre of Canada's foreign policy was necessarily its relationship with its southern neighbour, now elevated by World War Two to the status of a superpower. Politically, economically, and culturally, the U.S. republic now overshadowed the less populous constitutional monarchy to the north.

At home the 1931 census had long ago confirmed that a majority of Canadians now lived in towns and cities. Most of that urban majority had been renters, and it wasn't until after World War Two that a large number could afford to buy their first home. Prosperity and easier borrowing now rapidly made Canada a nation of homeowners (except Quebec, where renters remained in the majority). Home ownership also invariably meant new families. The birthrate, which had languished throughout the1930s, rose year after year and the number of Canadians coming into the world doubled (from under 250,000 to 500,000 annually). And more of those children were surviving. Canada's infant mortality rate dropped by 50% as a result of better housing, improved nutrition, and vastly improved drugs and access to medical facilities.

The resident population was now also joined by a massive influx of new immigrants. During the 1930s immigration had rapidly fallen off - and for a time had actually gone into reverse as 100,000 more people left the struggling country than entered it. All that changed after the war ended, with some two million immigrants arriving over a 15-year period. About a third of these new arrivals still came from Britain (it would prove to be the last great wave of immigration from the British Isles), but most of the remainder now came from elsewhere in Europe - many displaced by war or fearful of emerging Soviet control of much of the eastern half of the continent. A new immigration policy also finally ended the blatant discrimination against Chinese immigrants, although it still acknowledged the widespread view that "the people of Canada do not wish, as a result of mass immigration, to make a fundamental alteration in the character of our population." As a result, immigration focused on "the admission of relatives of persons who are already in Canada, and on assisting the resettlement of displaced persons and refugees." Mindful of concerns over a possible recession and unemployment, the government also assured Canadians that immigration would always be geared to prevailing "economic conditions".

However, the fears of renewed unemployment proved unfounded. The booming economy actually created a labour shortage, and newcomers poured in looking for a new life away from the devastation and political instability of Europe, primarily from Germany, Italy, Holland, Greece, Portugal, Poland, and Hungary. Unlike earlier waves of immigration, most of these newcomers settled in cities, and despite the official misgivings they did indeed change the character of urban life - adding a new cosmopolitan quality to Canadian communities. They not only brought with them valuable skills and capital, but their cultural and commercial energy added to the explosive growth of Canada's towns and cities.

At the beginning of the 1940s about 55% of Canadians lived in urban centres, but that would rise to 70% over the next two decades, with more than half of the population living in communities of more than 100,000 inhabitants. Montreal continued to be Canada's largest city, with a population topping two million, but it was now closely followed by Toronto at 1.8 million. Together these two cities now accounted for fully one fifth of Canada's population. The next largest city, Vancouver, was considerably smaller at 800,000 people. Contrasting with this impressive growth was the continuing depopulation of rural areas, in particular on the Prairies. The hardships of the 1930s were over, and throughout the 1940s there was substantial demand for Canadian grain, but the hardships had not been forgotten and the lure of urban life and well-paying jobs attracted many from the land, particularly the young. It was the beginning of a trend. Canada's farm population declined by about 20% during the 1940s and early '50s.

As the troops returned home, governments had promised better housing and more home ownership, and Ottawa delivered with legislation that made mortgages easier to obtain, and the provinces responded with regulations that tried to ensure new homes met minimum standards - including electricity and modern plumbing. In 1951 there were still 886,000 Canadian homes

The late 1940s and '50s would eventually develop an image of uptight reserve and conservative behaviour, but that's not how people living through those years saw them. This revealing swimsuit (opposite page), from an article in Weekend Magazine, was typical of the daring post-war styles that emerged. It was an age of colour, innovation, and new ideas.

Louis Jaques/National Archives of Canada

With most families now able to own a car, Canadians in the post-war years joined Americans in embracing the new mobility that came with vehicle ownership. It would be some years until Canadians could boast a national road system remotely comparable to the U.S. interstate highways, but other American innovations were adopted more rapidly - such as this Ontario motel: one of the first of its kind.

without indoor plumbing, and a great many without electricity, but increasingly these were in rural areas and as the decade progressed both amenities would become almost universal. With more buyers and more homes Canadian cities resumed the expansion dampened by the Great Depression. The country's largest city spread west across Montreal Island, creating the middle class suburbs of the West Island, and then steadily south across the St. Lawrence. In Toronto the expansion urbanized the townships surrounding the city and effectively created a single metropolitan area - a reality recognized by the province of Ontario with the creation of the Metropolitan Toronto federation of municipalities in 1953. The first suburban shopping centres (an idea copied from the U.S.) appeared, first at Norgate outside Montreal in 1949, followed a year later by Dorval (also in Montreal), and Northgate in West Vancouver. The new suburban homes were filled with new gadgets and appliances - everything from washing machines and clothes dryers, to refrigerators, and the first dishwashers. And of course these appliances - not to mention industrial expansion, new office buildings, schools, and hospitals - all required power.

Hydroelectricity was Canada's major home-grown source of energy, but the country was fast running out of easily accessible hydro sources, and despite the building of new dams (on the Columbia River in B.C., the Nelson River in Manitoba, and at Churchill Falls in Labrador), and the modernization of old generating equipment, at the end of the 1940s there were a series of ominous power cuts - primarily in southern Ontario. The major back-up to hydro was coal, with almost half of the demand being met from Canadian mines (most in Nova Scotia and Alberta). But the other half, including most of the high-grade anthracite used by industry, came from the U.S. Importing such huge amounts of coal (22 million tons in the late 1940s) meant an equally large flow of currency out of Canada, which increased Ottawa's already substantial concern about dependency on imported fuel. The only other energy alternatives were oil and natural gas, and although Alberta had both there was not enough to meet the demands of a prosperous and growing country - and Alberta's reserves (the amount of oil and gas estimated to be in the ground) were actually falling. A solution to this energy dilemma seemed remote - until a frosty day in February 1947, in a farmyard south of Edmonton.

Imperial Oil had given 48-hours notice to the media that something special was expected from a new well on farmer Mike Turta's land northwest of the town of Leduc. After a series of 112 dry holes this was either a display of supreme confidence or just plain foolhardiness. By noon on the appointed day - Thursday, February 13 - some 500 curious people had gathered in Turta's farmyard to see which it would be. The dignitaries and journalists in the crowd had been invited, but hundreds of ordinary folk simply turned up to see what all the fuss was about. The predicted time of the gusher, 1 p.m., came and went, and Imperial treated the restless onlookers to coffee, sandwiches and cake. By 3:30 a good many people were leaving, including Edmonton Mayor Harry Ainlay. It seemed as if Imperial had yet another dud on its hands. But the confident rig boss, the ominously nick-named Vernon "Dry Hole" Hunter, kept his crew working, and just before 4 p.m. there was a rumble which many later described a similar to an oncoming freight train. From 5,066 feet below, and 300 million years in the making, Alberta's future came snaking through a three-inch line to Imperial's well head - and erupted with a mighty "whoosh!"

Roughneck Johnny Funk had the honour of tossing a burning rag into the volatile mix spewing from the earth. The result, reported the *Daily Oil Bulletin*, was "a roaring column of burning oil and gas, shooting flames some 20 metres into the air, and clouds of black smoke hundreds of metres into the sky." As the astonished crowd watched, "The well belched a few times as it cleared itself," Funk recalled years later, and then a perfect circular smoke ring rose high into the frigid air. Old hands nodded that was a good omen, and many in the crowd surged forward with bottles and

In Canada's two largest cities, Toronto and Montreal, as the streets became more congested mass transit began to go underground. In this 1950 photo (opposite page) the street in front of Toronto's Royal York Hotel is being excavated during the construction of the city's subway system.

National Film Board/
National Archives of Canada

jars to scoop up a souvenir of the glutinous oil. There was a big party that evening at Edmonton's Hotel Macdonald, and bold headlines in the newspapers the following day, but it's safe to say that few people understood the full impact Leduc No. 1 would have on Alberta and Canada. Vern Hunter had some inkling. He quickly tested the flow-rate of the well and estimated it might produce an unheard-of thousand barrels-a-day. "I couldn't help but wonder whether the horizon would be dotted with flares before the next year rolled around." He wasn't wrong. Imperial had discovered a gigantic, multi-level oilfield in Canada's deep Western Sedimentary Basin. Within weeks dozens of rigs were pouring in as Shell, British American, California Standard, Gulf, and all the big players arrived on scene. The *Lethbridge Herald* sounded a note of caution: "We would not say that the great oil pool for which Albertans have been searching ever since John Lineham drilled at Waterton Lakes nearly 50 years ago has been found." But the paper did allow that, with luck, within a lifetime the population of Edmonton "might grow to 250,000."

The day Alberta changed forever. On the afternoon of February 13, 1947, muddy oil spews from the well in farmer Mike Turta's yard (below). The event drew a big crowd, but few present had any idea of the transformation that awaited the poorest Prairie province. There were so many vehicles cluttering the road to the farm that driller George Tosh (right) and his crew had to park a mile from the rig and walk in to begin their historic shift.

(Main) Provincial Archives of Alberta
(Inset) Glenbow Archives

Turta, the farmer on whose land Leduc No. 1 had been drilled, didn't own the mineral rights (in Canada those rights usually belonged to the province, or original landowners such as the railways), but after the well came in oil companies were paying hefty bonuses (as much as six figures) for leases to prospect for oil and gas. For the minority of landowners who did own the mineral rights to their property, a strike also meant regular royalty cheques which could turn into a small fortune. Turta's father, Anton, farmed two miles west of his son and assumed he also didn't own the mineral rights to his land - but he and his family became curious when no one came knocking on his door to ask about a lease. What did they know that he didn't? "We thought it

The mess tent (above) at an oil and gas exploration camp in the Brazeau area of central Alberta. There was renewed demand, domestically and internationally, for Canada's mineral wealth - but that wealth was often located in remote areas and those who searched for it often faced the same hazards and endured the same privations as earlier pioneers.

Glenbow Archives

was kind of funny," he said later. "People were drilling all around - except here. So we looked into it." It turned out that when the land had been sold by the Canadian Pacific Railway in 1908 a clerk had failed to reserve the mineral rights for the company. An employee in the land titles office had later corrected the oversight, but the Supreme Court of Alberta ruled that the original title was valid. So although the son made only a modest profit from the great Leduc strike, royalties from the oil beneath the father's land would eventually be worth an estimated $5 million, a huge amount of money at the time.

Over the next few years Alberta experienced a near frenzy of exploration and development of its oil and gas resources, with almost $2 billion being invested in the industry throughout the province. The boom was particularly apparent in Edmonton, with 68 new oilfield businesses springing up in 1947 alone. "The city still looked like the drab market town that was the capital of bankrupt Alberta in the 1930s," wrote Toronto journalist Blair Fraser. The capital had indeed seen hard times, but the city and the province would change rapidly. And it wasn't only Albertans who benefited. Author James G. MacGregor (*History of Alberta*, Edmonton, Hurtig, 1972) maintains that, in addition to the Marshall Plan, it was Alberta oil and the influx of American dollars it prompted that saved the country from a potential financial crisis. "Not only had oil... put a chicken on every Albertan's table but it had saved every Canadian's bacon," he wrote. "During 1947, just when Canada was running into one of its most serious financial crises,

Leduc No. 1 came to its aid." He was not wrong. The same year as the Leduc oil strike Canada had signed a new international trade treaty, the General Agreement on Tariffs and Trade (GATT), which set out trade rules in an effort to reduce import taxes, lower trade barriers, and avoid another depression. The same day the new treaty was announced in Ottawa, Canada invoked GATT provisions to protect troubled economies. Restrictions were placed on imports of all kinds from the U.S. in an effort to limit a yawning trade imbalance with the Americans. Thanks to Leduc, it was only a temporary measure, but during the winter of 1947-48 cabbage was often the only green vegetable to found in many Canadian grocery stores.

Ironically, the prospect of exporting huge amounts of natural gas sparked a fierce debate in Alberta, where opposition politicians, the major municipal governments, the media, chambers of commerce, and indeed many members of the public viewed such exports as a sale of Albertans' birthright. "Money realized from depletion of Alberta's natural resources should not be considered as race-track winnings," warned Liberal leader J. Harper Prowse. He suggested that at the very least a portion of energy revenue should be diverted to a trust fund for future use (an idea that would later be adopted by the government of Peter Lougheed as the Alberta Heritage Savings Trust Fund). Part of the opposition was due to sheer provincialism (why allow Americans access to Alberta oil and gas?), but there was also fear that Albertans would be called upon to pay world prices for their own resource (they would), and the hundreds of millions of dollars necessary to

An oil pump and storage tanks in the midst of fields outside Edmonton, Alberta. As Canada's economy expanded, Ottawa had worried about the rising cost of importing fuel - but beneath the Alberta landscape the Western Sedimentary Basin was about to give up its 300 million-year-old secret and solve that problem.

Glenbow Archives

build pipelines and other transmission facilities to export both oil and gas simply unnerved people. In a province so recently Canada's poorest, many recalled that Alberta had been bankrupted in the Great Depression by far smaller numbers. Still, cautiously at first, Alberta would begin exporting its energy resources. The first gas pipeline - just 110 km into Montana - would supply energy to the Anaconda Copper and Mining Company smelter. More would follow, and Albertans would gradually warm to the idea of U.S. energy revenues.

Culture Shock

The War Brides Arrive In Canada

The flow of immigrants to Canada was sharply reduced during the Great Depression, and dried up almost completely during the war years - with one notable exception. During the war Canadians in uniform spent more time away from home than any other Allied troops, and during their long sojourn in Britain thousands got married. Some spouses and their children came to Canada during the war, but as the conflict drew to a close the trickle became a flood as shipload after shipload of war brides, about half with children, crossed the Atlantic to join husbands they hardly knew, in a country they knew not at all. In all 48,000 women and 22,000 children would make the journey.

In *Promise Me You'll Take Care of My Daughter*, author Ben Wicks tells the typical story of Iris Hughes, who imagined her new spouse's Alberta farm would be something like those she knew in England, complete with roses, thatched roof, and picket fence. "What a culture shock," she remembered later. "The house was of bare boards, banked to the windows with manure and straw to keep the frost out in winter - as it wasn't insulated and every nail hole was as big as a quarter." Many war brides struggled at first,

but with the help of in-laws and neighbours they made the adjustment. Stella Chudleigh's husband, Rufus, had at least given her an unvarnished description of the life and climate in Brooks, Alberta, and she received a warm welcome from his family. "Mom treated me just like another daughter and was very patient with the green, 22-year-old English girl born and raised in town. I soon settled in, in spite of no electricity, gas, or plumbing of any kind. That first summer I had to learn how to wash clothes on a scrub board, clean coal-oil lamps, separate the cream, churn butter, can dozens of jars of fruit and vegetables, and cook on a coal and wood stove for the hay crews and threshing crews."

For war brides from occupied Europe, Canada was a haven of peace and security. When her father, a member of the Dutch underground, was captured and sent to a concentration camp, Ann Wood took his place. "If the underground took a stand and did some damage, the Germans would just take people off the street and stick them on a tree with a bayonet," she told Wicks. "We had been without food and water a long time when the Allied troops began attacking our city, Nijmegen, early in September 1944. They were bombing and shelling, and as I stuck my nose out of a foxhole

a Canadian soldier grabbed me and pushed me back in. That's how I met my husband, Ernest. Later that month the Canadians took the city, after a long, hard fight, and Ernest stayed through the winter. We had to get three sets of papers, and I married the same guy three times."

War brides were transported to Canada on huge troop ships specially outfitted for their use, and converted luxury liners. The most notable of these was the *Queen Mary*. Many war brides remember hanging diapers in the pool area, and sharing the ship with nearly 1,000 other women and hundreds of children. Among the youngsters was 14-year-old Evelyn Gooderham, whose mother had married a soldier from P.E.I. "The first time we all went down to the dining room, we couldn't get over the food. I had never seen that much food before in my whole life," Gooderham later wrote in her diary. "The white rolls and real butter, all kinds of meat. Our

bread in the war was kind of a grey colour."

Like immigrants before and after them, almost all the war brides vividly remember docking in Halifax, and passing through Pier 21. They were met there by Red Cross and Salvation Army volunteers, who offered the new Canadians a warm welcome and gifts of food and clothes for the children. They boarded special trains bound for various points across Canada. For most there were wedding and baby showers from welcoming communities. A few were not so lucky. The government had only undertaken to pay travel fares one way - so an unwelcome or unhappy war bride with no means of returning to her family faced a precarious situation. Some found help from the Red Cross, sympathetic neighbours, or local communities, and managed to return to their families in Britain. For the vast majority, though, it was the beginning of a new life in a vast country on the verge of unprecedented prosperity. ■

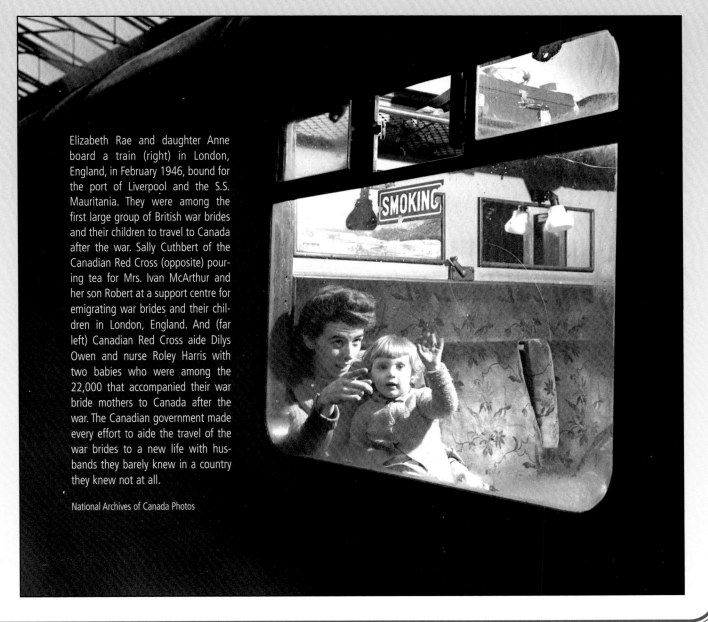

Elizabeth Rae and daughter Anne board a train (right) in London, England, in February 1946, bound for the port of Liverpool and the S.S. Mauritania. They were among the first large group of British war brides and their children to travel to Canada after the war. Sally Cuthbert of the Canadian Red Cross (opposite) pouring tea for Mrs. Ivan McArthur and her son Robert at a support centre for emigrating war brides and their children in London, England. And (far left) Canadian Red Cross aide Dilys Owen and nurse Roley Harris with two babies who were among the 22,000 that accompanied their war bride mothers to Canada after the war. The Canadian government made every effort to aide the travel of the war brides to a new life with husbands they barely knew in a country they knew not at all.

National Archives of Canada Photos

A blast furnace at the Steel Company of Canada plant in Hamilton, Ontario. In a bitter strike the company used boats and planes to bypass picket lines and keep production going. Despite rapidly improving wages and conditions, union membership boomed to about 30% of the Canadian workforce by the end of the 1940s.

National Film Board/National Archives of Canada

The Aluminum Company of Canada plant at Arvida, Quebec (below) in the 1940s. Canada had become the world's second largest producer of the metal, and the world's largest aluminum smelter was planned for Kitimat, B.C.

National Film Board/
National Archives of Canada

Despite the impressive growth of manufacturing during and after the war, Canada was still a country that mostly exported raw materials or semi-processed products, such as pulp and paper or lead and zinc - and increasingly oil and natural gas. The inflow of American capital (and American oilmen and their families) to Alberta was matched by the similar development of resources in other parts of the country. Rich mineral deposits were discovered in Ontario north of Lake Superior, and on the Ungava Peninsula on the Quebec/Labrador border. Uranium was found near Beaverlodge in northern Saskatchewan, and then again at Blind River and Elliot Lake in Ontario. In the Northwest Territories lead, zinc, gold, and silver deposits were found near Great Slave Lake, tungsten along the Yukon border, and oil along the lower Mackenzie River. Canada was now the world's second-largest producer of aluminum (with the world's largest smelter planned for Kitimat, B.C.), and the country supplied about half the world's newsprint. All this activity necessitated better transportation links, and there was a flurry of road, rail, and airport construction.

In particular the development of the iron ore deposits on the Quebec-Newfoundland border posed a problem. There was a ready market for the ore in U.S. and Canadian steel plants, and the Iron Ore Company of Canada spent hundreds of millions of dollars opening mines and building a rail link to the port of Sept-Iles on the Gulf of St. Lawrence. But the steel plants were clustered around the Great Lakes, and the canals and locks joining the lakes to the St. Lawrence were relics of the 19th century - too shallow and narrow to allow the passage of large ore-carriers. Plans to make the St. Lawrence navigable to ocean-going vessels were once again dusted off, and when it looked as if opposition from the U.S. railway lobby might delay the project once again, Ottawa announced that the Canadian government would go ahead with the project on its own. The U.S. government recognized that the St. Lawrence project could provide vital hydroelectric power to the bordering states and would be a much more efficient avenue for moving goods in and out of the vast manufacturing area that surrounded the Great Lakes. A treaty with Washington was signed in 1954 (the St. Lawrence is an international waterway), and the U.S. government paid for the building of its share of locks.

The influx of American capital had by now become an overwhelming national trend. At the beginning of the 20th century financing for Canada's first great boom and westward expansion had come from Britain (85%), then by far the wealthiest and most powerful country in the world, with the U.S. as a secondary source of capital. After World War Two that situation would be reversed, as Britain struggled to repair its own finances and shed its far-flung empire. Foreign investment in Canada tripled after the war, and most of that investment came from the U.S. At the same time cross-border trade with America came to dominate the Canadian economy. This sparked a debate in Canada about the nation's increasing economic dependence on the U.S., but C.D. Howe, Canada's practical, American-born minister of trade and commerce, argued that the country should "sell as much as possible wherever possible" and enjoy the resulting prosperity! Howe reminded Canadians of the positive contribution of American investment. "Had it not been for the enterprise and capital of the United States, which has been so freely at our disposal in the post-war years, our development would have been slower, and some of the spectacular projects about which we are... so rightly proud, since they are Canadian projects, would still be far in the future." He was right, but for some Canadians it was an uncomfortable truth.

Continental integration also appeared to make sense politically and militarily. Britain was fading as a world power and could not be relied upon to protect Canadian interests in the post-war era. Canada's neighbour, by contrast, had emerged from the war as the wealthiest and most powerful nation in the world, and had shed its traditional isolationism to assume leadership of the Western democracies and oppose the Soviet Union in its quest for global dominance. A close relationship with the U.S. was clearly in Canada's interest, but it was also clear to the King government that this relationship had to be balanced by an active demonstration of independence in international affairs. This balancing act would prove to be difficult, and at times divisive, but in response to the realities of the Cold War, Canada for the first time proved willing to extend its influence into the arena of international relations.

Meanwhile, the bustling economy and labour shortages proved to be a boon to organized labour in the post-war years, with union membership passing the one million mark by the end of the 1940s (about 30% of the workforce). The growing confidence and bargaining power enjoyed by industrial unions allowed Canadian workers to negotiate better pay and working conditions, but it also resulted in a flurry of strikes. In a bitter and dramatic dispute involving the Steel Company of Canada plant in Hamilton, Ontario, management used planes and

A female worker handles asbestos fibre (opposite page) at a plant in the Quebec town named after the fireproof mineral. The violent 1949 strike at Asbestos pitted the workers against the authoritarian Union Nationale government of Premier Maurice Duplessis. The health hazards of asbestos dust were first documented at the end of the 19th century, but it would continue to be used as a building and industrial material until the 1980s.

National Film Board/
National Archives of Canada

Construction of the St. Lawrence Seaway in 1952. Canada took the lead in getting the mega-project built, primarily to ease the shipping of iron ore from Labrador to the steel plants of the Great Lakes. In 1954 the American government became a partner and the seaway was officially designated as an international waterway.

National Film Board/National Archives of Canada

boats to avoid picket lines and keep production going. But the most famous and politicized industrial dispute of the period took place in Quebec, where in February 1949, 5,000 asbestos miners went on strike against their American-owned employer, the Johns-Manville company.

The miners wanted a wage increase of 15-cents-an-hour, and improved working conditions (asbestos dust posed a serious health threat to the miners), while the company offered 5-cents-an-hour.

The strike became political when Quebec Premier Maurice Duplessis weighed in on the company's side, and the strikers blocked roads into the town of Asbestos to press their claims. "This is about an admitted attempt, encouraged from the outside, to challenge and break the state's authority," thundered Duplessis. He sent in 400 police armed with tear gas and guns, which unsurprisingly resulted in a violent confrontation with the miners. The Archbishop of Montreal, Joseph Charbonneau, angrily denounced the government's involvement and called it a "conspiracy aimed at crushing the working class".

The bitter and violent strike at Asbestos lasted five months, with the miners eventually becoming the best paid in Canada, but the dispute is often identified as the beginning of a Quiet Revolution that would forever change Quebec politics and culture. It was a landmark victory for opponents of the dictatorial Duplessis and his Union Nationale government, and in particular for the left in Quebec politics. It also solidified an anti-Americanism that would become a fixture among Quebec intellectuals, and signalled a change in the traditionally close relationship between the government and the Catholic Church. (Archbishop Charbonneau resigned and spent the rest of his life as a hospital chaplain in Victoria, B.C.) There were also repercussions for the rest of Canada, not the least of which was the appearance among the strikers of 29-year-old Montreal lawyer Pierre Elliott Trudeau. The miners nicknamed the bearded Trudeau "St. Joseph", but when he talked at their meetings they listened attentively. For the future prime minister it was a first taste of social activism, and a tentative road test of what would prove to be his considerable political charisma.

Chalk River Secret

Canada Joins The Nuclear Club

In September 1945 a cryptic telegram arrived at the Ottawa office of C.D. Howe, Canada's wartime minister of supply. It said simply, "Operational condition reached." What it signified was that barely a month after the U.S. dropped nuclear bombs on Hiroshima and Nagasaki to end World War Two, Canada had become the second member of the global nuclear club with the successful initiation of a top secret nuclear reactor at Chalk River, Ontario.

The establishment of Canada's nuclear program owed much to the fact the country had ample uranium, power - and a long-standing nuclear science pedigree (established before the turn of the 20th century when Ernest Rutherford set up a laboratory at McGill University to study radioactivity and probe the structure of the atom). But the events that conspired to centre wartime nuclear research on the banks of the Ottawa River read more like a Hollywood script - and indeed they were the basis for a successful motion picture!

In the popular 1965 movie *The Heroes Of Telemark*, actors Kirk Douglas and Richard Harris destroy a Norwegian plant producing "heavy water" critical to German nuclear weapons research. In real life Lew Kowarski, a Russian-born scientist, escaped the Nazi occupation in 1940 with almost all of the Norwegian heavy water (about 200 litres in 26 cans - virtually the entire world supply at the time). For good measure, the Norwegian plant was eventually destroyed by British commandos, but that didn't happen until 1943.

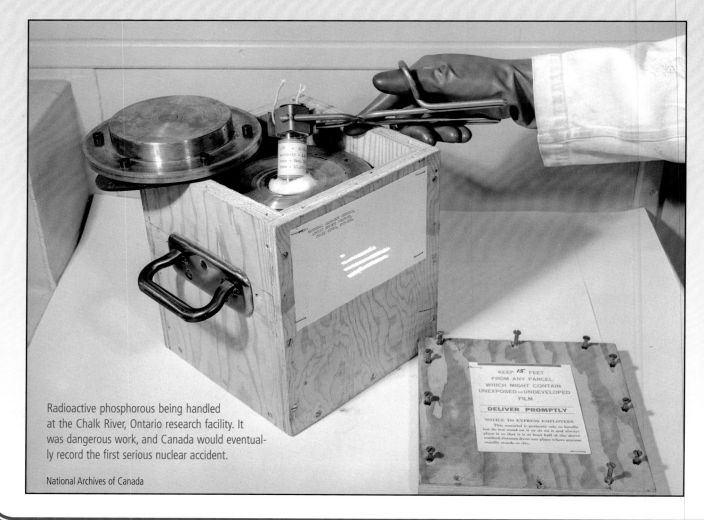

Radioactive phosphorous being handled at the Chalk River, Ontario research facility. It was dangerous work, and Canada would eventually record the first serious nuclear accident.

National Archives of Canada

The second reactor built at Chalk River (above). Completed in 1947 it was the most powerful in the world, and it put Canada at the forefront of research into nuclear energy.

National Archives of Canada

Once in Britain, Kowarski and fellow refugee scientist Hans von Halban continued to experiment with uranium and heavy water and became part of Britain's nuclear program. Meanwhile, across the Atlantic in Ottawa, nuclear researcher George Laurence followed Kowarski and Halban's work. By day Laurence was an adviser to Canada's wartime aircraft industry, but in his spare time he worked towards building a nuclear reactor.

With nightly bombing raids and the very real prospect of a German invasion, the British offered to move their nuclear program to the U.S. - and were flatly refused (the Americans wanted to keep their research to themselves). Howe and the Canadian government were more receptive, and in the fall of 1942 the research being done at the Cavendish Laboratory in Cambridge, England was moved to Canada. The British group was assigned to the National Research Council (NRC) and was joined by a number of Canadians led by Laurence. Their goal was designing a pilot heavy-water nuclear reactor to produce plutonium - a miracle fuel that was also the key to creating a nuclear weapon. Prior to the war plutonium had only existed in trace amounts, and could only be created in sufficient quantities within a nuclear reactor.

The research had obvious military significance, but NRC President C.J. Mackenzie later claimed the deciding factor in Canada's interest was the social and commercial potential of atomic energy. In July 1944 - a month after D-Day - a site for the pilot plant was chosen about two hours west of Ottawa, near the village of Chalk River. A secret research facility was built from scratch, along with a town site - Deep River - to house its workers. Among them was Lew Kowarski and his heavy water.

Construction at Chalk River continued through the final days of the war. Germany, it turned out, was never close to building an atom bomb, but by July 1945 the Americans had made enough plutonium to test the world's first atomic weapon. In August the second and third U.S. atomic bombs were dropped on the Japanese

Nobel Prize laureate Bert Brockhouse (above), builder of a sophisticated neutron spectrometer that provided mankind's first look inside the structure of many minerals.

National Archives of Canada

cities of Hiroshima and Nagasaki. Canada's test reactor, the first one outside the U.S., started up a month later. Born out of wartime expediency, Canada's nuclear program became a peacetime gift, fully staffed and ready to go. Already under construction at Chalk River was a second, larger reactor. Completed in 1947, it was the most powerful reactor yet built and put Canadian nuclear science at the forefront of global research.

Among the gifted scientists working at Chalk River after the war was Bert Brockhouse. Born in Lethbridge, Alberta, he began his education in a one-room schoolhouse a few miles from the family farm. Completing high school at the height of the depression, he took evening courses in radio design and repaired radios to supplement the family income. In 1939 Brockhouse enlisted in the Royal Canadian Navy and went to sea as a sonar operator. He left in 1945 as a sub-lieutenant, and took advantage of a veterans' program to enrol at the University of British Columbia. After university Brockhouse went to work for the NRC and became part of the group at Chalk River.

Brockhouse combined his scientific and engineering expertise to build the world's most sophisticated neutron spectrometer: a kind of flashlight to see inside the structure of metals, minerals, gems, and rocks. Brockhouse was also a religious man, his fascination with physics coexisting with his spiritual beliefs. "Science is an act of faith," he insisted, arguing that without faith, how can understanding atomic structure help with the larger moral issues in life? His work on the spectrometer would eventually earn him the Nobel Prize in Physics. (Brockhouse, later professor emeritus at McMaster University in Hamilton, Ontario, died on October 13, 2003.)

After the war Canada did not pursue the development of atomic weaponry, despite being one of only three countries with the know-how to do so (the U.S., Britain, and Canada). That did not mean, however, that there were no nuclear weapons in Canada. On the afternoon of November 10, 1950, St-Alexandre-de-Kamouraska,

A model (above) helps demonstrate the use of radiation therapy in the treatment of cancer. Medical uses for radiation were pioneered at Chalk River and the University of Saskatchewan, and in 1951 the Victoria Hospital in London, Ontario, became the first in the world to use radiation to treat a cancer patient.

National Archives of Canada

on the south shore of the St. Lawrence River near Quebec City, was rocked by a powerful explosion. Townsfolk saw a thick cloud of smoke rising above the middle of the river, which is 20 km wide at that point. It was four decades before officials finally admitted to what had happened: a U.S. Air Force plane had accidentally detonated an atomic bomb.

Fortunately, the weapon's plutonium-uranium core was not present. What exploded so dramatically over the St. Lawrence was a 2,200-kg chemical charge used to detonate the bomb. It had been dropped by a U.S. Air Force B-50 bomber that had run into trouble during a flight from Goose Bay, Labrador. A bogus cover story was concocted about a smaller bomb being jettisoned into the river as a safety measure. (The truth came to light from top-secret documents declassified in the 1990s.)

The reactors at Chalk River did turn out a small amount of plutonium for U.S. military use, but the goal set by Ottawa for the NRC was development of commercial uses for nuclear power. One

thing the Chalk River reactor could do better than any other was making radioisotopes; radioactive materials used for industrial, medical, and scientific purposes. In 1949, Dr. Harold Johns of the University of Saskatchewan asked the NRC to make some radioactive cobalt for use in cancer therapy. The idea was novel at the time: the powerful energy from radioactive cobalt used to kill cancerous cells. But on October 27, 1951, the cancer clinic at Victoria Hospital in London, Ontario, became the first in the world to treat a patient with radiation. The Saskatchewan team followed 12 days later, and would treat almost 7,000 patients over the next 21 years.

Canada would become the world leader in the production of medical radioisotopes and radiation therapy devices, (and is still responsible for 80% of the world's radioactive cobalt for industrial and medical use, as well as producing many other important medical isotopes). The heavy-water reactor pioneered at Chalk River would eventually make Canada a leader in nuclear power generation and a major exporter of reactor technology. ■

Above, U.S. President Harry Truman (left), British Prime Minister Clement Atlee (centre), and Canadian Prime Minister Mackenzie King (right). The three leaders met to discuss the post-war uses of nuclear power. Both the U.S. and Britain would develop arsenals of nuclear weapons, but the third member of the exclusive nuclear club, Canada, would opt to concentrate on the peaceful uses of the new source of energy.

National Archives of Canada

A car hauls silver radium ore from the depths of the Eldorado Mine at Great Bear Lake, NWT. Canadian mines had been producing radioactive minerals for decades, but with the onset of the cold War and the nuclear age they would take on a new, strategic importance.

National Archives of Canada

Despite sporadic labour unrest, across Canada working conditions and social welfare were undergoing a dramatic shift as a result of expanded government programs and a raft of new legislation and regulation. Fearing a post-war recession, Ottawa had brought in an unemployment insurance system in 1940, and in 1944 created the first family allowances - paid directly to mothers. As the war ended, Parliament had passed the Veteran's Charter, which provided educational grants for returning servicemen, and even seed money to help them get established in farming and business. There was money to help businesses make the shift from wartime to civilian production, money for new housing, and a host of public works projects. At a time when Britain was rejecting its wartime leader, Winston Churchill,

The Sigvaldassons (above) issuing family allowance in the form of powdered milk, in their store at Cape Smith, N.W.T., in 1948. A national system of family allowances - paid directly to mothers - had been introduced four years earlier. It was one of the first social welfare programs instituted by Ottawa after the war.

National Archives of Canada

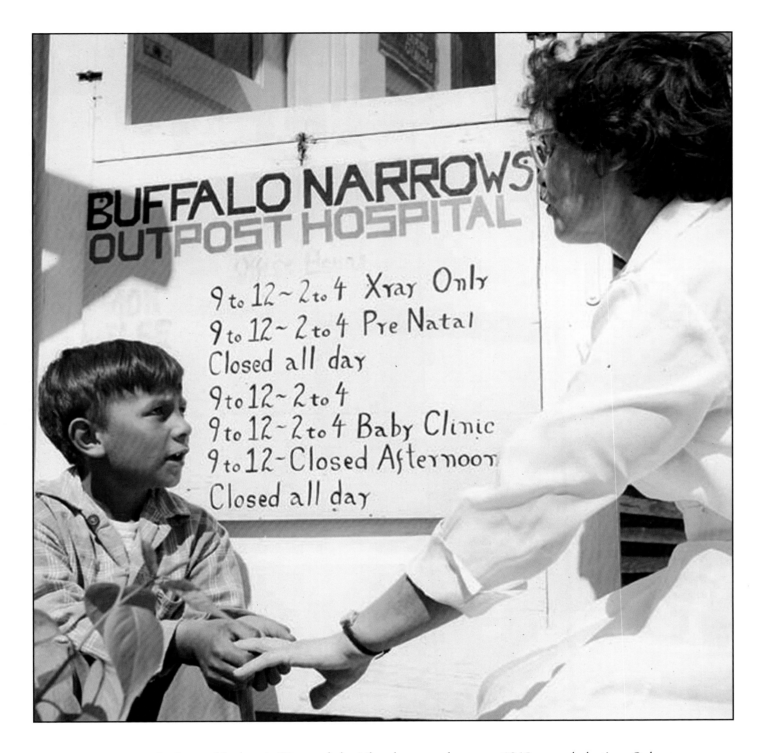

The sign reads:

BUFFALO NARROWS
OUTPOST HOSPITAL

9 to 12 ~ 2 to 4 Xray Only
9 to 12 ~ 2 to 4 Pre Natal
Closed all day
9 to 12 ~ 2 to 4
9 to 12 ~ 2 to 4 Baby Clinic
9 to 12 ~ Closed Afternoon
Closed all day

Health nurse Margaret Schindler with a young patient (above) outside the nursing station at Buffalo Narrows, Saskatchewan, in 1949. With increased accessibility by air and road, public services in many northern communities were steadily improving.

National Archives of Canada

Mackenzie King and the Liberals narrowly won a 1945 general election. Only a year or so before the left-wing CCF had been leading in opinion polls, but the party's agenda of government activism was undercut by King's expansive program of public spending. The Conservatives, whose commitment to the new welfare state and interventionist government was half-hearted at best, went nowhere. In truth, many people saw little reason to change the government. The economy had doubled in size during the war, and had kept on growing after it. There were jobs and prosperity, and suddenly it seemed to many Canadians that the country was on the verge of becoming the roaring success its founding fathers had long ago predicted it would be.

The Conservatives had changed leaders three times since the departure of R.B. Bennett and had been reduced to little more than an Ontario regional party. Federally, support for the CCF and Social Credit didn't extend much beyond Saskatchewan and Alberta respectively. Only the Liberals could claim broad support and representation across the country, and it was a claim they made often and loudly. At the provincial level, however, Canadians seemed more inclined to balance Liberal domination in Ottawa with governments of a different stripe. In 1943 George Drew inaugurated 42 years of Conservative control of the Ontario legislature (he was succeeded by Leslie Frost in 1949). The provincial Conservative revival continued with Hugh Flemming's victory in New Brunswick in 1952, followed later by Robert Stanfield in Nova Scotia, Duff Roblin

in Manitoba, and Walter Shaw in PEI. The Socreds continued to govern Alberta under the new leadership of Ernest Manning, and in 1952 W.A.C. Bennett led Social Credit into government in neighbouring British Columbia. In Quebec Maurice Duplessis's controversial but populist Union Nationale remained entrenched. Only in the new province of Newfoundland did the Liberals retain provincial power under the last father of confederation, Joey Smallwood.

Saskatchewan proved to be the first Canadian province to embrace the policies of the CCF, electing in 1944 a government led by the redoubtable Tommy Douglas - the last of the fiery social gospel political leaders. The Scottish-born Baptist preacher - and former boxer - was a gifted speaker who entertained as much as informed. A Douglas speech from the 1944 campaign gives some idea of his compelling oratory. "Mouseland was a place where all the little mice lived and played. And every time on election day they used to elect their government, a government made up of big, fat, black cats. They were nice fellow. They passed good laws - that is laws that were good for cats. When the mice couldn't put up with it any more, they decided something had to be done. They voted the black cats out - and they put in white cats. But you see my friends the trouble wasn't the colour of the cats. The trouble was that they were cats. Presently there came along one little mouse who had an idea. And he said to the other mice: 'Look fellows, why don't we elect a government made up of mice.' Oh, they said, he's a Bolshevik. Lock him up. "Douglas was duly elected, forming North America's first socialist administration and beginning two decades of CCF government in Saskatchewan.

The post-war years also saw the emergence of a new, politically savvy breed of social activists who became critics of the rapidly expanding array of government programs and services. One of the most notable was Charlotte Whitton, a crusader for child welfare and women's rights who had been a consultant to the King government in Ottawa (and would later go on to be the capital city's first female mayor). The Edmonton chapter of the Imperial Order - Daughters of the Empire (IODE) hired Whitton to report on the state of welfare services in Alberta. The province's Social Credit government was generally impervious to criticism from nosey social activists, but the upright ladies of the IODE were hard to ignore. And as a committed Anglican who was on record as preferring "the power of the Holy Spirit to psychiatry" Whitton was a tough adversary for a party that generally assumed God was a card-carrying Socred. Before she had even completed her probe, Whitton did an admirable job of getting the media on side. The *Albertan* newspaper lauded her in a headline as "Canada's First Lady of Social Service Work." *Time* magazine's Canadian edition described her as "one of the most determined women in the Dominion," while the *Calgary Herald* followed her lead in producing its own expose headlined "Children In Iron Cages."

Whitton's report, after three months of investigation, castigated Alberta's welfare services as "centralized, bureaucratic, unresponsive, secretive, and tainted with authoritarianism." And that was just for starters. She charged that children in care were routinely maltreated, placed in inadequate foster homes, and even indentured to farmers as veritable serfs! Single mothers and poor families were pressured into giving up babies for adoption, and the infants were often shipped to other provinces or the U.S. Outside her report, she also claimed that such babies could be bought on a black market. "Little girl babies are worth from $200 to $300 more on the black market in the United States than male babies," she declared. Twins were worth even more, and Whitton claimed that the province had created sets of false twins to meet the demand. Reporter Harold Dingman wrote that her report detailed "One of the blackest and ugliest chapters in the development of modern government." It was, he claimed, an "unparalleled story of a government trafficking in illegitimate babies," and of "providing unjustifiably harsh and delinquent care of

A patient being transported to hospital in rural in Alberta using a railroad "speeder" (opposite page). The photo, from the late 1940s, was actually set up for a National film Board documentary, with an employee of Alberta Health playing the part of the patient. Whether many patients were actually transported using such quaint methods is doubtful.

National Film Board/National Archives of Canada

A Spy Story

The Cold War Comes To Ottawa

Among the hundreds of thousands of new Canadians in the 1940s was Igor Gouzenko, although his route to Canadian citizenship was considerably more unorthodox than most. It also had profound political implications. Gouzenko was a cipher clerk at the Soviet embassy in Ottawa. In 1945 he was ordered to return to Russia, but decided he would much rather remain in Canada. With more than a hundred classified Soviets documents stuffed under his shirt, Gouzenko visited the offices of the *Ottawa Journal* newspaper and announced he had proof of a Soviet espionage operation in the Canadian capital that included a number of civil servants and politicians. It took two visits before he could get anyone to listen to him. His allegations were eventually relayed to the government, but no one seemed in any particular hurry to act. After all, at that time the Soviet Union was still a Canadian ally and Prime Minister Mackenzie King was preparing to meet with the Russians and Canada's other wartime allies to map out the hard-won peace. "It was like a bomb on top of everything," wrote King.

Gouzenko, meanwhile, was wandering the streets of Ottawa, unsuccessfully trying to seek political asylum and wondering if he'd made a very serious mistake. He later said he'd even contemplated suicide. His former colleagues at the Soviet embassy were by this time aware of the missing documents and attempted an unsuccessful late night abduction of Gouzenko and his family. Police were called and after a noisy confrontation the Soviets left, without their clerk or their documents. There followed a secret five-month investigation into a ring of 22 suspected Canadian spies, with 19 eventually being arrested and charged. Eleven were eventually convicted of treason, including MP Fred Rose, who was sentenced to six years in prison, and physicist Alan Nunn May, who received a 10-year sentence (and served six). The Gouzenko affair effectively ended the polite fiction that, on the surface at least, had governed relations between the Soviet Union and its wartime allies. Soviet duplicity had been suspected, but the existence of the Ottawa spy ring proved it beyond any doubt. As a result the RCMP conducted discreet security checks on 70,000 Canadians (an operation in sharp contrast to the full-blown "Red Scare" that was to erupt south of the border), and the Cold War became a disturbing reality.

Gouzenko retired to the Ontario countryside and live in quiet anonymity under an assumed name - apart from a few public appearances where he appeared with his head covered. Gouzenko and his wife eventually had eight children. He wrote two books, an account of his defection (*This Was My Choice*), and a novel about life in the Soviet Union - *The Fall Of A Titan* - that won the 1954 Governor General's Award for Fiction. He also painted the portraits of his security detail. The man who, more than any other, had first made the Cold War a reality for Canadians, died of a heart attack in 1982, and was initially buried in an unmarked grave. His family put up a headstone in 2002 - after the death of Gouzenko's wife, Svetlana. ■

Igor Gouzenko (above, hooded) during a television appearance in the 1960s. The Soviet cipher clerk's defection in Ottawa brought home the reality of the Cold War to a country that still tended to view Russia as a wartime ally.

Montreal Gazette/National Archives of Canada

A civil defence exercise (above) in Lethbridge, Alberta. Similar exercises had taken place during World War Two, when the actual threat to Canadians had been almost non-existent, but the advent of the Cold War and long-range bombers meant Canada's remoteness from the world's trouble spots was no longer a guarantee of security.

Glenbow Archives

Alberta's very young and very old." The Manning government responded by establishing a Royal Commission to examine the allegations - and also charged Whitton, Dingman, and magazine publisher Jack Kent Cooke with criminal libel (unlike regular libel, an indictable offence punishable by jail time).

The Manning government's denunciation of Whitton's claims was seriously undermined by several scandals that soon surfaced from within the welfare system (foster children had in one instance been whipped, and a toddler killed by his adoptive mother), and the criminal charges against Whitton and the journalists were stayed. When the Royal Commission issued its report it debunked Whitton's wilder charges, including the allegations of baby trafficking, but it did find serious weaknesses in Alberta's child welfare system and endorsed recommendations that welfare workers be given professional training, adoptive and foster homes be better supervised, and out-of-province adoptions be ended. The province instituted many of the recommendations, but Health and Welfare Minister W.W. Cross studiously avoided giving Whitton any credit for the changes. The controversy successfully revived Whitton's career, which had been flagging, and her media tactics and the success of her campaign in Alberta would prove to be a blueprint for many future assaults on government.

As it had after the Great War, Canada emerged from World War Two with the self-assurance and confidence that flowed from its considerable contribution to the Allied victory. Despite having fewer than 12 million people, the country had made a huge contribution in manpower and materiel to the war effort and had developed a host of new and durable industries in the process. However, the cost of its participation in the war had been great: 43,000 men and women had died and the national debt had quadrupled. Yet those casualties were much lower than they had been during the earlier conflict. Moreover, most of the wartime spending had been in Canada, resulting in a doubling of the gross national product. Economically, Canada was in much better shape in 1946 than it had been in 1918. It had also treated its returning veterans much better than after that earlier war. Indeed, the very word "veteran" was a new and consciously more honourable way to describe those who had served in uniform. The government made a real effort to avoid the indifference that had greeted returning servicemen after the Great War. The Veteran's Land Act provided loans to more 140,000 soldiers, sailors, and airmen to buy farms, start a business, or build a home. Thousands more took advantage of financial assistance available for college or vocational training. The result was a bolstering of Canada's middle class that helped reverse the ravages of the Great Depression and changed the social fabric of the nation. The great conflict had also compelled the country to grow up technologically. Forced by wartime conditions to reduce dependence on European and American imports, Canadian businesses had become more innovative and self-reliant. As a result, the range and volume of Canadian industrial production had expanded dramatically. By war's end the country's steel-making capacity had increased by more than 50%, and Canadian factories were producing many items—aircraft, plastics, diesel engines, electronic equipment—that they had not previously made.

The Statute of Westminster (1931) had accorded final legal recognition to Canada's status as a self-governing dominion with full control over its own foreign relations. A dozen years later the war seemed to have confirmed Canada's place of influence in the world. A majority of Canadians believed that the war had truly confirmed Canada as a sovereign, independent nation, and as a result the remaining emblems of colonialism would be removed and the symbols of independent nationhood substituted. It would be a slow process. Not until 1949 would Canada abolish the practice of appealing the decisions of Canada's Supreme Court to the Judicial Committee of the Privy Council in London. In 1952 the country would acquire its first Canadian-born Governor General (Vincent Massey, a scion of Canada's greatest manufacturing dynasty), but it would be two decades before a new Canadian flag made its debut. However, one significant symbol of independent nationhood - separate Canadian citizenship - would find legal recognition in 1947, less than two years after the end of the war in the Pacific. Up until that point, Canadian nationals had been legally defined as British subjects, both in Canada and abroad. Liberal Cabinet Minister Paul Martin Sr. apparently first conceived the idea of a separate Canadian citizenship during the war, but it was not until he had made an emotional visit to the military cemetery at Dieppe that he determined to push the idea within government.

It was certainly time for an overhaul of Canada's naturalization laws. There were three confusing and sometimes contradictory pieces of legislation governing who was and wasn't considered a Canadian national (the Immigration Act of 1910, the Naturalization Act of 1914, and the Canadian Nationals Act of 1921). The result, Martin told the House of Commons, was "unending confusion and embarrassment" for Canadians. Married women, for example, did not have full control over their nationality and in most instances were classified together with minors and the mentally handicapped. There was also no single set of rules for immigrants wishing to become naturalized Canadians, with clear discrimination between those who were already British subjects

After a hiatus during the Great Depression and the war, immigration surged in the post-war years - particularly from the devastated countries of Europe. These new arrivals (opposite page) are from Holland, which had been liberated by Canadian forces. The Dutch would remember their debt to Canadian soldiers, even when such remembrance fell out of fashion at home.

National Archives of Canada

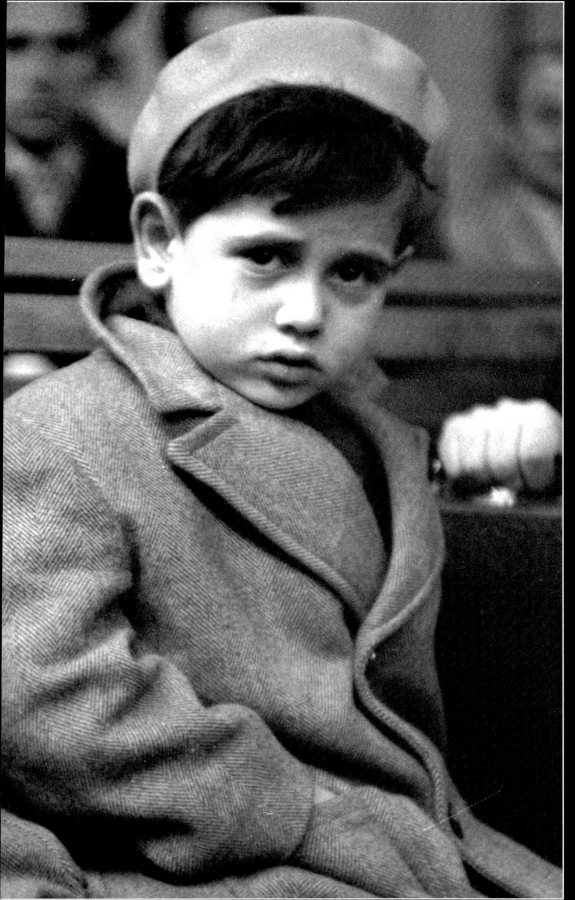

A pair of new arrivals waiting in the immigration hall at Halifax's Pier 21. Most immigrants from Europe still arrived by sea, at Halifax, Quebec City, or Montreal. From 1928 to 1971, Pier 21 was the entry point for a million new Canadians.

and those who weren't. "For the national unity of Canada and for the future and greatness of this country it is felt to be of utmost importance that all of us, new Canadians or old, have a consciousness of a common purpose and common interests as Canadians," argued Martin. "That all of us are able to say with pride and say with meaning: 'I am a Canadian citizen.' "

The Canadian Citizenship Act came into force on January 1, 1947 and for the first time created a common Canadian citizenship for all naturalized Canadians, regardless of where they had been born. It contained a number of significant citizenship rights we now take for granted, including automatic right of entry into Canada, and full control over nationality for married women. Immigrants who had served in the Canadian armed forces during the two world wars (and there were many) could also apply for fast-track naturalization. Canada became the first Commonwealth country to create its own class of citizenship (although Canadians would remain British subjects for another three decades). On January 3, in a ceremony held in the Supreme Court chamber in Ottawa, 26 people were presented with citizenship certificates.

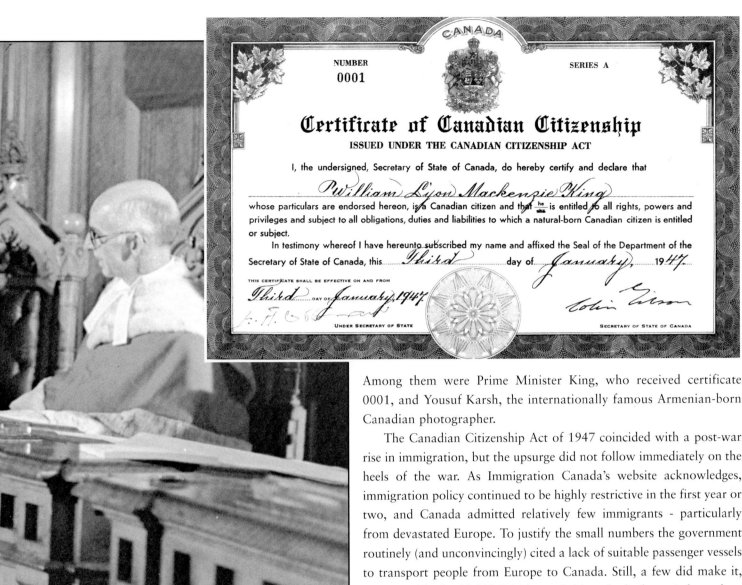

CANADA

NUMBER
0001

SERIES A

Certificate of Canadian Citizenship

ISSUED UNDER THE CANADIAN CITIZENSHIP ACT

I, the undersigned, Secretary of State of Canada, do hereby certify and declare that

William Lyon Mackenzie King

whose particulars are endorsed hereon, is a Canadian citizen and that _he_ is entitled to all rights, powers and privileges and subject to all obligations, duties and liabilities to which a natural-born Canadian citizen is entitled or subject.

In testimony whereof I have hereunto subscribed my name and affixed the Seal of the Department of the Secretary of State of Canada, this *Third* day of *January*, 19*47*

THIS CERTIFICATE SHALL BE EFFECTIVE ON AND FROM

Third DAY OF *January* *1947*

UNDER SECRETARY OF STATE

SECRETARY OF STATE OF CANADA

Supreme Court Chief Justice Thibaudeau Rinfret presents a citizenship certificate to Prime Minister Mackenzie King (above) during the first citizenship ceremony, on January 3, 1947. King received certificate number one (pictured top right) as Canada became the first Commonwealth country to establish its own citizenship law.

National Film Board/National Archives of Canada Photos

Among them were Prime Minister King, who received certificate 0001, and Yousuf Karsh, the internationally famous Armenian-born Canadian photographer.

The Canadian Citizenship Act of 1947 coincided with a post-war rise in immigration, but the upsurge did not follow immediately on the heels of the war. As Immigration Canada's website acknowledges, immigration policy continued to be highly restrictive in the first year or two, and Canada admitted relatively few immigrants - particularly from devastated Europe. To justify the small numbers the government routinely (and unconvincingly) cited a lack of suitable passenger vessels to transport people from Europe to Canada. Still, a few did make it, most notably the 48,000 British war brides who had married members of Canada's fighting forces. Eventually, the requirements of a booming economy, and mounting pressure from business groups, churches, and returning diplomats who had seen first-hand conditions in Europe, forced the government's hand. Slowly the King government began to open Canada's doors to Europe's homeless.

Polish war veterans were among the first beneficiaries of Canada's tentative move towards a more liberal immigration policy. They were admitted beginning in 1947 with the arrival of some 3,000 Polish Free Army veterans who had refused to be repatriated from Great Britain to a homeland now occupied by the Red Army. With hindsight, the restrictions placed on them look onerous indeed. Each Polish veteran was bound by contract to serve on a farm for one year, after which he was free to renew or discontinue the contract. Not surprisingly, when their term was up the majority chose to head for Canada's cities in search of better-paying jobs.

After three decades in politics, 22 of them leading the country, Prime Minister King finally retired in 1948. Despite his determination to avoid radical change and foreign entanglements, this puzzling politician had presided over Canada's full independence from Britain, its recovery from the Great Depression, the great crusade against fascism, the negotiation of Newfoundland's entry into confederation, and finally Canada's emergence as a prosperous and re-energized country.

He was replaced by the man who more than any other had shaped Canada's new international image as a staunch member of the Western Alliance, External Affairs Minister Louis St. Laurent. A former corporate lawyer, the second French Canadian to lead the country was already widely respected and credited with the national vision that King had never fully articulated. St. Laurent shared few of the isolationist, anti-British, or anti-American views popular among Quebec's intellectual and political elite, but most ordinary Quebeckers seemed not to care. He was one of theirs. In June 1949 the St. Laurent Liberals were re-elected with a record majority - 193 out of 262 seats in the House of Commons. The new prime minister was a clear and gifted speaker, a courageous policy maker, and above all a determined anti-Communist. But undoubtedly his biggest political asset was the fact that Canadians were comfortable with the easy-going, affable image projected by St. Laurent that quickly earned him the nickname Uncle Louis.

Perhaps the most famous nation-building event of the 1940s had nothing at all to do with citizenship or politics. It was the Grey Cup game of 1948, which pitted the Calgary Stampeders against the Ottawa Rough Riders in a game held in Toronto. Thousands of Calgarians descended on Toronto in late November and with their energy and enthusiasm turned a football game into a national spectacle. Special trains had been arranged to accommodate an expected deluge of western supporters, but nobody in Toronto was ready for the full blown party that arrived at Union Station and immediately took over the city centre's hotels and watering holes. The fact that some Calgarians had brought their horses, and proceeded to ride them through the lobby of the staid old Royal York Hotel, caused a sensation. Eastern fans had never seen anything like it. The good-natured westerners partied and sang from dawn to dusk, for an entire week, and in the process captivated the media and citizens who had never shown the least degree of interest in the senior football championship. Calgary vanquished Ottawa 12-7 in front of a crowd of about 20,000, which sent the Stampeder fans home happy, but more importantly the Grey Cup as we know it had arrived. It would be another eight years before the Canadian Football League would be formed, but by that time its championship game was already well on the way to becoming a national institution.

The fact that famously up-tight Toronto embraced the 1948 Grey Cup party was undoubtedly an indication of something else that was changing. Wartime restrictions on dress were abandoned as women adopted a billowy New Look that flaunted the availability of cloth, and men did the same with the big lapels, baggy pants, and ample jackets of the "zoot suit." Moral attitudes were also loosening and nowhere more clearly than in the sale of liquor. The pre-war temperance movement was in full retreat, with every province moving from dry to wet (even Prince Edward Island stopped insisting on a doctor's prescription before residents could buy a bottle from the province's new government liquor stores). Early in 1947 Ontario passed Canada's most progressive liquor legislation, which even allowed for American-style cocktail bars. As author and journalist Pierre Berton noted, "The public went mad. When my wife and I arrived in Toronto from the West that June, we found we had to struggle to make our way through the block-long crowds that waited outside the Silver Rail on Yonge Street - one of the first bars to open in the city." In his 2001 book, *Marching As To War* (Anchor Canada, Toronto), Berton recalls the comments of bartender Eddie Paltry. "People here don't really know how to drink yet. They are learning slowly. At the beginning, they come in here, some of them, and they try to start at the top of the (bar) menu and work right down. It's all so new you see. One fellow, he'll come in and order whiskey, then rye, then a gin drink, they maybe a bottle of beer, then he'll have a crème de menthe, then an eggnog, then another beer... What that does to the stomach I don't know, but it's not good."

Louis St. Laurent (opposite page) during the 1949 federal election campaign. The former minister of external affairs became only the second French Canadian to lead the country, and shared none of the isolationist, anti-British, and anti-American views that were popular among Quebec's opinion leaders. Unlike his predecessor, St. Laurent was a clear and gifted speaker, and a decisive policy-maker.

National Archives of Canada

The Calgary Stampeders celebrate their victory over the Ottawa Rough Riders in the 1948 Grey Cup. More than the game itself, the enthusiasm of Western football fans turned the championship into a truly national celebration that transcended Canada's formidable geography.

Alberta Sports Hall of Fame

Then We Were Ten

Newfoundland Enters Confederation

In Newfoundland the end of World War Two meant a resumption of the debate over the colony's future. Britain had rescued it from bankruptcy and assumed direct political control a decade earlier, but faced with war debts and the need to rebuild its own economy and cities, the London government didn't relish a continued responsibility for maintaining its last North American possession. A convention was held to decide whether Newfoundland should resume its independence, remain a Crown colony, or even become part of Canada. Most delegates favoured independence, but one who did not was a former pig farmer and radio broadcaster named Joseph Smallwood, who proposed that a delegation be sent to Ottawa to explore the possibility of union with Canada. His suggestion was defeated, but within months it became clear that Britain was in a position to offer little

support for the colony and that independence would likely mean continued poverty for the vast majority of Newfoundlanders. A delegation did go to Ottawa, and received a warm reception from Prime Minister Mackenzie King, who saw an opportunity to complete the nation building of Macdonald and Laurier. "I believed some day - the dream of a great country, a British country, extending from the waters of the Atlantic to the Pacific, all one, united - would come to pass," he wrote in his diary. He was not sure Newfoundlanders would agree, but King pledged to absorb most of the colony's debt and offered an immediate $15 million in capital. There was also the attraction of joining a country that was booming economically, and which could afford social programs, pensions, and public spending beyond Newfoundland's reach. In the event, King's caution was well-placed, since union with Canada

Joseph Smallwood (above) signing the agreement admitting Newfoundland into Confederation. A majority of Newfoundlanders had originally favoured remaining a British colony, or taking another try at independence, but the determined Smallwood had insisted that union with Canada be considered an option.

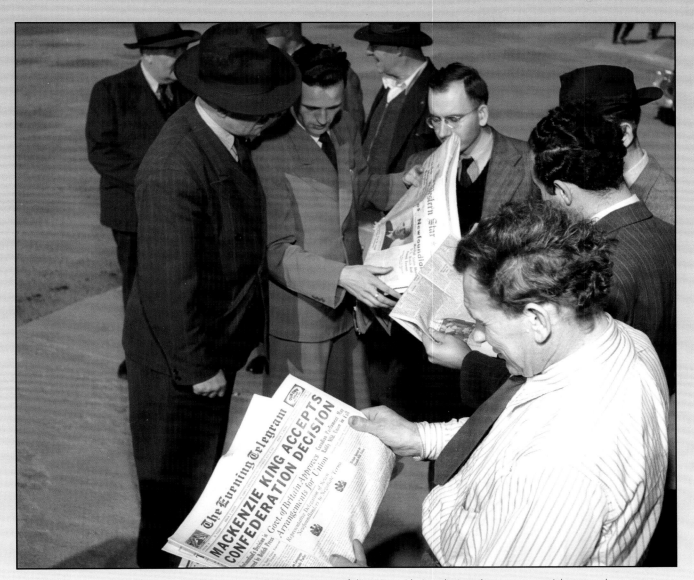

Residents of Corner Brook, Newfoundland, reading news reports of the union with Canada. It took two controversial votes and a very slim majority of 52% in favour, but the country now had 10 provinces.

National Archives of Canada

wasn't originally on the ballot for a June 1948 referendum on the colony's future.

But Smallwood was not a man easily deflected, and he launched a petition urging that the option of union with Canada be added to the ballot in addition to independence and continued colonial status. With the support of almost 50,000 Newfoundlanders he was successful, and then set off on a tour of the colony to sell the merits of joining Canada. When the votes were counted none of the three options had majority support, but having polled the least votes the idea of remaining a colony was removed from the next referendum - leaving a clear choice between independence and union with Canada. The campaign for the final vote was bitter and divisive. Irish Catholic Newfoundlanders overwhelmingly opposed joining Canada, while those of English

Protestant heritage generally supported the idea. The colony's business and professional class was staunchly against, concerned that Newfoundland would have to cede too much power to Ottawa. As the chief promoter of union Smallwood was either loved or vilified, and sometimes threatened with violence. "We can resolutely decide to be poor but proud," he warned. "But if such a decision is made it must be made by the 60,000 poor families, and not by the 5,000 families who are confident of getting along pretty well in any case." As he travelled from meeting to meeting he hired bodyguards and took to carrying a gun. The referendum produced a slim majority - 52% - in favour of joining Canada. The debate would continue for a generation, but on March 31, 1949, Newfoundland became the country's 10th province. ■

As the 1950s began Canadians were buying homes and home appliances as never before, but the one consumer item most emblematic of that thrusting decade is the automobile. From the 100 horsepower, black and basic utility vehicles of the Depression and war years, the automobile morphed into huge, 300 horsepower, chromed and candy-coloured behemoths. These now became much more than conveyances, mere transportation. They were an extrovert statement of personality, exuding confidence and power. An ad for the Dodge Custom made the point with typical overkill: "It's a dream. Wait 'till you get the full glistening impact of its low, sweeping lines, its jewel-like accents of bright metal, its high-soaring tailfins that dramatize its forward-thrusting look, its wide, gracefully curved expanse of windshield and rear

Thelma Anderson (below) working on refrigerator motors at the Westinghouse Electrical plant in Hamilton, Ontario. Electronics and home appliances had proliferated through the 1920s and 1930s, but it wasn't until after the war that most Canadians could actually afford to buy them.

National Archives of Canada

window, its distinctive twin lights that accent the massive bumper grille..." During the early 1950s vehicle registrations doubled, and soon one in every five Canadians would own a car. By now the factories that made these vehicles were all owned by U.S. companies - Ford, General Motors, and Chrysler.

Whoever made them, all these new cars needed roads, of course, and the 1950s saw the foundation of Canada's modern road system. The Americans had been building multi-lane roads since the 1920s, and by this time were busy linking them into a national system of interstate highways. Alberta had the worst roads in the country, but the state of Canada's inter-provincial highways was summed up in an editorial in the *Calgary Albertan*. "This country greatly needs a good

national highway. Each of the provinces has some good roads, but they are entirely inadequate for inter-provincial travel. Motoring from Alberta to the Pacific Coast is a chore and a hazard much of the year, except by going through the U.S. The highways from Calgary and Edmonton to Winnipeg are little more than good market roads for most of their distance." Many of the major provincial highways were, in fact, gravel roads that had been "paved" with a layer of tar - an economical process known as "blotter". Winter maintenance of major roads was sporadic at best. Bus companies very often had to provide their own snow plows if they wanted to ensure continued service. During the 1930s governments could with some justification claim they didn't have the money or resources to upgrade highways, but in the post-war boom - with government revenues and road traffic increasing - road improvement became a priority for the provinces.

Ottawa was predictably slow to appreciate the need for a Trans-Canada Highway, but both the Liberals and opposition Conservatives endorsed the idea at their 1948 national conventions and a federal-provincial conference was convened in Ottawa that December to discuss the proposal. Much to the surprise of the provinces, the federal government agreed in principal to provide an unstated amount of money for the project, and left the provinces to decide on the route. There was much lobbying by communities that wanted the new highway, but amaz- ingly most of the route had

A group of intrepid automobile pio- neers (below) in the foothills of the Rockies, west of Rocky Mountain House, Alberta. Vehicle registrations quickly doubled after the war, and by the early 1950s there was great pub- lic pressure for more and better roads.

Provincial Archives of Alberta

been agreed by 1949. It would not, however, be officially opened until September 1962.

Canada's railways had suffered along with other businesses during the depression, but freight doubled during the war and passenger travel quadrupled. At its peak, Canadian Pacific's wartime traffic rivalled the glory years of the 1920s, but the situation would not last. The railways remained the primary means of moving people and goods through the 1940s, but despite the poor condition of many Canadian highways, trucks were gaining an ever-larger slice of the nation's commercial transportation business. There was a railway strike in the summer of 1950, which even a few years earlier would have rapidly developed

An earth mover at work on the Trans-Canada Highway, east of Banff, Alberta. By the late 1940s the idea of a coast-to-coast highway was endorsed by both major political parties and supported by the provinces, and construction began in 1950. But it would be a dozen years before the route was officially opened.

National Archives of Canada

An early CBC portable television camera unit (left) in the 1950s. The first CBC television stations opened in Montreal, Toronto, and Ottawa in 1952 and '53, but strict government control meant the rest of the country had to wait in line for access to the most influential medium of the 20th century.

National Archives of Canada

into a national crisis. This time businesses adapted and although there were difficulties, the economy kept going. The railways kept most of traffic in low-cost, bulk commodities such as ore, lumber, and grain, but higher value cargos - in particular manufactured goods - were increasingly transported by truck. Passenger traffic increased from 761 million miles travelled in 1938 to almost three billion by 1945, but the total was no longer keeping up with the growth in population. It was already apparent that, given the choice, for medium-length journeys and travel within their own province, Canadians preferred the freedom of their own automobiles. Airlines had not yet begun to take a significant portion of long-distance passenger traffic, and in the early

1950s both Canadian Pacific and CN Rail introduced a new generation of locomotives that could cut as much as 16 hours off the trip from Halifax to Vancouver. These new Super Continentals were less luxurious than the grand trains of the 1920s, but they offered reclining seats, observation cars, and a high level of service. The railways that had bound Canada together for seven decades and made settlement of the vast country possible would continue to fight for their share of the transportation business, but it was already quite clear that their dominance was at an end.

As far as international travel was concerned, at the beginning of the 1950s North America was still very much isolated from the rest of the world. Long-distance aircraft now existed, but international travel was still a luxury experienced only by those with money and time. At the end of the age of ocean liners it was still expensive and time-consuming to get to Europe, and the other continents seemed a world away. To be sure, a large number of Canadians had served in Europe during the war, but that continent was still in the process of rebuilding and was not the tourist draw it would later become. Citizens of Canada and the U.S. mostly visited each other. Canadians did not need a passport to visit America, and they didn't as yet even need a visa to immigrate there. As a result a lot of people had relatives to visit in the U.S. - where Canadians were the third largest "ethnic group" according to the U.S. census. Whenever they had the opportunity, those Canadians who lived close enough also began to shop south of the border, where there was a greater choice of goods and - thanks to the absence of Canada's substantial import tariffs - prices were invariably lower. They were also familiar with what was available in American stores because in most respects consumers on either side of the border had become a single market driven by common advertising in print and radio - and also lately by the new medium of television.

The most influential medium of the 20th century had been invented in 1929, commercially available in Britain since 1935 and in the U.S. a decade later. A 1950 survey discovered that about 20% of Canadians had first seen television while travelling in the U.S., where there were already 108 stations. Around the same time Canadians living close to the border were for the first time able to buy one of the original eight-inch sets, put up the gigantic metal aerials necessary to receive the signal, and watch programs at home. On September 6, 1952 the first CBC television station went on air in Montreal, and two days later Toronto also had its own CBC station. CBC Ottawa television went on air in 1953. That November *Maclean's* magazine had a reporter watch Toronto television for a week to get a feel for this revolutionary new medium. There were 25 hours of Canadian programming, nine British and the rest, 31 hours, were American. After watching the Jackie Gleason and Milton Berle shows, the anonymous author "almost decided to borrow some money and buy a television set." The rest of the country could only read about all of this, because Ottawa was adamant that CBC television would only expand to "the regions" after it had proved itself financially in Ontario and Quebec - which after 18 months of operation seemed as if it might take a while. When CBC expansion did come, the government decided it would happen in an orderly, bureaucratic fashion, with Vancouver and Winnipeg first in line. Edmonton and Calgary were classified as "secondary" markets, along with Kitchener, Ont., and Chicoutimi, Que. The federal government decided that in these lesser markets the CBC stations could be privately-owned affiliates, which immediately caught the interest of several entrepreneurs and marked the beginning of Canada's independent television industry.

The first television sets were expensive, $200 to $400 (a quarter the cost of a car), and usually offered a single channel with about 40 hours a week of black and white programming. Reception, via a roof antenna, was usually snowy and sound reproduction tinny. Compared to radio, an established and sophisticated medium with worldwide connections, or the movies,

which by now offered lush, widescreen colour productions with stereo sound, early television appeared rather primitive and amateurish. Yet within a handful of years it would be embraced by Canadians and come to dominate daily life in a way nothing ever had before. Movie attendance dropped by almost half, and restaurants noticed that their evening rush was happening earlier, as people brought meal times forward so as not to miss the prime time shows. People started staying home on Saturday nights to see what Sid Caesar was up to. Radio drama and variety shows began disappearing in favour of hours of recorded music hosted by "on-air personalities" who rapidly became known as disk jockeys. By 1954 television would become the most lucrative advertising medium in North America.

Early Canadian television was determinedly up-market and patterned very much along the lines of the British Broadcasting Company, with theatre productions - everything from Shakespeare to Harold Pinter - dominating. But there was also Canadian content, and perhaps not surprisingly the most successful early television broadcasts were NHL tilts starring the Montreal Canadiens and Toronto Maple Leafs. For years Canadians had heard and read about Maple Leaf Gardens and the Montreal Forum, but now they could actually see them. Hockey was not the only sport to benefit from the arrival of the new medium. The 1948 Grey Cup game between the Ottawa Rough Riders and the Calgary Stampeders had been the most successful - and talked about - national football championship of all time, thanks in large part to the enthusiasm of the Calgary fans. Television now helped make the Grey Cup a truly national institution, and a good excuse for a party. American shows would dominate Canadian television, but at the same time hockey and football became staples of Canadian visual entertainment.

Not surprisingly, everyone from politicians and the clergy to newspaper editorialists fretted about the impact of this new phenomenon. William Tomyn, who represented an Edmonton constituency in the Alberta legislature, was in no doubt where he stood on the issue. "Only morons, with no sense of moral values, could produce such trash and drivel," he told the Alberta legislative assembly. "Judging by some of the recent productions I sometimes wonder if these individuals need psychiatric care." Calgary pastor Frank Morley thought that television was probably more dangerous than the atom bomb, noting that in one week of TV shows viewers witnessed "91 murders, seven stagecoach hold-ups, three kidnappings, 10 thefts, four burglaries, two cases of arson, two jail breaks, a terrorist attack which killed 20, two suicides and dozens of assaults." It was a complaint that would be heard often over the years, without any discernable impact on television producers.

The *Calgary Herald* optimistically hoped that television might prove to be at least a mixed blessing, particularly where the young were concerned. "In the United States is has been found that whereas the automobile shattered family life, the television set is restoring it. Young people stay home evenings instead of gadding around and getting into mischief. Children wander the streets less. But this is not an unadulterated blessing. Children also get less sleep, less than they need. Many of the programs are definitely harmful to their receptive and undiscriminating young minds. People read less. They make their own entertainment less. They are becoming illiterate. It is still not settled whether television is a good or a bad thing, on balance, but the right of people to view it must not be denied." It was a debate that would continue as television itself continued to grow in influence and diversity, leading the way towards what Canadian media guru Marshall McLuhan called the "Global Village." The only certainty being Canadians' seemingly unquenchable appetite for the new medium.

Future Quebec premier Rene Levesque (opposite page with microphone), at the time a war correspondent, interviewing Private Lawrence Hall in a mortar position near the Imjin River, in August 1951.

National Archives of Canada

It was widely recognized by Canadians that Russia had borne the brunt of the war against Nazi Germany. In the midst of prosperity, and with the Depression a fading memory, few people took seriously the suggestion - popular as ever among intellectuals and left-wing politicians - that Canada should emulate the centrally-planned Soviet economic system. Yet there was considerable public sympathy for Canada's wartime ally and admiration for the long-suffering Russian people. Then Soviet spies were discovered in Ottawa, of all places, as a result of the defection of Igor Gouzenko, a cipher clerk at the Soviet embassy. Moscow also showed no inclination to allow the liberated nations of Eastern Europe to determine their own futures, and Russian representatives at the new United Nations began to sound ominously threatening. World War Two, it seemed, was hardly over before the Cold War began.

The Soviet Union successfully detonated its first atomic weapon in 1949. Barely a year later, in June 1950, Communist North Korea invaded its democratic neighbour, South Korea, with Moscow's blessing and the promise of support and weapons. It was a clear test of international resolve by the now nuclear-armed Soviet Union, and the United Nations - of which the Soviets were a member state - quickly condemned the invasion. The U.S. offered naval and air support to the South Koreans. Lester Pearson, a former ambassador to Washington, was now Canada's external affairs minister. He was approached privately by his American counterpart, Secretary of State Dean Acheson, who asked for Canadian military support. Ottawa originally displayed no such willingness, debating what to do for three weeks. It was not until August 7 that Prime Minister Louis St. Laurent, under intense international pressure, announced that Canada would send a volunteer brigade to Korea. The response was immediate, with hundreds of men lining up outside recruiting centres before they opened. The Canadian Army Special Force (soon to become the 25th Canadian Infantry Brigade Group) received its training in Alberta at Wainwright and Calgary, but as the first Canadians sailed from Seattle on November 25, it actually looked as if the war might soon be over.

Led by American General Douglas MacArthur, the American, South Korean and other UN forces had pushed back the North Koreans and were on the border with China. The following day six Chinese armies crossed into Korea and entered the war on the North Korean side. By the time the first Canadians landed in Pusan on December 18th, much of the north of the country was back under Communist control - and the capital of Seoul would fall for the second time on January 4, 1951. The Canadian brigade saw action through a campaign of attacks and counterattacks during the spring of 1951. By the end of June the fighting resulted in a virtual stalemate along the old border between the two Koreas. The war would grind on in this way for another two years, before a ceasefire was concluded on July 27, 1953. The ceasefire would remain in place until the end of the century and beyond, but the democracies had proven their willingness to fight, if necessary, to block Communist aggression.

The fighting ended, but there was no permanent resolution of the conflict and the Korean peninsula was effectively divided along the lines of East and West Germany. The country had become part of the Cold War stalemate, which would continue for more than three decades, More than two million Koreans had died in the fighting. Nearly 27,000 Canadian soldiers fought in Korea, and 516 lost their lives there. In stark contrast to the scenes at the end of World War Two, there was no official welcome for returning Canadian troops, and little public interest in what was euphemistically called a "police action". Ottawa treated the entire episode with mild embarrassment. "You'd think we were criminals, or something," one chagrined Korean vet told the *Calgary Herald*. The lack of public recognition for those who fought in Korea would linger for decades and continue to be a serious disappointment for the veterans of the conflict. Fifty years on, it would remain a forgotten war and only in a new century would Canada's Korean soldiers finally begin to receive the recognition they deserved.

Korean youngsters (right) being fed by a soldier of the 2nd Battalion Princess Patricia's Canadian Light Infantry. As the war swept up and down the Korean peninsular, the civilian population faced displacement and starvation. At least two million civilians died during the three-year conflict, many of starvation and disease, but also from bombing and reprisals (at Taejon, North Korean forces executed 5,000 people).

National Archives of Canada

Pilots of the RCAF 403 Squadron, based in Calgary, Alberta (left to right, Gordie McLaws, Cal Taylor, George Grainger, George Kelly). Although Canada did not send any fighter squadrons to Korea, 23 RCAF pilots served on "exchange" with the United States Air Force. These pilots were awarded seven U.S. Distinguished Flying Crosses, one Commonwealth Distinguished Flying Cross, four U.S. Air Medals, and flew a total of 1,036 sorties in Korea. Canada also supplied the USAF with 60 F-86 Sabre fighters.

Glenbow Archives

Korean refugees receiving food and clothing from the crew of HMCS Crusader. The destroyer was one of eight Canadian warships that saw service in Korea. The Crusader's speciality was destroying North Korean supply trains as they made their way through the coastal mountains. With five to her credit, the ship was the "top gun" of the UN naval blockade.

National Archives of Canada

The War That Wasn't

Canadians Join The UN 'Police Action' In Korea

Barely five years after the end of World War Two, Canada did not have enough fighting soldiers to support military involvement on the ground in Korea. The 600,000 men and women in uniform in 1945 had been swiftly reduced to just 20,000, based on the thinking that any future conflict would be in Europe where Canada's major commitment would be from the navy and air force. It was in many ways a return to 1938, with defence policy based more on wishful thinking than hard reality. And it puzzled

Canada's allies. Ottawa had been a strong voice in the new United Nations assembly, and the secretary general, Trygve Lie, assumed that meant Canada would provide practical support for UN military involvement in Korea. Canada had offered three destroyers, but clearly Lie thought troops would follow - and on July 14 made public a letter to the St. Laurent government that said as much. The problem was that in the summer of 1950 Canada didn't have troops to send, and in any event the government was on holiday. The prime minister was fishing, and when

February 1951: Men of the 2nd Battalion, Princess Patricia's Canadian Light Infantry (above) during a rest period. That month the PPCLI became the first Canadian unit to see action in Korea, defending Hill 444.

National Archives of Canada

Private Jim O'Neil of the Princess Patricia's Canadian Light Infantry watches for a possible ambush as soldiers of the PPCLI move into position near Miryang, Korea, in February 1951.

National Archives of Canada

the media tracked him down he gave them the brush off. "I wish reporters wouldn't bother me when I'm on my holidays," he complained.

Lester Pearson, the foreign affairs minister, was dispatched to the U.S. for talks with Lie and the American government. Pearson returned to Ottawa to deliver the opinion that Canada's commitment to the UN required that the country do more to support the UN-backed intervention in Korea. The UN forces were, of course, led by the U.S. and made up primarily of Americans, and the government wished to avoid the impression that Canada was fighting for U.S. foreign policy goals. Pearson

offered the obligatory fig leaf: "We fight only as a result of UN decisions, and with other UN members." The prime minister was not yet persuaded, and discussions went on until August 6, when St. Laurent finally acquiesced. The following evening he went on radio to inform the nation that Canada was embarking "on a police action intended to prevent war by discouraging aggression." Anything less, he suggested, would amount to the same sort of appeasement that had encouraged Hitler during the 1930s (and which his predecessor had wholeheartedly supported). Canada would supply a special brigade for one year only, and to be used only in Korea.

The war that Canada's involvement was wishfully supposed to discourage was, in fact, already well underway - and looking more and more like a rout. Some 135,000 troops of the Soviet-trained and equipped People's Army of North Korea swept the South Korean and American forces before them as they rampaged down the peninsula. The poorly equipped South Koreans had been particularly badly mauled, with thousands killed and wounded, and tens of thousands of troops deserting. For their part, the Americans were rushing clerks, cooks, electricians - any men in uniform they could find - from Japan to the South Korean port of Pusan, where American and South Korean forces regrouped to defend their last toehold until major reinforcements arrived. Many of the Americans had received no more than basic training, and hundreds were killed as they were rushed into the front line at Pusan. *Herald Tribune* reporter Marguerite Higgins wrote "I saw young Americans turn and bolt in battle, or throw down their arms, cursing their government for what they thought was embroilment in a hopeless cause." Such was the preventative "police action" Canada was now entering.

The Pacific may have seemed a long way off to the government in Ottawa, but it appeared considerably closer from Alberta and British Columbia, where enlistments had doubled

Company Sergeant Major, Lew Burke
(opposite page), of the 3rd Battalion,
Princess Patricia's Canadian Light Infantry,
in Korea during 1953. And Gerald
Lapointe and Maurice Ethier of the Royal
22nd Regiment, the VanDoos, in a fortified
position overlooking enemy-held country.
By this time both sides were dug into
trench systems that more resembled a
World War One battlefield than the mobile
warfare the Canadians had trained for.

P 262 Glenbow Archives
P 263 National Archives of Canada

even before the announcement of Canada's troop commitment
to the UN action. By September 1950 almost 13,000 men had
volunteered for the special brigade. Half were veterans of World
War Two, and of those about 40% were either former officers
and NCOs or had specialist military training. They were joined
by thousands of younger men, raised on a diet of patriotic war
movies and the exploits of their fathers or older brothers, who
wanted to experience warfare for themselves. Among them was
Galt, Ontario's Don Hibbs. "All I knew was I'd missed out on
the war, and I wanted to be a soldier. You know, pulling pins out
of grenades with my teeth like I'd see in those John Wayne war
movies... I thought it'd be great to be a real soldier. I wanted to
be a hero."

It should have been the most experienced and motivated
group of soldiers Canada had ever sent overseas. Unfortunately,
competition between recruiting offices, particular in Montreal
and Toronto, was so fierce that enlistment procedures were
sometimes sidestepped and less than prime candidates slipped
through the cracks. They included a 75-year-old, a veteran with
an artificial leg, and a host of men who were either medically or
mentally unfit. It took months to weed out the rejects, which
eventually amounted to an astonishing 25% - double the rate in
the first year of World War Two. Perhaps the most notorious
recruiting slip-up involved Frederick Waldo Demara, a U.S. citizen who posed as a surgeon named Joseph Cyr when he enlisted
at a naval recruitment office. He made it to Korea and actually

Men of the Royal 22nd Regiment in action in Korea. Canada's commitment to the conflict was much smaller than its involvement in World War Two, but for the men who fought in the Korean "police action" there was absolutely no question that this was war.

National Archives of Canada

performed operations on a number of wounded before being identified as a charlatan. He was later portrayed by Tony Curtis in the Hollywood movie *The Great Pretender*.

The Canadian Army Special Force (soon to become the 25th Canadian Infantry Brigade Group) received its basic training in Alberta, at Wainwright and Calgary. It was made up of recruits from three permanent force regiments: Princess Patricia's Canadian Light Infantry, the Royal Canadian Regiment, and the Royal 22nd Regiment (the Van Doos). The commander was John Meredith Rockingham, a towering Australian immigrant with a stellar wartime record who was a senior executive with Pacific Stage Lines in Vancouver. When he got the call from Ottawa he accepted the job on the spot. He chose as his battalion commanders three seasoned veterans, all of whom had been decorated in the 1939-45 conflict: Jacques "Mad Jimmy" Dextraze would command the Van Doos, cigar-chomping Robert Keane would lead the RCR, and ex-farmer Jim Stone would command the PPCLI battalion. Edmontonian Lt. Col. Jim Stone, had joined the PPCLI as a private at the outbreak of World War Two and had risen through the ranks. As the regiment passed through his home town on its way to becoming the first Canadian army unit to leave for Korea, Stone was asked by an *Edmonton Bulletin* reporter why he had volunteered to go overseas. "I think we're just at the commencement of the biggest war in history," he said. "That's why I joined up."

Stone was not alone in his reasoning. It was widely believed that defeat in Korea could open the way to full-scale conflict with the Soviet Union and China. But by the fall of 1951 the rout in Korea was over, and it looked as if the war might soon be won. General Douglas MacArthur's U.S. forces had landed at Inchon in September, split the North Koreans and pushed them back across the border. It seemed as if the UN goal of defending South Korean sovereignty had been all but achieved, without the active involvement of Canadian ground forces - which produced a mixture of relief and self-satisfaction in Ottawa. MacArthur confidently informed a senior Canadian liaison officer that hostilities were likely to be over by the time the Canadians arrived, but he suggested it might be wise to send at least a token force across the Pacific - "to show the flag." Stone and his 1st Battalion PPCLI were the token... but by the time they sailed from Seattle the Korean conflict was about to experience yet another dramatic u-turn.

MacArthur had argued for, and was given, permission to cross into North Korea to destroy the enemy forces - a move that was supposed to end the North Korean threat without provoking a wider conflict. There were warnings from the Chinese that they would intervene if UN troops moved into North Korea in force, but these were ignored as mere sabre-rattling. They were not. Some 130,000 Chinese troops crossed into North Korea without being spotted, to be followed by six entire Chinese

armies, pushing back South Korean and American forces. Then they stopped, for 19 days! Convinced this was a sign of weakness or lack of resolve, MacArthur launched what he believed would be the final offensive to end the war. Two days later - 24 hours after the PPCLI sailed from Seattle - the Chinese launched a massive and ferocious counter-attack. By the time the Pats landed in Pusan on December 18, much of the north of the country was back under Communist control.

As the Canadians walked down the gangway from their ship, a band began playing *If I Knew You Were Coming I'd Have Baked A Cake*. It seemed appropriate, since Jim Stone quickly discovered that his American senior officer, General Walton Walker, was desperate for reinforcements and expected the PPCLI to be in the front line within three days. After more than three debilitating weeks at sea Stone was adamant that he would not put his troops into combat until he deemed them ready. He wanted time to train his soldiers on the rugged Korean terrain - something the Americans tried to avoid, preferring to rely on their vehicles and roads. The Americans insisted he move the PPCLI into the front line right away. The impasse was settled when Stone produced a written directive from the Canadian government, which had been forwarded to MacArthur, that ordered him not to engage in offensive operations "until you have complete the training of your command and are satisfied that your unit is fit for operations." Prime Minister St. Laurent had wanted to ensure that Korea was not a repeat of the tragedies at Hong Kong and Dieppe. Stone was not to be rushed. Not wanting to provoke a political fuss, Gen. Walker relented. Several days later he was killed in a vehicle accident. His replacement, Gen. Matthew Ridgway, was an infantry officer with much the same off-road approach to soldiering as Stone.

While still training, the Canadians began reconnaissance and anti-guerrilla operations early in 1951. They joined the British Commonwealth Brigade at the front on February 19, and in bitterly cold weather D Company of the PPCLI made the first contact with the enemy and dug in. The following day the Canadians suffered their first casualties of the war, four dead and one wounded. The conditions in Korea were indeed brutal, alternating between scorching heat and freezing cold, and the tactics of the Chinese horrified the Canadians. Heavily outnumbering the UN forces, the Chinese would often attack in "human wave" assaults designed to overwhelm their opponents. The result was slaughter on an appalling scale. There were also rats "so big you'd swear they were wearing combat boots."

The PPCLI saw action through the spring of 1951, most famously at Kapyong, a small village northeast of the capital city, Seoul. There, towards the end of April, the Pats were called upon to cover the withdrawal of UN forces in the face of yet another large scale attack by the Chinese. Together with American and Australian troops, the Pats occupied high ground overlooking the Kapyong Valley and were given the task of slowing the Chinese advance. After 18 hours of fierce fighting the Americans and Australians on the Canadian flank were forced to withdraw, and the Pats knew they would now be the focus of the full Chinese assault. Throughout the night of April 24, and into the next day, the isolated Pats repulsed attack after attack. Supported by New Zealand artillery, they held their ground. The unit was eventually relieved by British troops, but they had successfully halted the Chinese advance (and for their efforts would be awarded a U.S. Presidential Citation). The rest of the Canadian brigade arrived shortly after, and on May 28 they fought for the first and last time as a single unit in an unsuccessful attack on Kakhul-Bong - or Hill 467. Early in June the Chinese met with UN negotiators to discuss terms for a ceasefire. Yet again it seemed this unglamorous war might soon be over.

It wasn't of course. As negotiations dragged on the Korean conflict bogged down into a static war of trenches and patrols into no-man's land. It began to resemble the Great War more than the mobile fighting the Canadian brigade had trained for. Far more Canadians were wounded and killed after the armistice talks began, in what the troops called the "twilight war." Their greatest challenge came in November, when a Canadian battalion became isolated in an area known as Little Gibraltar. The Chinese took the high ground overlooking a position held by the 2nd Battalion of the Royal 22nd. Refusing to withdraw, Col. Jacques Dextraze told the Canadian headquarters "We will hold out positions. We will fight to the end." Massively outnumbered, the Van Doos fired their mortars until the barrels glowed red hot, and a single platoon went through 40 cases of grenades. Some troops endured 48 hours on open ground, constantly under fire and exposed to snow and freezing cold. Others were forced to call in artillery fire on their own positions to avoid being overrun. But they held their ground, at a cost of 63 dead and wounded. The attacking Chinese are thought to have suffered 1,400 dead and an unknown number of injured. Historian David Bercuson has called it "one of the finest defensive actions in the history of the Canadian army." Eleven months later the Royal Canadian Regiment would again heroically defend the same ground, this time at a loss of 67 dead and wounded. Ottawa might regard it as a "police action," but to the troops on the ground this was warfare as fierce as anything Canadians had been involved in during the world wars.

The static war dragged on and men continued to die as the on-again, off-again search for a political solution to the conflict went on. The veterans went home, to be replaced by much younger soldiers. The average age in many platoons was no more than 20, with soldiers in their late 20s being regarded as "grandfathers" in some units. The patrols into no-man's land continued

until the spring of 1953, when the newly-arrived 3rd Battalion of the Royal Canadians lost 23 men killed in a single, devastating clash with an attacking Chinese force. A Canadian patrol ran into an unexpected Chinese assault. They retreated back to the Canadian forward defences, but the Chinese were only prevented from overwhelming the position when a platoon commander decided on the desperate tactic of calling in friendly artillery fire on the Canadian trenches.

The early enthusiasm for the war had vanished and the flow of volunteers had slowed to a trickle. Rockingham's brigade was by now under strength by 400 men. The final months of the war were fought mostly by the artillery, with the UN forces firing 4.5 million shells at the Chinese positions, and the Chinese answering back with 1.5 million. When the armistice was finally signed on July 27, the Canadians emerged from their positions to find the surrounding hillsides covered with a mass of Chinese troops, many waving banners while loudspeakers blared out messages encouraging the UN soldiers to come forward to greet them. The Canadians were dumbfounded to see that they had been outnumbered by four or five to one - but it was all a propaganda ploy. The Chinese had brought forward their reserves - many more men than could have been accommodated in their frontline positions - for what looked like a victory celebration.

But the frustrating, unheralded "police action" in Korea was far from being a victory for the Chinese army or Communist ideology. The unglamorous conflict served notice to the Soviet Union and China that the democracies were indeed ready to fight. Despite the original miscues and MacArthur's chronic misreading of the Chinese, the resolve ultimately demonstrated by the UN forces surely discouraged Communist aggression - and may well have prevented a much wider conflict. In unwarlike Canada, Korean and the Cold War meant that defence would remain the single largest item in the federal budget for a decade and a half after World War Two. Almost 22,000 Canadian soldiers, sailors and airmen served in Korea, and 312 gave their lives there. Sadly, their sacrifice was widely unappreciated. Korea didn't generate the same level of public support as the world wars (for several days in 1951 the *Vancouver Sun* ran the same two-paragraph story on the fighting, without getting a single comment from readers). Distracted by expanding prosperity and growing materialism, a war-weary nation had turned its mind to other things. That lack of public recognition and the official insistence that the war had been no more than a "police action" would sting Korean vets for decades to come. Not until the end of the 20th century would they receive the recognition they so clearly deserved. ∎

Calgary, June 20, 1953: K.A. Pickering of Lord Strathcona's Horse (Royal Canadians) is reunited with his wife and young child after a year of serving in Korea. The war likely prevented a wider conflict with the Soviet Union and China, but lack of recognition - official and public - would hurt Korean vets for decades to come.

Glenbow Archives.

Official and public ambivalence to Canada's role in Korea was emblematic of the new international image the Ottawa government was attempting to forge: that of an independent, reasonable, middle power. For a country so entwined economically and militarily with its powerful southern neighbour, this was a difficult and sometimes contradictory goal. The politician who, more than any other, would come to be associated with attaining it was Lester Pearson. He had served in the Great War as a medic and pilot, and after studying at Oxford became a professor of history at the University of Toronto before embarking on a career as a diplomat. As Canada's U.S. ambassador in 1945, he was an observer at the San Francisco conference that created the United Nations. Pearson was acutely aware of what he called "the deviousness" of Soviet policy, but he also fretted about Canada's relations with an America transformed by the war into a new superpower. "We are constantly faced with the problem of trying to influence the United States in a manner which will protect our interests and our conception of what is good for the world," he wrote, "but which will not involve us in public quarrels with a great and friendly neighbour."

Such a public quarrel was not long in coming. One of the names thrown up by the defection of Ottawa-based Soviet intelligence officer Igor Gouzenko was that of Canadian diplomat Herbert Norman. Norman was cleared by an RCMP investigation, but since he was running the U.S. desk in Ottawa's external affairs ministry the Americans were concerned that he might have access to classified material. External Affairs Minister Pearson came to Norman's defence, and also refused to allow Gouzenko to testify before the U.S. Senate, saying Canada wanted no part of "the black madness of the witch hunt." That raised the ire of FBI chief J. Edgar Hoover, who apparently already had a substantial file on Pearson (indeed, Hoover seems to have had files on many prominent people), and the publisher of the *Chicago Tribune* denounced the foreign affairs minister as "the most dangerous man in the English-speaking world".

In the decade after World War Two Canada's population rocketed from just short of 12 million to 16 million, an astonishing increase - even taking into account the 345,000 Newfoundlanders who arrived with the stroke of a pen on March 31, 1949. The country's increasing wealth more than matched the growth in population, with the value of goods and services produced by Canadians more than doubling. Compared to the depth of the Great Depression the transformation was even more astounding. As a result pride and confidence in Canada and its future resonated through political debate and the media in a way that hadn't

New arrivals (above) enduring the inevitable paperwork in the immigration hall of Pier 21 in Halifax, Nova Scotia. The Canadian government had originally been concerned about immigrants taking jobs, but the postwar boom actually created a labour shortage - and Canada gradually began to open its doors to a wave of new immigration.

National Film Board/National Archives of Canada

happened since before the Great War. Everywhere Canadians looked there was material progress: new homes, schools, hospitals, and a host of impressive new products - everything from aircraft to refrigerators - that were now "Made In Canada". Later generations would sniff at these years as being predictable, traditional, and dull, but at the time people who had endured war and economic depression relished the mood of stability and certainty. For the first time in the memory of most Canadians the times were changing for the better. There was renewed optimism, and, yes, excitement.

Unemployment was low in the post-war years, settling at 3.4% by 1956 despite a brief recession in 1953-54. The workforce was still overwhelmingly male - 77% - but that meant almost a

German immigrants in Kitchener, Ontario. Wartime hostilities were quickly forgotten, and thousands of German immigrants joined the exodus from Europe to Canada. Coming from a continent where scarcity and rationing were still the norm, Canada and the U.S. seemed to be islands of abundance.

National Archives of Canada

quarter of working Canadians were women, a huge increase over pre-war numbers. The federal government ran budget surpluses most of the time, amounting to a healthy 15% of total revenue between 1948 and 1953, and could afford to lower personal and corporate taxes. Ottawa's wealth did have a downside. Relations between Ottawa and the provinces remained strained over what the provinces viewed, quite reasonably, as an inequitable division of tax revenue. Ottawa had most of the money, while they had the responsibility to deliver most government services. The provinces also continued to complain about the intrusion of Ottawa into areas that were clearly provincial responsibilities. In 1948 the federal government enacted a national health program, which provided federal grants for improving hospitals and other health facilities. The provinces appreciated the money, but less so the fact Ottawa wanted to determine how it was spent.

FRESH FRUITS AND VEGETABLES

FOOD FLOOR ENTRANCE

Supermarkets like this one (above) first appeared in the 1950s and would gradually replace many smaller grocery stores. As the world watched in awe, the hardships of the Great Depression and the shortages of the war years were replaced in North America by unprecedented prosperity and abundance. The Age of Everyman had arrived, or so it seemed.

Provincial Archives of Alberta.

It was the same story with old-age pensions (instituted in 1951 as a $40-a-month payment to those over 70) and unemployment insurance (1956). These initiatives were popular with most Canadians, who didn't much care which level of government did what, and were already showing signs of succumbing to the view - by now prevalent in the media - that constitutional arguments were either just too boring or entirely the fault of provincial greed.

In Quebec a Royal Commission of Inquiry on Constitutional Problems (the Tremblay Commission) called for a return to "true federalism" and an end to Ottawa's "imperialism". In setting up the commission the Quebec government had identified a problem that would fester and do enormous damage to federal-provincial relations. It pointed out that "the constitution of 1867 grants to the provinces, and to the Province of Quebec in particular, rights, prerogatives and liberties,

By the mid 1950s post-war prosperity, the Baby Boom, and the influx of immigrants from
around the world was beginning quite literally to change the face of Canada. It was a process
that would continue and intensify over the coming decades, redefining Canada.

National Archives of Canada

scrupulous respect for that which is intimately bound up with national unity and the survival of confederation, and it imposes upon them responsibilities and obligations... The Province of Quebec intends to exercise and discharge these rights and obligations, to which end it must safeguard the fiscal resources which belong to it and preserve its financial independence as well as its legislative and administrative autonomy. "Most provincial governments agreed, but as for halting the increasing imbalance of federal-provincial power, it was a voice in the wilderness.

Since the onset of the Great Depression the political authority of the provinces had been steadily eroded. Even as late as the outbreak of World War Two the opinion of provincial governments had mattered substantially. Quebec Premier Maurice Duplessis's attempt to undermine Canada's war effort had been taken very seriously in Ottawa, and had required an enormous political effort by federal ministers from Quebec to derail it. The same had been true of Ontario Premier Mitch Hepburn's criticism of what he viewed as the King government's "half-hearted" prosecution of the war. In 1940 a motion by the Ontario legislature censuring Ottawa's handling of the war effort had been viewed as a serious threat to the credibility of the government and the prime minister - triggering a federal election (which the King Liberals handily won). By contrast, the Tremblay Commission's pointed challenge to federal encroachment on provincial authority provoked little serious concern in Ottawa. Yet over the coming decades, continuing tension over this festering issue would serve to undermine the cause of national unity - particularly in Quebec and the West.

On November 1, 1952, the U.S. successfully tested a new weapon in the South Pacific, a hydrogen bomb that was a thousand times more powerful than the nuclear bomb dropped on Hiroshima. The Soviet Union shortly tested its own hydrogen bomb. The Cold War conflict of ideologies and the alarming arms race that now accompanied it would dominate global affairs for the next four decades. For Canada, the oversight of the British Empire in international affairs was gone and Canadians were now masters in their own house, yet more and more the country's economic and political destiny was linked to the new superpower to the south. The new Canada would find itself increasingly in the shadow of its more populous neighbour. Yet this was hardly a time for dark thoughts, as the great post-war boom continued, producing a generation of Canadians for whom the economic hardships of the 1930s and the terrible sacrifices of the struggle against Nazism were increasingly remote - almost unthinkable. "Progress" was now the universal watchword, and this favoured generation would have its own ideas about Canada, the world, and traditional values. The Baby Boomers would enjoy the benefits of perhaps the most privileged and secure upbringing in human history... and much to the horror of their parents, would eventually have the temerity to challenge the fundamental beliefs and social mores of the society that had provided it. ■

Scourge Of The Boomers

Polio Is Finally Vanquished By The Salk Vaccine

Better diet and advances in public hygiene and medicine had by mid-century transformed the health of Canadians, particularly the young. Previously devastating diseases were being controlled and eradicated, the almost miraculous "sulfa drugs" (early antibiotics) were curing infections and aiding recovery from injuries, and people were living longer and healthier lives than ever before. But there was one disease which appeared almost impervious to medical

advances, and indeed seemed almost to thrive with improvements in hygiene. The perverse irony of polio, or "infantile paralysis" as it was commonly known, was that without some exposure to the virus in infancy, children often failed to develop immunity and stood at greater risk of later infection by more virulent strains.

The polio virus had first been identified in 1908, and throughout the 1930s and '40s there was research to find a cure for the disease. The most famous case of polio in Canada during these early

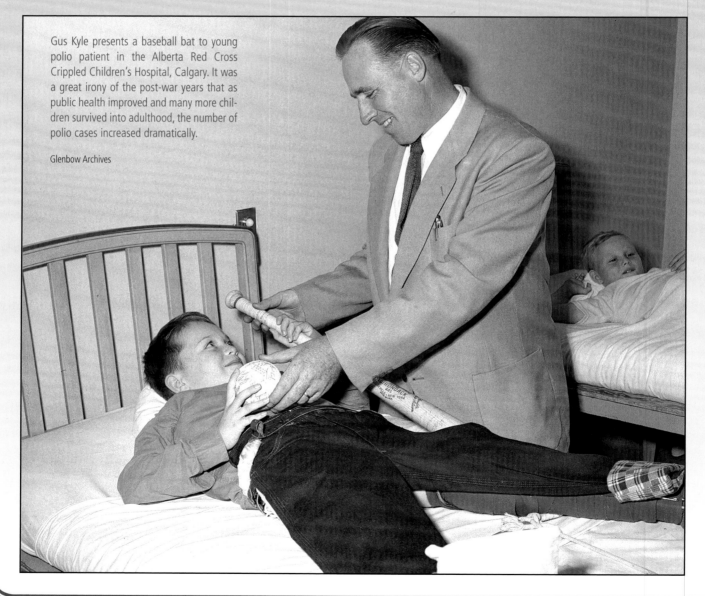

Gus Kyle presents a baseball bat to young polio patient in the Alberta Red Cross Crippled Children's Hospital, Calgary. It was a great irony of the post-war years that as public health improved and many more children survived into adulthood, the number of polio cases increased dramatically.

Glenbow Archives

Two-year-old Gifford, a polio victim, works with a physiotherapist (above) at Sudbury General Hospital in Ontario. The photo was taken in March 1953, only a short time before the development of a vaccine that would rapidly eradicate the scourge of polio from the developed world.

National Archives of Canada

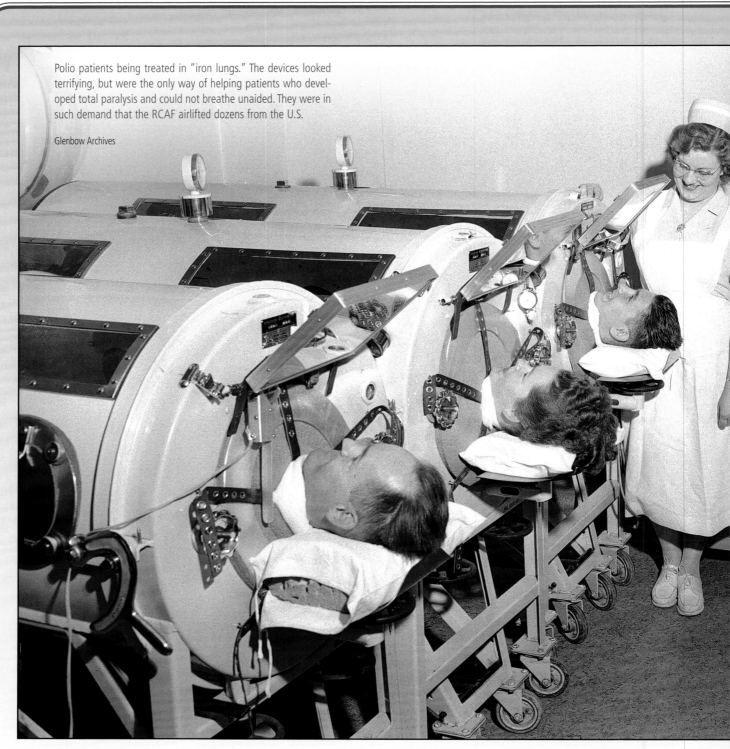

Polio patients being treated in "iron lungs." The devices looked terrifying, but were the only way of helping patients who developed total paralysis and could not breathe unaided. They were in such demand that the RCAF airlifted dozens from the U.S.

Glenbow Archives

years actually involved an American: wartime U.S. President Franklin Delano Roosevelt, who contracted the disease in childhood at his family's summer home in rural New Brunswick. So great was the fear of polio that the very sick Roosevelt was at first refused re-admission to the U.S. His family's connections eventually enabled them to transport him to New York for treatment, barely in time to save his life.

Ottawa resident Barbara Bondar grew up in Toronto during the war years and contracted polio in October 1947, two months before her 12th birthday. She recalled her experience with the disease for the Polio Canada website. "I had been home from school for several days because of a sore throat and cold. When I did not seem to be getting better our family doctor prescribed a sulfa drug. One night my temperature soared and I became delirious. During

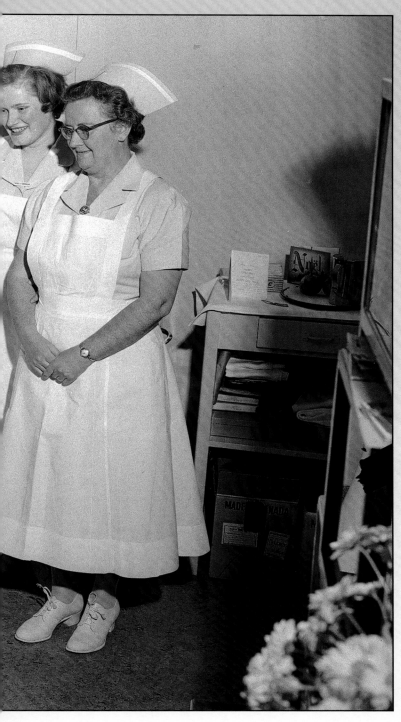

and it was very painful. Some days I was taken to a swimming pool in the basement of the hospital and lowered into the water by a large lift. It was in that pool that I took my first steps since polio. I was quite excited but I would have to wait a month before I could try walking on the floor."

The number of cases of polio actually began to trend upwards during the post-war Baby Boom, and in 1952-53 Canada faced its worst outbreak with thousands of youngsters falling prey to the disease and 1,400 dying from it. On the Kowalski farm near Millet, Alberta, two of the family's four children became sick. Deanna, 12, got it first and was hospitalized at Wetaskiwin. During a visit to the hospital, her 15-year-old sister, Connie, complained of feeling tired. Within days the two girls were sharing a room in the isolation ward. Deanna's case was relatively mild and she soon recovered, though with a permanent minor disability in one leg. Connie was hit much harder, becoming totally paralyzed. She spent the next 18 months in an iron lung (an artificial breathing machine), and the rest of her life as a quadriplegic.

Across Canada panicked health officials closed swimming pools and movie theatres to children under 16. Many schools were also closed. When it appeared as if there might not be enough nurses to care for all the victims, retired nurses were urged to return to work. Many did, although polio represented a significant risk for the doctors and nurses treating patients. Donna Graham, a nurse at the isolation hospital attached to Edmonton's Royal Alexandra Hospital, contracted the illness and was totally paralyzed for the rest of her life. Iron lungs were airlifted from Boston by the RCAF, and in an unprecedented move in the days before publicly-funded health care, governments agreed to pay almost all the medical bills of those stricken by polio.

In 1954 a vaccine developed by Dr. Jonas Salk at the University of Pittsburgh, with significant help from the University of Toronto's Connaught Laboratories, was hurriedly tested on almost half a million American children (including Salk's two sons). When the test proved safe, and 80% successful, some vaccine was shipped to Canada where it was tested successfully in Alberta, Manitoba, and Nova Scotia. A year later the mass immunization of children began across North America. Despite some serious setbacks in the U.S. (Canadian-made vaccine proved to be more reliable), the number of polio cases fell dramatically throughout the 1950s, and by the 1960s the disease would be mostly eradicated in the developed world.

the night I could no longer sit up or raise my head. By morning I could not even swallow my own saliva. That night marks the dividing line between pre-polio and post-polio in my life." Bondar survived, while many did not, but her recovery was a long and painful process. "I was fitted with splints and forced to sleep in them. My upper arms were strapped at a 90 degree angle from my sides and the forearms were raised. The muscles had tightened considerably

With physical therapy most polio survivors did well and many went on to live full and active lives, but sadly their ordeal was not over. As the survivors reached middle age about 60% were stricken with what became known as post-polio syndrome: brittle bones, difficulty breathing, and a general weakness in the arms and legs. The scourge of the Baby Boomers had returned. ∎

A nurse with young polio patients at the University Hospital, in Edmonton, Alberta. During the epidemics of 1952-53, thousands of Canadian children contracted the disease - and 1,400 died as a result. The development of a vaccine tamed the disease, but tragically a significant percentage of those who survived would by middle age be stricken with "post-polio syndrome" - an echo of the disease they had faced in childhood.

National Archives of Canada

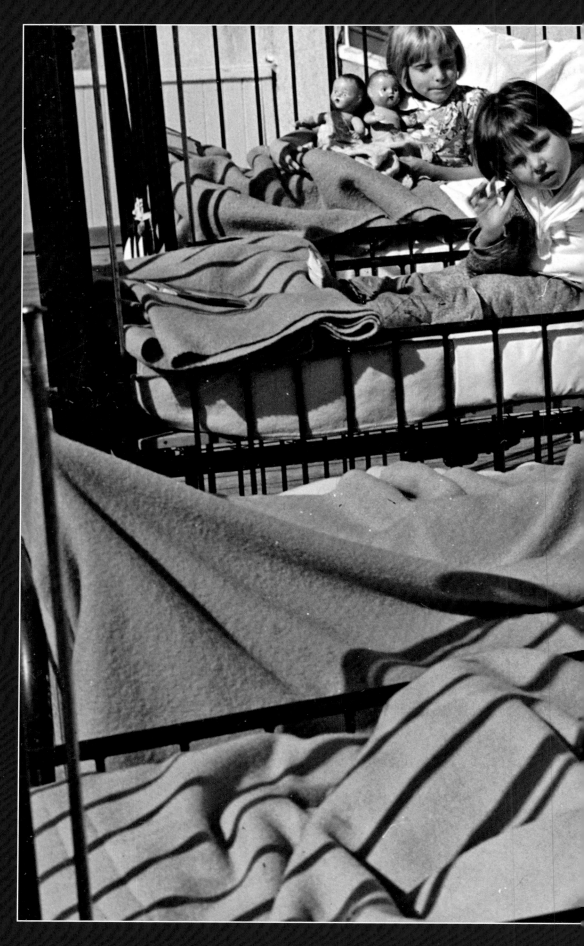

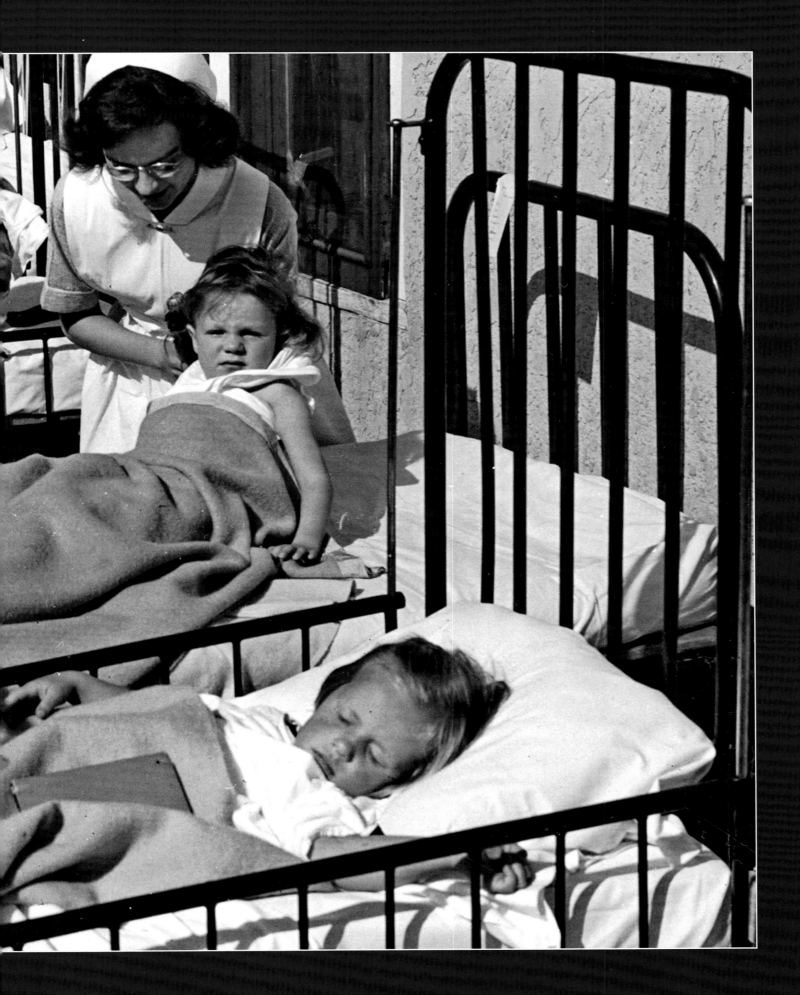

About the Author

Veteran journalist, editor and author Paul Stanway is a regular columnist for several daily newspapers across Canada. His first book, *The Albertans*, was published in the spring of 2005 to coincide with Alberta's centennial. His second, *Birth Of A Nation* - a history of Canada from 1900 to 1929 - was published in 2006. Paul was born in Manchester, England, and worked for several British newspapers before immigrating to Canada in 1976. He covered politics for *The Winnipeg Free Press*, before spending a year in Ottawa freelancing for *The Toronto Sun* and other publications. He was a member of the start-up team that launched *The Edmonton Sun* in 1978, and served the paper in several senior positions before being appointed Editor of *The Calgary Sun* in 1988. In 1989 he was appointed European bureau chief and columnist for the Sun Media newspaper chain, based in London, England. From 1992 until 2001 he was Editor in Chief of *The Edmonton Sun*. In addition to his writing, he also works as an editorial consultant.

Photo and Archival Sources

The publisher and author gratefully acknowledge the generous assistance of the sources of the photographs and archival material contained in this volume: The National Archives of Canada, the National Library of Canada, National Film Board of Canada, Veterans Affairs Canada, Heritage Canada, Glenbow Museum and Archives, the Ontario Provincial Archives, Provincial Archives of Alberta, Alberta Sports Hall of Fame, British Columbia Archives, City of Toronto Archives, University of Toronto Library, University of Manitoba Library, City of Edmonton Library, Department of National Defence, The Montreal Gazette, The Calgary Herald.

INDEX

Note: Numbers in italics refer to photographs or captions.

spectrometry, 222
speed limit, 137
spies. *See* expionage.
Squires, Richard, 20
Stalin, Josef, 77
Stanfield, Robert, 228
Stanger, William Samuel. *See* Stephenson, William.
Stanley Cup, 52
Star Weekly, 58
Statute of Westminster (1931), 18, *19*, 87, 233
Steel Company of Canada, Hamilton, ON, *214*
Stephenson, William, 140-141
Stettler, AB, 151
Stevens, Harry, 52, 67
stock exchanges, 46
Stone, Lt. Col. Jim, 265
Stratford, ON, 33
streetcars, 137
strikes. *See demonstrations, strikes and protests*
Stuart, Pte R.M., *154-155*
submarines, 118, 125. *See also* U-boats.
suburbs, 204
subways, *205*
Sudbury, ON, 28, 53, 277
supermarkets, 273
Supertest Gas, *196*
Supreme Court of Canada, 233, 236-237, *236-237*
mineral rights decision, 209
swimming, 76-77
Sydney, NS, 138

T

Taejon, Korea, *255*
tanks, *142, 143*
tariffs, 13-15, 30
Taverner, Ben, Harold and Stanley, 139
taxation, 13, 46, 103, 272
Taylor, Cal, *256-257*
Taylor, E.P., 107
teacups, 136
technology. *See* science and technology.
television, *230*, 250, 251-253
temperance movement, 239
Terreti, Italy, *154-155*
Thousand Islands Bridge, *83*
Thunder Bay. *See* Fort William, ON.
Time magazine, 229
Tip Top Tailors, 132
Tojo, Hideki, 121
Tomyn, William, 253
Toronto, ON, 18, *21*, 73, 83, *134*
1948 Grey Cup, 239
arrival of television, 251
enlistment in Mackenzie-Papineau Battalion, 68
enlistment in World War Two, 112, 147, 148
expansion, 204
Maple Leaf Gardens, 52
population, 201
relief system, 22, 104
transportation, *205*
Toronto Globe, 13
Toronto Maple Leafs, 52, 253
Tosh, George, *207*
tourism, 37, *47*, *192-193*, *202-203*, 246-247, 251. *See also* Niagara Falls, ON; Quintland.
trade, 18, 63, 209-210
Canada-Great Britain, 30
Canada-U.S., 217
Canada-Soviet, 77
trade unions. *See* labour, organized.
Trans-Canada Airlines, 76
Trans-Canada Highway, 246-248, *248-249*
transportation, 13, 27, *43*, 44, 215. *See also* aviation; ferries; railways; roads; streetcars; subways.
treaties, Canada-U.S., 217
Tremblay commission (Royal

Commission of Inquiry on Constitutional Problems), 273-275
Trenton, ON, *22*
truck transport, 250
Trudeau, Pierre Elliott, 137, 219
Trudel Furs Ltd, Edmonton, *60-61*
Trueman, Ernest, 125
Truk (Pacific Island), *184-185*
Truman, Harry, *224*
tuberculosis, 23
tungsten, 215
Turner, Percival Stanley "Stan", 112
Turta, Anton, 208-209
Turta, Mike, 204, *206-207*, 208
"twilight conflict", 266

U

U-boats, 118-120, 138-139, 150, *160*, *161*, *175*
Ukraine, Ukrainians, 33
unemployment, 13, 27, 32, 49, 62, 73
during World War Two, 130, 132
post World War Two, 201
unemployment insurance, 58, 80, 226, 273
Ungava Peninsula, 215
Union Nationale, 44. *See also* Duplessis, Maurice.
Union of Soviet Socialist Republics. *See* Soviet Union.
United Farmers of Alberta, 43, 44. *See also* Brownlee, John Edward.
United Kingdom. *See* Great Britain.
United Nations (UN), 199, 254, 260
Canada's role in, 261
creation of, 268
Korean conflict, 265-266
United States, 89, 115
arms production, 142
awards and citations, *256-257*, 266
Canadian emigration to, 32, 87
census, 251
economic interventionism, 61
economy, 13
espionage, 140
investment in Canada, 13, 217
Korean conflict, 254, 262, 265-266
loans to Great Britain, 197
nuclear power, 275
relations with Canada, 97, 106, 129, 199, 261, 268
Senate hearings (McCarthy), 268
trade with Canada, 15, 204, 209
World War Two, 96, 106-107, 140
world power, 217
See also Alaska Highway; Roosevelt, Franklin Delano.
United States Air Force, 224
University Hospital, Edmonton, AB, *280-281*
University of Alberta, 155
University of British Columbia, 222
University of Chicago, 80
University of Montreal, *105*
University of Oxford, 268
University of Pittsburgh, 277
University of Saskatchewan. *See also* Johns, Harold.
University of Toronto, 80, 83, 140, 277, 268
University of Western Ontario, 141
Upper Brockway, NB, 72
Upper Canada, 80
uranium, 215, 220
urbanization, 9, 18, 201
Utrecht, Holland, *182*

V

vaccines. *See* immunization, 277
Val d'Or, QC, 79
Valcartier, QC, 27
Valois, Fr Odias, *134*
Van Doos. *See* Royal 22nd Regiment.
Vancouver, BC, 18, 102, 117, 265
arrival of television, 251

demonstrations, 33, 64
population, 201
relief system, *22*, *29*
Stanley Park, *59*
Vancouver Island, 125
Vancouver Maritime Museum, 103
Vancouver Sun, 266
Vegreville, AB, 53
Verdun, QC, 116
veterans, 188
citizenship and naturalization, 236
education, 222
Korean conflict, 254
Polish, 237
Spanish Civil War, 68
reintegration into civilian life, 183, 188, *194*, 226, 233
Veteran's Charter, 226
Veteran's Land Act, 188, 233
Vichy government, France, 110
Victoria, BC, 68, *118*, 219
Victoria, Queen, 151
Victoria Cross, 104, 151
Victoria Island, BC, 102
Victorian Order of Nurses, *50-51*
Victory Bonds. *See* war bonds.
Virden, MB, *113*
von Halban, Hans, 222
vote, right to, 124-125

W

Wageningen, Holland, *183*
wages and salaries, 52
government cutbacks, 18
minimum wage, 58
wartime, 130, 132
Wainwright, AB, 254, 265
Walker, Gen. Walton, 265
Walker, George, 111
Walsh, James "Red", 67
war. *See* casualties of war; Great War; Korean conflict; Spanish Civil War; World War Two.
war bonds, 116, 117, *134*, 136
war brides, 212-213, 237
war cemeteries, 183
War Savings Stamps, 135-136
Wartime Prices and Trade Board, 130
Waters, Stanley Charles "Stan", 155-156
Waterton Lakes, AB, 206
Watson Lake, YK, 128
Watson, Patrick, 149
Wayne, John, 263
Wayne, John, and Shuster, Frank, *137*
Webster, George, 71
Weekend Magazine, 200
welfare, 23, 103. *See also* relief.
Wells, Annie, 52
Wernham, James, 149
West Germany, 197
Westinghouse Electrical Company, Hamilton, ON, *244-245*
Wetaskiwin, AB, 277
Whitaker, Capt. Denis, 151
Whitby, ON, 140
Whitecourt, AB, *143*
Whitehorse, YK, 128
Whitton, Charlotte, 229-231
Wicks, Ben, 212
wildlife conservation, 74
Wiley, George, 149
Wilkie, Agnes, 139
William the Conqueror, *170*
Wilson, Cairine, 98
Winch, Ernie, 43
Winnipeg, MB, 18, 32, 56, 64, 140
arrival of television, 251
doctors' strike, 48
Winnipeg Free Press, 31-32, 87
Winnipeg General Strike, 39
Winnipeg Grenadiers, 121
women
demonstrations, *59*
employment, *119*, *120*, *122*, *131*, 134-135, *143*, *216*, *244-245*, 272

legal positon and rights, 229, 233, 236
war service, 115-116, 139, 165
Wong, Agnes, *143*
Wood, Ernest and Ann, 212-213
Woodsworth, J.S., 41, 101
Woodward, W.C., 125
work camps. *See* Japanese-Canadians; relief system.
workers. *See* labour, organized.
World War One. *See* Great War.
World War Two, 80, 92-190
air war, 112
Canada's entry into, 101
Canadian support for, 96-99, 101
costs, 233
enlistment, 104, *108-109*, *184-185*
home front, 130, 132, 134-137
Italian campaign, 153-161
Normandy invasion, 151, 157, 162-165, *162-163*, *170*
public support for, 96-99, 104, 120, 136
shortages, 136. *See also* rationing.
See also armed forces, Canadian; Battle of Britain; Battle of the Atlantic; conscription; rationing.

XYZ

York, Isabel, 135
York, ON, 18
Young Men's Christian Association (YMCA), 101
Yukon, 215
Zeidman, Rev. Morris, 104
"Zombies", 174
zoos, 43

CANADA IN THE 20TH CENTURY

To order additional copies of this book, or the upcoming two additions in the series please call CanMedia at 1-888-301-2664 or visit our website at **www.cdnhistory.com**

BIRTH OF A NATION
1900 TO 1929

The tumultuous story of Canada's emergence as a modern state - from a frontier of empire to the 20th Century's first economic tiger. The horrors of the Great War, and the forging of a national identity as troops of the young Dominion lead the Allied forces to victory on the battlefields of Flanders, the social and political turmoil of the Roaring 20s, and the looming economic crisis that would end Canada's first great boom. Veteran journalist and author Paul Stanway brings to life the leaders, heroes, villains, and celebrities who left their mark on the on a developing country. All beautifully illustrated with hundreds of rare photographs, many reproduced here for the first time in decades.

TRAGEDY & TRIUMPH
1930 TO 1953

Ravaged by the unemployment and misery of the Great Depression, Canada is once again called upon to stand with Britain in a global war - this one more terrible than any conflict in human history. Punching far above its weight, the country plays a central role in the defeat of the Axis powers, and emerges from the challenges of World War Two reinvigorated and united as never before. The onset of the Cold War and the Korean conflict cast a pall over the post-war years, but the hard times finally give way to an unprecedented period of prosperity that transforms the lives of ordinary Canadians. The tragedies and triumphs that shaped a maturing nation are recalled in vivid detail and lavishly illustrated with unique photographs.